Natural Progression

A Lifetime of Skiing the World's Greatest Ranges

Michael Marolt

with
Cameron M Burns

ISBN: 978-1-7168-9319-3 (sc)
ISBN: 978-1-7168-9320-9 (hc)
ISBN: 978-1-7168-9318-6 (e)

Library of Congress Control Number: 2020910520

Because of the dynamic nature of the Internet, any web addresses or links contained in this book may have changed since publication and may no longer be valid. The views expressed in this work are solely those of the author and do not necessarily reflect the views of the publisher, and the publisher hereby disclaims any responsibility for them.

Any people depicted in stock imagery provided by Getty Images are models, and such images are being used for illustrative purposes only. Certain stock imagery © Getty Images.

Lulu Publishing Services rev. date: 06/19/2020

To Talulah, Flora, and Shelly for putting up with my expeditions. Also, to my mother, Betty Marolt, who gave me my fortitude, toughness, and faith

Foreword

In the spring of 2019, I went to Alaska with three friends—Linus Platt, Jeff Rogers, and Rich Page—to climb and ski Mount Sanford by its easiest route, the Sheep Glacier. I'd never done a big so-called "skimo" (ski mountaineering) trip, and I was curious to understand why it had become such a popular activity over the past two decades.

Linus, Jeff, Rich, and I plodded up the hill, foot by foot, hour after hour. I'd done this on big mountains around the world, under the guise of "climbing," and while it was fun, plodding along in big boots grows very old very quickly. But Sanford was different. After we'd dropped a load of food, fuel, and gear, we clicked into our bindings and schussed down the mountain. It was nothing short of a revelation. Here we were gliding across the snow and ice as if we were flying, as if we'd been untethered from gravity. As if we were free. Yup, sounds corny—but the feeling was fantastic.

As we swooshed into a lower camp, I could feel the biggest grin my face had hosted in thirty years crack across my face. *That sure beat the hell out of tromping back down*, I thought.

My interest wasn't just because of the recent explosion of skimo on mountains around the world. It was partly driven by the fact that two years earlier an Aspen skier named Mike Marolt had asked me to help him with a book project (the stack of bound paper you now hold in your hand). This book project was basically a recounting of some of his ski mountaineering trips of the past thirty years. As I dug into the manuscript and googled Mike online, it became apparent that this guy was the real deal. And a *big* deal.

Mike, along with his twin brother, Steve, and childhood friend Jim Gile, had done nearly sixty ski mountaineering trips to the high peaks of Asia and South America's Andes. They'd skied all over Alaska and Colorado and had done trips to other areas of the Mountain West.

And yet, if you asked me who they were before Mike got in touch, I'd have been hard put to tell you. There were a few articles about them, but nothing put them into perspective the way Mike's humble narrative did. These guys were, and remain, a phenomenon.

More specifically, their résumé includes thirteen Himalayan ski expeditions and several dozen ski expeditions to Peru, Bolivia, Ecuador, Chile, and Argentina. They are pioneers in winter Himalayan skiing, with two world altitude-record ski descents. They possess arguably the greatest résumé in the history of ski descents from the world's five-thousand- to eight-thousand-meter peaks. They climb and ski "pure" style, without the aid of supplemental oxygen or porters, or altitude drugs, something that if you've ever been to altitude you know is an incredible accomplishment. To climb the highest peaks in the world in pure style is limited to the greatest elite climbers in history. To climb the highest peaks in the world in pure style *and carry skis*—as the Marolt brothers, Gile, and a small group of their friends have done—is almost beyond comprehension.

Coming from a place in the climbing world, where "spray"— that is, talking about your achievements—is more than annoyingly present, Mike, Steve, and Jim offered a refreshing reprieve. Apparently, they'd just been doing their thing, on their own, with no hoopla, for three decades.

Their incredible humility and unconcern with ski mountaineering fame comes from their humble roots. Starting when they were just children, Mike and his group of friends started skiing "off-piste" (in the backcountry, not on resort trails) in the mountains of central Colorado. Their abilities and their achievements grew in tiny increments, hardly enough for an outsider to notice. But season by season, year by year, decade by decade their exploits become more and more impressive. To Mike and his friends, though, the incremental growth was holistic, natural. They were skiing Colorado's fourteen-thousand-foot peaks then running off to ski Everest. They spent three decades learning how to, when to, where to, and, most importantly, why to. They turned around on dozens of peaks, in many instances when they were tantalizingly close to the summit. These turnarounds might seem to the casual observer unnecessary and a waste of time and money getting to a particular high point. But they stuck with the lessons learned over those three decades and achieved so much that the many "near misses" were an acceptable tally in their ski mountaineering career.

The lesson in their careers as ski mountaineers is take it easy, grow slowly and at a natural pace, and don't push anything. In doing that, they've gained remarkable insight into the mountain world, their abilities, and themselves as individuals. They've brought those qualities back to their families, friends, and communities, and in the process, they've become the most accomplished ski mountaineers in American history.

Their story is a natural progression, a story of how to grow, how to learn, and how to get as much as you can out of life.

Cam Burns,
Basalt, Colorado, July 2019

Preface

This book is a project that started merely as my effort to practice writing for a request I received several years ago to be a writer for a national ski magazine. I always loved to write but never imagined myself to be a writer. I'd be lying if I said I didn't wonder what went through a writer's mind as he stamped that last period in a completed book. And while I didn't set out to write a book, I knew eventually I'd write something to see what that was like. But this project was not ever something I envisioned to be that experience. So, in life, timing is everything. As my editor provided me with his third round of edits and questions, it allowed me to read my own book for the first time (keep in mind I started compiling this seven years ago). As I paged through the words and stories over the past year, it coincided with all the questions this notion of being a Hall of Famer brought up, and it refreshed my memories of how it all fell into place. When I started writing this piece, I didn't even think about needing a title. But then, as I recollected the last stories, it became clear. This book is an account of how a couple of brothers from Aspen, Colorado, followed their passion, and how by doing that, they naturally progressed. Bingo, the title popped up. This book is a compilation of stories and personal thoughts that illustrate how we progressed naturally from our back yard to climbing and skiing the highest peaks in the world. It really is our natural progression in that it was not influenced by anything other than finding out what gifts we were presented with, realizing those gifts were ours for the taking, and utilizing them for the pure purpose of experiencing what they allowed us to do.

My hope for you as a reader is to understand that we all have been given gifts. They are often not easy to find, and once you find them, even more difficult to cultivate and appreciate. But they are there. It is our lives' mission to find them, use them, and be thankful for them. Life is a process and a progression. For us, what we realized is that it truly is about the journey. If you learn this and live it, you will find yourself living in the moment and seeing that this is always the ultimate reward.

Introduction

I was sitting in my office working, and my phone rang. "Hello, Mike, this is Justin at the USA Ski and Snowboard Hall of Fame. I am very excited to let you know that our esteemed members and voting panel have elected you and Steve to be inducted as members of the Hall of Fame. Congratulations!"

Several years prior, I was made aware of a group of people that came up with the idea to nominate Steve and me. We were flattered, enhanced by the experience of personally accepting my father's induction to the Colorado Ski Hall of Fame shortly after he passed away. That was for Colorado; this call was from the national Hall of Fame. But outside of this congratulatory call, I always deemed it to be far-fetched. At that moment I thought this was my brother playing a cruel joke on me.

I quickly gathered my senses and looked at the caller ID and realized it was no joke. Steve and I had been elected to the USA Ski Hall of Fame! I thanked the voice on the phone and excitedly hung up the phone and called Steve. "Is this Steve Marolt, USA Ski Hall of Famer?"

Steve was well aware that an application was in the works but never paid much attention to the matter, not knowing the people submitting it as well as I did. Casual conversation at best kept him in the loop. His response was blunt: "Are you fucking kidding me? We were inducted into that thing?"

So Steve's response and our general sense of overwhelming disbelief with the induction message that day needs a bit of background not fully expanded upon in this essay if only because during the years that I wrote it, the notion of being a Hall of Famer was not remotely anticipated. My initial reaction that this was a joke and Steve's dumfounded amazement were more logical than anything.

For starters, the activity of ski mountaineering is not by most definitions even a sport. It's very athletic and takes enormous dedication and training both mentally and physically, arguably more than most sports, but it's the antithesis of competition. Especially as was the case for Steve and me, our ski mountaineering came in earnest long after our days of youth when we competitively took part in sports, including ski racing, which drove us to be our best. For us, ski mountaineering started to extend our love of skiing past the day the lifts closed and allowed us to capture what any competitive skier will tell you is the purest form of the sport, "free skiing." The term free skiing is used for all skiing beyond competition where you can go where you want, how you want, and when you want to experience the exhilaration and sensation that ultimately makes skiing the desirable sport that it is for so many. Free skiing is the essence of the activity. It doesn't matter if you are a tourist hitting the bunny slopes for the first time or the greatest ski racer of the day, it all begins and ends with free skiing.

For Steve and me, skiing was no different than it was for so many who ever clicked into their bindings for the first time. After the initial learning curve, we were hooked. But what made skiing different for us was that in the Marolt family, skiing was the very fiber of family life. Not only was it the catalyst for my parents to meet, it was the means to an end financially for how my father supported the family. In short, skiing was a way of life. For Steve and me, this was enhanced by the reality that Dad was not just a skier; he was an Olympic skier. His brothers were also Olympians, and their friends were generally world-class skiers. Aspen was a mecca for world-class skiers in all aspects of skiing, and being a generational family in the town put the Marolts in the center of things. Growing up in these shadows was akin to the kid that grew up as a bat boy hanging around the clubhouse at Yankee Stadium because his dad was the manager. Our notion of what a world-class skier amounted to was just one of Dad's buddies and something that just happened to old people.

As Steve and I grew up, however, and developed as skiers ourselves, the true nature of the sport set in. Steve and I were not the greatest athletes by the definition we found ourselves surrounded by, and the reality not just in skiing but every sport we ever played began to manifest itself in a deep respect and appreciation for what the term "world class" actually meant. This was not a negative thing, and, in fact, it created a situation in which Dad was not only what every good man is to his son, but it left us with a sense of awe in who our father was as an athlete; we worshiped Dad. But the experience also left us with role models— people we aspired to be but could never really match. Despite being surrounded by all these gifted skiers, we realized probably more than most the disparity that existed between the true greats of the sport and all the rest. Later in life when the terms "pro" and "world class" were thrown around for any substance of success, we often found ourselves cringing. Those were terms used for Olympians, major league athletes, and the likes. The notion that one of these world-class athletes was in the Hall of Fame took the concept of world class to the ultimate level. Steve and I grew up knowing who had made it, and we were in awe of these world-class athletes. Ski mountaineering was not remotely, in our minds, part of the plot.

The nature of this upbringing combined with the nature of how a young person perceives the world through life's experiences allowed us to get on with our lives and appreciate these things for what they were but also to leave them behind. As we aged and gained life experience, we detached from sports and competition like all people do and set out to make our lives. In that process, however, it also opened the doors to other passions and experiences. For us, ski mountaineering provided an avenue to see what lay beyond the next ridge, then the next peak, and so on and so on. Skiing was always at the heart of it, but with no goals or ambition, the driving force was the enormous fun and satisfaction that came with literally getting away from life.

But we did bring along all the attributes we learned trying to aspire to the greats; we were tireless with our training. It became a passion. We put that effort into pushing ourselves farther and farther into the backcountry. We wanted to experience the great outdoors, and our penchant for training allowed us to pursue more peaks and places. That developed into a passion to complete one adventure and wonder what we could do on the next. The paths of our lives to earn a living played a role because it generated financial and personal freedom to do what we wanted. It all played into a progression of sorts that allowed us to create our own lives, which were enhanced by growing up with great skiers who were also role models. They taught us by example what it takes to be successful without us even realizing it.

Shortly before my father passed away, and several years after our initial achievements skiing the highest peaks in the world, he passed on some of his last words of wisdom. He said that we all are provided gifts. "Some obtain the gift to hit a fastball out of Yankee Stadium. Others the gift to ski race in an Olympic Games. You guys were given the gifts that allowed you to excel at skiing where not many people have or can. But the key in life is to understand that often for so many, their gift is something they never realize. They perceive themselves as ordinary, and they give up on life. They never find their gift. You guys were given the gift of passion. Through that passion you found all the other physical and mental gifts that allowed you guys to accomplish what so few others have. In turn, that has allowed you guys to create lives on your own terms—how you want to live, doing what you truly want to. At the end of the day, how we realize the gifts presented is all that matters. The battle is to find them and to never give up until you know you have."

As I write this, I am a year into the process of being inducted into the USA National Ski and Snowboard Hall of Fame. In fact, in a week Steve and I will experience the final aspect of the process with an enshrinement ceremony. Yet for us, we still don't perceive ourselves to be world class or even of the caliber we find ourselves surrounded by in the process. It's humbling to say the least and difficult to comprehend at best. We didn't ask for it, or remotely anticipate it. The application process was awkward for us to accept—that others thought how they did about what we had accomplished. And it's not that we question the accomplishment either. We don't. We know what we did, and we are extremely proud and thankful. So, the process has generated more questions than answers, and we are left to humbly accept the accolade, which we will do proudly. But this is where things have become clear in my mind.

1

Growing Up in Aspen

July 4, 1976—5:00 a.m.

"Wake up, guys. You need to get some breakfast, and we need to get moving."

My identical twin brother, Steve, and I shared the same room, and Dad was eager to start the day. I heard him walk down the hall to get our older brother, Roger, out of bed. Getting up was the last thing I wanted to do, but then I remembered that the night before we had loaded up the Ford LTD station wagon with all our ski gear. We were going skiing!

Just the day before we had been on the baseball field playing ball in sunny, eighty-degree weather, so reconciling that with the notion of going skiing was hard. I sat up, not having a clue what to expect, but the excitement in Dad's voice made me realize I needed to move.

At the dinner table the night before, Dad had brought up the idea of heading up Independence Pass, which reaches twelve thousand feet at the Continental Divide twenty miles east of Aspen. The peaks were a small hike off the road and had snowfields that would allow us to ski during the height of summer. The specific run we were headed for even had a name—Fourth of July Bowl—and that alone was enough to get us excited. Strong mountain winds would blow winter snow off a nearby ridge, coating the bowl with snow that would last until July and allow us to ski the hard, smooth corn—an icy form of snow—from about thirteen thousand feet to around eleven thousand feet throughout the summer. For a handful of local skiers, skiing the run as late as its namesake was, and remains, a tradition—the last gasp of the ski season, which in Aspen ends each year in mid-April.

Dad made it clear that we needed to "fuel up." At 5:00 a.m., eating was the last thing we felt like doing, but he insisted. We choked down our cereal, gulped down an extra glass of water, and headed to the car, where we promptly returned to sleep. With the headlights on, Dad steered the vehicle east. After a forty-five-minute drive, the car stopped and Dad said, "Okay, guys. Let's go skiing."

I will never forget getting out of the car as Dad started to unpack the skis. The sky was a soft blue with the horizon toward the sun taking on a magenta hue. We gazed at it for what seemed like the first time. This was the first moment of many that would become a large part of my passion to climb and ski.

I have vivid memories as a toddler of the hard blue sky, the bright white snow, and the contrast of the green pine trees while skiing in the winter. But nothing compared to what I was looking at standing beside the car that day. The entire Rocky Mountain range seemed to fan out below us. Most twelve-year-old boys are more concerned with playing baseball or eating pizza than the great outdoors, but that moment stands out in my memory as my first realization of the extent of God's great natural world. The quiet of the morning, the crisp cold biting my cheeks, and this vast panorama took my breath away. Dad shouldered his skis and directed us toward the high hills that rolled gently upward. At just over twelve thousand feet, with the cold seeping into our ski boots, we started the slow march onward and upward, experiencing altitude for the first time.

As I walked, I felt the skis dig into my shoulder. This was the first time I'd had to carry my skis for any length of time. I felt slow. Dad kept saying, "Take your time, guys. We are higher than home, and the air is thinner." This didn't register with me as I had no concept of altitude and its effects, but I noticed I felt oddly weak. My excitement forced me to walk faster than normal, faster than I should have been walking, and Dad's warning was more of an annoyance to me than sound advice. Dad took the lead to slow us down, and soon I found myself in what I would later know as the climber's trance—a meditative state of mind that people achieve when exercising in the great outdoors. My mind wandered as I looked for the next place to put my foot, and we all found a rhythm. There was not a lot of looking around—just walking, following my brother who was a couple of steps ahead of me. The discomfort I felt at first faded with the proper pace, and methodically, we marched higher.

After a half hour, we arrived at a high spot. The sun was not yet cresting the horizon, and Dad told us we needed to sit down and rest. He pulled a canteen of water out of the backpack he was carrying. It was still cold, and the last thing we all felt like doing was drinking, but he insisted. He explained, "We are high, guys, and when you are exerting yourselves up here, water will make you feel much better. We need to wait a few minutes for the sun to warm up the slope." He then gave us our first lesson on backcountry skiing. He told us that the slope was very steep. As we looked down, the slope rolled over, and all we could see was the road far below. "We need to wait for the sun to melt the hard snow, so we have softer conditions. When you get to the roll, I want you guys to stop. You can't afford to fall here because if you do, you will slide down the slope into the rocks and get hurt. So, go slow and be careful."

This didn't register in our young minds at all. All we wanted to do was ski. The slope was glass smooth, and while we were hanging out waiting for the sun, looking over the Elk Range to the west, Dad started to point out the various peaks. He pointed out Castle Peak on the horizon and said if we liked what we were doing that day, we would head up to Castle Peak next week. I didn't think about it at the time but looking out over the peaks made a big impression. Sitting there waiting, talking with Dad and my brothers, was my first taste of mountain camaraderie. Only later would I really appreciate it; at the time, I just remember it being a lot of fun.

Suddenly, the sun came through the peaks to the east, and its warmth was immediate. We watched the sun gradually light up the tips of all the peaks, bringing an odd sensation of pure pleasure. Dad commented, "Just think, boys: Aspen is still in the dark, and Mom and Marlis (our sister) are still sleeping." This just clicked in my head, and I knew I didn't want to be anyplace else! Even today, forty years later, that is one of the most vivid memories I have. As the sun continued to illuminate the slope below us, Dad got up and told us to get our skis on. "Be careful, guys. Don't lose your skis here." We stood ready to go for a few moments, and then Dad took off toward the lip of the face and stopped. Our legs were stiff from the walk and sitting. We all had to find our ski legs on the gentle slope, since it had been months since we last skied. We all stopped at the lip and looked down at the slope below. It was steep, smooth, and by this time had a thin layer of soft snow. Roger took off as if he had just skied off the ramp of the ski lift and arced in beautiful turns down the face. Steve followed, and when he made a few turns, I followed. Dad waited for us to get off the steep section.

My skis bit into the soft, smooth snow, and I let out a whoop that could not be contained. The warnings about being careful disappeared completely, and I focused on the effortless nature of skiing on perfect corn snow. It was beyond my wildest imagination. We had experienced corn snow on Aspen Mountain during the closing months of the ski season, but we had never experienced corn snow this smooth and consistent. We watched Dad and just started laughing. This was the greatest thing any of us had ever done!

We skied the final slopes to the rocks. Near the bottom of the snowfield, the snow was rough and sun cupped, forcing us to slow down. Dad found a snow bridge that we skied over to cross the river, and we hiked back to the highway where he thumbed a ride from a passing vehicle back to our car at the top. Mom and Dad had told us to never hitchhike and to never get into a stranger's car, so this struck us as odd.

The three of us sat there waiting and relishing our first taste of ski mountaineering. There were no other skiers up there, and to be standing on the side of the road with skis and ski boots was an enormous point of pride. We gazed at our tracks in amazement at what we had just done, and we could barely contain our excitement. We wanted to do more. Soon Dad arrived, and we loaded up. We wanted to do another run, but Dad gave us another lesson in backcountry awareness. He said that once the sun hits the slopes, you have a small window of time before the snow gets too soft. When it gets too soft, you must be careful about it sliding. Avalanche danger was something he drilled into us when it snowed heavily, but this was the first time we realized that avalanches were something to be aware of on any slopes at any time of the season. Again, at age twelve, it didn't really register. Later I would come to understand what he was talking about.

As we drove home, our excitement was huge. The term "backcountry skiing" had not yet been coined, and we had never heard of "ski mountaineering"; for us, it was just "skiing." We wouldn't come to terms with those concepts for another decade. We were just kids that loved to ski, and this experience offered us a way of extending the ski season. It also planted a seed for everything that would come in the following decades. All we knew was that we wanted to do this kind of skiing more. A lot more.

We would head up to Fourth of July bowl a few more times that summer, but Dad also started to take us up to Montezuma Basin, a cirque in the Castle Peak massif that he had pointed out on that first day. We had a 1948 Willys Jeep, and we would pile into that and drive the rough roads to Montezuma Basin, which boasted a permanent snowfield at about twelve thousand feet and where Dad had a ski racing camp in the mid-'60s. We spent hours hiking up the snowfield and skiing down for the half dozen or so summers that followed—until we had driver's licenses and could go whenever we wanted. Dad often joined us, and along with teaching us the basic skills needed to climb and ski safely, he taught us how to drive the Jeep without rolling it. The inherent dangers of everything, from the driving to the climbing and skiing—including discussions about avalanches, rock fall, and falling—were always on our minds. Beyond the passion that we were developing, these forays provided a basic platform about how dangerous this stuff really was, a notion that we would carry with us in later years. We developed an ability to look ahead and to anticipate the dangers that came with being in the backcountry. We started to analyze the weather, the timeframes, and the conditions in general. Through trial and error, we developed a deep respect for how powerful and unforgiving the mountains really were.

Our lifelong buddy John Callahan was always part of the equation, and his father would tell us stories of his experiences as a mountain rescuer. He was constantly telling us: "Not one of the bodies I hauled out of these mountains set out thinking they were going to die." He told us horrific stories of his work and gave us examples of the consequences of not taking the mountains seriously. Bluntly, he scared the hell out of us. But both our father and John's also encouraged us with our newly found passion and told us that with care, we could really have a great time. In retrospect, by starting out doing this stuff as youngsters, we had the opportunity to be exposed to the power of nature and the mountains that can only be attained by growing up in the mountains.

When you grow up in Aspen, you start out with a big advantage toward respecting nature and the mountains. It begins with the outdoor education program that has been part of the public schools since 1967. When kids enter eighth grade at Aspen Middle School, outdoor education is required, and students participate in what has become one of the longest-running public school outdoor education systems in the world. The program starts with a three-day hike from Aspen over the Elk Range to a base camp high above the town of Marble, Colorado. Outward Bound established a climbing school in Marble in 1962. Teachers and climbers from the community meet the students, and the kids spend the week learning rock climbing, basic survival skills, team building, and all about the local ecology. You can talk to anyone who ever went through the program, and they will almost always tell you the week was one highlight, if not *the* highlight, of his or her youth. It changes everyone who goes through it.

The program includes a solo night in the woods, often the first time that students have been completely alone. No food, no company, not even any books—just a pencil and paper to record your feelings, and twenty-four hours of pure nature that humbles anyone who experiences it. For most eighth-graders, it's a scary proposition. It was for me. But it was also the first time that I really connected myself to the mountains, and it made me realize how small and insignificant I am. It taught me how few things one needs to survive in a world that is filled with seemingly endless distractions from what is real. As I gazed out across the valley, I saw how beautiful the world really is, but I also experienced the fear of being alone in an environment that really didn't care about me or my well-being.

We learned the basics of rock climbing, including how to tie a bowline with one hand. The skill to safely belay instilled in us an appreciation of our mates. Eventually, everyone graduates to a massive 150-foot-high and overhanging rappel. A rope course involves getting your team over a twelve-foot wall without aids. Walking through a cube-shaped spider's web of line without touching the ropes is an extreme test reminiscent of the game Twister. In all, the program is designed to make you understand that you can't climb alone and to appreciate your friends as resources. Often a meek or loner kid would rise to the top, and it showed everyone how little we know about each other as human beings because we don't take the time to incorporate everyone into our lives.

This was my first lesson in what it means to be humble. But it was also a very critical point of reference that I would take with me for the rest of my life. While the experience registered as remarkable for anyone who went through it, for a handful, it was a launching pad to follow our passions in the mountains. Looking back, it was the combination of camaraderie, team building, and technical skills that gave us the ability to appreciate and deal with all that the natural world offers. Everything we learned was pointed toward the reality that the big, wonderful, great outdoors was poised to bitch-slap the crap out of us if we didn't take it seriously. We were simultaneously learning to respect nature and how to deal with it. For my brothers and me and our friends, it became a prescription for more. In the mind of an eighth-grader, the message was simple: "Take this nature stuff seriously, or it will kill you dead, and here's how to stay alive … and enjoy it. This is your world. Respect it."

Even with the environment and culture in place, growing up in Aspen for my brothers and me was enhanced by the influence of our father. Not only was he the initial catalyst to take us out into the mountains, Dad was our hero. He grew up in a much different Aspen than we did. As a kid, school was almost secondary. In the 1920s, his father and uncles purchased what today is the municipal golf course for pennies, and through the late '50s, operated the Marolt-Holden ranch. They raised cattle and farmed potatoes. Life on the ranch was hard.

As a toddler, Dad started working on the ranch picking the main crop—potatoes. As he grew up, he took on all the normal duties of a working ranch hand, and he hated every moment of it. At that time, the glory days of Aspen and the silver rush were a distant memory, and skiing was not yet an industry. I remember my great-uncle, Steve Marolt, describing Aspen as a prison. There wasn't a whole lot going on for adults or kids, and even ranching offered barely enough money to eke out a living.

To my father's last breath, he couldn't look at a trout, and eating anything other than beef was never an option. When I was a kid, my family couldn't afford to slaughter our own cattle, much less buy it at the grocery store. We relied on hunting and fishing to put food on the table. We were typical meat-and-potatoes ranchers and ate literally what we shot. So, as an adult, Dad wanted nothing to do with hunting or fishing. He hated the "game" taste and had butchered enough wild animals to resign himself to the fact that the world was a better place with wild animals living in the forest.

I vividly remember one family meal where a neighbor brought over a handful of trout. When mom put them on the table, Dad politely excused himself—the only time we ever witnessed such a thing. The moment was augmented by the fact that my mother dropped an F-bomb—the only time I ever heard her do so—when she suggested, "Cook your own fucking dinner next time!" Clearly, trout was never going to be on the table again.

As my great-uncle told me, "Aspen was a damn tough place to earn a living, Mikey," and the kids of my father's generation were hell-bent to get out. However, by the 1930s Aspen wasn't totally awful for the first generation of skiers. Pioneers like André Roch, a Swiss mountaineer and skier, were engaged by the US Army to train troops in winter warfare. Roch and other European skiers and mountaineers trained their protégés just over the mountains from Aspen, at Camp Hale near Leadville. They brought the latest skiing technology with them and, before long, discovered Aspen. Roche even cut one of the first runs on Aspen Mountain in 1946.

My father's uncles and aunts were soon making their own skis from slats of wood pilfered from abandoned buildings around town, screwing on metal edges, and utilizing seal-skin pelts in what amounted to the first generation of backcountry skis. They set out and climbed and skied all the nearby peaks. They would drive their old Jeeps on the mining roads and take turns ferrying each other up to ski Colorado powder. Before long, they built a rope tow on the face of Aspen Mountain. They ran cables up the mountain in huge loops and attached sleds resembling boats; then they took an engine and a wheel out of someone's Jeep to pull the sleds full of people and skis up the mountain. Organized skiing had arrived. The technology developed, new lifts were installed, and by 1950 Aspen reached its zenith in North American skiing when they hosted the FIS (Fédération Internationale de Ski) World Championships.

Beguiled by the new sport, Dad and his brothers started skiing for the same reasons anyone does—it's fun! As the area developed, they started racing and, as he said, just messing around. There was nothing else to do, and skiing was a diversion. When the World Championships hit the slopes, the lights went on for the kids. There were men and women in town from distant places where they spoke funny languages, and skiing was their platform. In their young minds, skiing became literally the only way out.

At the age of twelve, Dad was an obvious potential athlete for future FIS races, and skiing became all he wanted to do. Every day that there was snow on Aspen Mountain, from sunup to sundown, Dad was out skiing. He missed work, he ditched school, and he made his relatives mad. Despite the success of the world championships, for the locals, skiing was still perceived as a passing fad. Dad's mother and father soon realized that there wasn't a whole lot they could do to change my father's mind, and as the training and hours manifested themselves in his talents, they slowly came to understand what he did. Maybe this kid can get out of here with this nonsense, they figured. So, they supported and encouraged Dad and did everything in their power to help him. And it paid off.

By 1953, Dad had made the list for the US Ski Team and was on the road, ski-racing full time. His travels were mostly in the States, as the team didn't have a lot of money, but by the end of that year, they told him that he would be headed to Europe to compete with the best in the world—"if you can find the money to go." Dad went door to door in Aspen to tell the community of his situation and slowly raised what he needed. By this time, Aspen was on the map as a world-class ski resort, and people were coming to town to see what the place offered. So, while many of the old locals were hesitant, there were enough "skiers" in town to appreciate what was available, and they saw the vision of Aspen's first generation of ski racers as a tool for promotion.

By 1954, Dad was well established with the US Ski Team and was named to the Olympic team. An injury kept Dad out of the races, but ambition fueled his efforts to train and go for the next round. In 1960, Dad headed off to Squaw Valley for the Olympic Games. By this time, even the old locals were sold that skiing was for real. Aspen was a quickly growing ski resort. Property prices rose, and money talked. The Marolt brothers had by then sold the ranch for what at the time was a big pile of money—a whopping $157,000. Today, it would be worth a hundred million, but back then that was an enormous amount of money. Everyone was happy. Skiing was, in fact, a way out in more ways than my father and his contemporaries ever imagined.

Dad continued to ski race through the early '60s, and he eventually retired from racing, but he kept his foot in the door as a coach, as a promoter of the sport, and as a gear rep. But in the process, he became a local legend. He was the first native-born kid to ski in an Olympic Games—his brother Bill was the second—and when combined with Aspen becoming the center of skiing in North America, he was a bit of a rock star. The family name became a recognizable institution of American skiing.

My sister was born in 1961, and then came Roger in 1962. Steve and I, twins, were born in 1964. By then the rock star was a full-fledged father and husband. He was constantly on the road with his ski business, which for the winter season made mom a saintly single parent, but when he was home, Dad was our hero. Flat-out, we grew up in the shadow of a man that we wanted to be like. We worshiped him. Dad also had a strong connection with young people in general and knew all the kids in town by their first names. Our friends were just as in awe of him as we were. And in winter, life in Aspen was about skiing. Dad would take the family out to Highlands Ski Area, and we would ski. He loved to ski with the family, but he also loved skiing by himself. We would ski all morning, but afternoons were his time. When I would get tired and cranky, suddenly there'd be a big arm wrapped around me. I'd look over to see Steve or Roger under the other arm, and we were off. Dad would pick us up and carry us under his arms to the bottom of the slope—it was as much fun as the skiing. He'd drop us off at the ski hill day care and say he'd see us in an hour.

As we grew older and set off to ski with our friends, we'd always run into Dad, and we would all stop and watch in wonder at his grace on skis. He skied with his legs together, with power and speed that even later in his life held strong. Dad was an amazing skier. He loved the steeps and bumps and often told us that "if you can't ski bumps and crud, you can't really ski." This mantra has followed us with our skiing to this day, and it is a huge part of why we love skiing the highest peaks. The higher you go, the worse the snow gets, but I know Dad's insistence that we learn to love tough conditions has followed us ever since. The days of swooping us up under his arms declined as we got better at skiing, and a life of skiing was set.

Dad obviously had a huge influence on our careers, which started that day on Independence Pass. But Dad was not a dominating father and in fact realized better than we did at that time that we were growing up in a shadow of a great skier in the mecca of American ski towns; he understood this could cause a distraction for us. While we skied often with Dad as kids, as we grew older, it didn't go unnoticed that he never once went to one of our ski races. He encouraged us, supplied us with all the gear imaginable from his work as a ski industry representative, and would train with us from time to time, but he was steadfast in never watching us race or critically talking about how we skied beyond general comments of how to be smooth and fast. Taking us up to ski that day was simply his way of sharing his passion for skiing, and it allowed him to pass that passion on without the tick of a clock or pressure. Had we not reacted to that day the way we did, it would have simply ended then and there with a fun day in the mountains as a family. For us, however, the fire was lit!

We ski-raced through our high school years, which amplified our passion and ability to ski, but the whole time, it was always about just skiing. As Dad introduced us to climbing to access our skiing, we also came to love the physical aspects of "earning our turns"—a term that wouldn't become common for years. In high school, we would train after school, but it was always after the lifts had closed. We had to hike for our training, something that we had no choice about, and it was an aspect of development that most of the kids dreaded. Not Steve and me. We would shoulder our skis and lap our teammates to try and get in a couple more runs than everyone else. Our coaches often joked that if we could ski down relative to how we hiked up, we'd be world champions. It wasn't so much that we liked hiking; rather, it was simple reality. We were limited by daylight, and the faster we hiked, the more skiing we could get in. This often irritated the coaches who would freeze while standing around watching and coaching, but they respected our efforts so much that they would stay around long after most kids had headed home just so we could get in one more run. By the end of a winter, we'd be in the best shape of our lives, allowing us to hike and ski well into the summer. With the introduction provided by Dad to the backcountry and our driver's licenses, we were constantly heading up into the mountains.

Our desire to ski was originally limited to the spots we were familiar with—Independence Pass and Montezuma Basin, for example. They were close and had guaranteed skiing, but we didn't comprehend the vastness beyond these slopes. Over time, however, we started to notice what was around us. One afternoon, we climbed to the top of the headwall of Montezuma Basin, and while taking a break, someone mentioned the top of Castle Peak, a nearby fourteen-thousand-foot mountain that we could see from Montezuma. Suddenly, the lights went on. There was no skiing off the peak at that time of year, but we wanted to see what the view was like.

The concept of climbing one of Colorado's fifty-four fourteen-thousand-foot peaks, or "fourteeners," was not part of Colorado pop culture as it is today, and for us, our field of vision was limited to only what we knew and enjoyed—skiing. We didn't even know how many fourteeners there were. But that day, we had to check this one out.

We secured our skis in a small bergschrund where the snow met the rock, and in our alpine ski boots, we started to climb. The summit became a magnet of sorts that pulled us upward. Walking on the rock was awkward, and the going was slow. We had no concept of time other than the impression that we were going terribly slow; the peak didn't seem to be getting any closer. But a funny thing happened. As we crested to the top of a small col, the view to the west came into sight, and with it, an excitement that I can feel even here writing this.

Before us was the Western Slope of the Colorado Rockies, and beyond, the vast landscape of the western desert. Our field of vision was entirely unobstructed, and we noticed the slight curve of the earth. We'd never seen anything like it, and for the first time in our lives, we were struck with summit fever. As we climbed the steep and rough ridge, we also had a view of the side we had climbed. Looking down at the Jeep in the valley far below, we had our first real sense of accomplishment; the Jeep was a tiny dot. We could see our tracks in the snow leading all the way up mountain, with the entire range as a backdrop. Our adrenaline spiked, and we climbed in a trance-like state to the top. Almost racing, we clicked into high gear. Suddenly we found ourselves standing on the summit with no more mountain to climb. We stood looking in all directions as far as our eyes could see. It is not an overstatement to say that at that moment, climbing had become part of our physiological and spiritual fiber.

The magnitude of what we experienced that day could not be overlooked or underappreciated. Since the beginning of time—since the first time a human climbed a mountain—there has always been an ambiguous sense of purpose and meaning that is burned into your mind as you take your first steps to that tiny chunk of earth called "the summit." From a modern climbing perspective, people have experienced what I refer to as summit fever as far back as 1492, when Antoine De Ville and a team mounted the first organized attempt to climb a high peak in the French Alps. Their big climb was Mont Aiguille in France.

But the act of mountaineering has been around—and evident— for thousands of years. In biblical terms, mountains were regarded as special places where man would go to get away from society and bridge the gap between the physical world and God. Jewish prophets including Moses climbed. Christ himself took to the mountains more than a few times. Greek mythology uses Mount Olympus as the penultimate sacred place and focal point of life's journey. Often not included in the history is the Inca contribution of the late 1300s. The Incas developed climbing shoes made from cotton and hemp as well as climbing tools made from sticks and rocks to help them achieve summits throughout the Andes, summits that they used for human sacrifice. A definitive yet ambiguous connection exists between mountains and spirituality. Whether figuratively or actually, world history is dotted with examples in which mountains are a place to go to get closer to God and to find oneself. But that history includes a few men climbing mountains for unknown reasons and documentation that leaves modern archeologists pondering unanswerable questions.

I believe that mountains are simply not a place where human beings are designed to be. But with enough effort and a bit of planning, they are places humans can go. The process of wondering, and then acting, and the fact that something so useless in practical terms is so satisfying in spiritual terms, are almost impossible to describe to most people that have never climbed. But I also think that the same reasons Moses and Christ set off to the mountains is applicable. Because these mountain places are so practically useless and difficult to attain, people that choose to experience them are almost guaranteed a place to be alone. Mountains distill the human experience to the bare necessities—just like our eighth-grade overnighters in the woods.

You need the clothes on your back and a bit of food (enough to just get up the peak), and at the end of the process you are left with a feeling of being a tiny nothing in the grand scheme of things. The vistas, the effort, the solitude, and the mass beneath you add up to a feeling of utter insignificance. When you find yourself standing on the precipice, even if you're not cognizant of it, you are standing in a place that has existed for millions if not billions of years and taken on all the beauty and harshness of nature relatively unchanged. When you experience the exertion of getting to that place, the magnitude of the energy, the disparity of time, and the wonder of nature—even if subconsciously—leaves you humbled. Without going to the tops of the mountains or the middles of the oceans or any of these wild places, it's difficult to be humbled like that. So, the feeling you are left with is somewhat ambiguous, but it gets burned into your very fiber. The feeling is like a drug, leaving a climber wanting more.

We stood on the top of Castle Peak in pure amazement. The normal buzz and hum of activity while we clicked into our skis was gone. Everything was quiet. I don't say this lightly, but the events of the day, the location, the view, and the realization of what we'd done all had a massive impact on us. To that point, it had always and only been about skiing. I'd go so far as to say the climbing, while exhilarating, was a means to an end, often accepted as an unfortunate reality. To that point, we often discussed how incredible it would have been to be up there when Dad had his rope tow running. At one point we even explored the possibility of putting another one in, but that day, we understood the power of climbing. This was a critical point in our young lives; it opened the door to the vastness of what we could do. Again, without even knowing it at the time, climbing had become a ticket to go wherever we wanted, to do whatever we wanted, and to do it nearly whenever we wanted—plus, we had the entire Elk Range as our playground. Our eyes and hearts were opened to unlimited places, but more importantly, they were opened to an experience that fueled the roots of what would become our lives' passion.

Our enthusiasm must have been something for Dad to witness as we talked endlessly about our day. In his mentoring way, he carefully reeled us in so we wouldn't let our excitement get the better of us. He encouraged us in the direction we were headed, but he always tempered it with the overreaching theme that we were entering into a vast wilderness that had a zillion ways of killing us. I look back at his excitement for us and marvel at his unique ability to balance our enthusiasm with the realities of how dangerous the mountains were. More importantly, though, he showed us how with a thoughtful and reasonable approach, they could become an incredible source of joy, beauty, and endless fun.

When we spoke of the possibility of putting in another rope tow, Dad kind of laughed in a mild way we never understood and suggested that the idea was not only not possible but not a good idea. After standing on Castle Peak, we started to understand his lack of enthusiasm. Along with our first sense of freedom in the hills, we also got our first sense of the fragile ecology. We didn't just give up on the notion of the rope tow, we found ourselves practically and factually knowing we didn't need one. And more importantly, we started to see the mountains as a place where they didn't belong. The sense of accomplishment and the satisfaction of climbing for our skiing, combined with the notion of achieving a summit, established in our young minds the reality that there was more to life in the mountains than just the skiing.

In a sense, there was a reward for the hard exertion involved with the climb, but for us it created something that just skiing doesn't offer. There is no arguing that skiing is fun. The great outdoors, the wind in your face, and the pure rush of controlling a free fall down a mountain has created an industry with equipment and amenities that appeals to millions of people. But when you climb what you ski, you develop an appreciation for the energy that is displaced, especially when you click into your skis and point them downhill. You understand, even if only subconsciously, how remarkable it truly is to ski. When you climb a peak, make the effort to carry your gear, put one foot in front of the other, and consider the enormous exertion expended, you appreciate the few minutes of skiing it generates in a way that you wouldn't otherwise appreciate. So not surprisingly, now when I look at lifts taking people to the top of a ski resort, I look at that differently, marveling at the power of the motors.

One expression coined in the 1970s by the first modern backcountry skiers was "earn your turns." This is a skiing metaphor that means that you get out of life what you put into it. It's one of those messages that we hear often in sports, in motivational books, and in lectures, from our parents and mentors, and so on— from people who have experienced the notion. No one would ever argue the concept to be nonsense, but until you experience it, it generally goes in one ear and out the other. For skiers, the concept is something of an afterthought. Skiing is intrinsically so much fun that, initially, as was the case for us, the only time we would ever consider climbing with all our gear would be where there was simply no alternative. In today's culture of health and awareness, there is an incentive for hiking uphill. But a funny thing happens to people who decide to pick up their gear and take the first step. As was the case for us on Independence Pass, and on countless days after that, including the moments we spent on top of Castle Peak, the act of "earning your turns" became something desirable.

I have described what happened to us in detail, but the reality is, again, that you get out of life what you put into it. All this needs to be put into context. To that point, our love of skiing was developed with little or no hiking, and as I have described, hiking for skiing was seen as an inconvenience more than anything of value. But by progressing slowly, all the hiking—all our initial backcountry activity as well as our hiking after school "for a couple more runs"—contributed to something that, for lack of a better term, was just better. While the initial reward was simply skiing, hiking led us to new places, new ways of looking at what we loved, and new feelings of accomplishment. In short, we experienced what it really means to get out of life what you put into it. The difference between being at the stage where you think you know that "you get out of life what you put into it" and actually experiencing it is obvious by what the actual experience does to a person.

We did come to realize that there were men out there doing this in our town—guys like Lou Dawson, Fritz Stammberger, Chris Landry, and a handful of others—but the activity still didn't register as anything other than a tremendous amount of fun. I remember reading about these men who were out skiing the backcountry, and in 1980 an article was published in *Sports Illustrated* on backcountry skiing, specifically on a guy, Chris Landry, who skied a peak we were very familiar with—Pyramid Peak. I had heard of the man and knew that he lived in Aspen. As I read the article, there was no relating it to what we had experienced in our initial pursuit of skiing the local peaks. The article referred to the notion of "extreme skiing," something we had never heard, and by reading about it, we decided the activity had been well named. Pyramid Peak is a fourteen-thousand-foot peak that I could see from my back yard. While I still had no concept of altitude, the familiar look of the peak and the article struck a chord. It is definitely a pyramid-shaped mountain. It is massive and, practically speaking, vertical. At the time, it was simply not something many if any people would have considered a ski peak. Also in the article, Chris was quoted as saying, "If you fall, you die"—putting a term to a concept that was obvious but never conceptualized in words like that. Ironically, the article was not a source of inspiration, but rather a testament to stupidity. Our limited experience and background, as I've mentioned, was enough to give us a healthy respect for the backcountry, but this article was about such an outlandish form of skiing that there was no reconciliation of what Chris had done with what we had experienced. Immediately, these men were not a source of inspiration but rather examples of everything we had no intention of emulating. Later in life, after getting to know these guys, they would admit that they felt like the dregs of the ski world. They were greatly underappreciated, totally misunderstood, and often publicly chastised for lacking even basic ski skills and common sense. As teenagers growing up in the shadow of an Olympian, in a ski town that was put on the map via ski racing, this was simply not real skiing, and these guys were perceived as reckless hippies with little athleticism or experience to understand what they didn't know. Little did we or anyone we knew understand how things would change. These guys were breaking trail for not only us but for a completely new breed of ski mountaineers.

For my brothers and me, and our buddies, life went on. We passed the time like normal kids, messing around in the local rivers, playing golf, and enjoying our first passion—baseball. Our homes were in the vicinity of the municipal golf course, and we spent countless hours playing golf but also shagging fly balls and playing catch on the seventh hole. We all came from good middle-class families, we were above average students for the most part, and we did everything together. The Marolt brothers and the Callahan brothers and Jimmy Gile grew up in houses within shouting distance of each other, all of us figuring out life in Aspen. But Aspen in the 1970s and '80s was not what it is today. Aspen was an adult playground not entirely conducive to kid activities. It was a cosmopolitan town trying to define itself with a superior culture, and money talked. Consequently, we didn't have what we have today: a $300 million school campus and a curriculum that included thirty-plus athletic sports to choose from. If you were an athlete, you had skiing, the basic ball sports, and hockey. The sports had limited seasons, and when they were over, you waited for the next season to start. There were no youth centers or recreation facilities whatsoever. It was all we knew, and the upside to life as a teen in the valley was that it forced us to get creative with our time outside of the sports we played. We were constantly outside looking for things to do. With this newly established "backcountry skiing," we found something we could do all year. Montezuma Basin had a miniglacier that never melted, so while we were limited in where we could ski from late summer into fall, it was still skiing, and it was fun.

Long before any of us could drive, Dad had purchased an old 1948 Willys Jeep. He completely overhauled it and created what would become "the kids' car." Callahan had a Willys, and between the two old rigs, we had enough capacity to load everyone and their gear into them and head for the hills. We never had enough money to buy tops, so they were basically four-wheel-drive dune buggies. Anyone who has ever owned an old Willys Jeep knows that while they are in running condition, they will take you anywhere, and the engineering involved in the creation of these vehicles is minimal. They were designed literally overnight in the early 1940s for the war effort, and in the beginning, an entire Jeep could be manufactured and put together in less than a day. Between watching Dad work on ours and reading the bible for Jeep owners (Chilton's how-to book on Jeep maintenance), we became mechanics. We also had a great auto garage and class in high school, and we studied how to fix problems. During our high school years, our mother cringed at the loss of her garage; we were constantly jacking up the old Jeep and tinkering. Over the years, except for the engine block, we replaced every part on that bucket of bolts. We were all on a first-name basis with the owner of the local auto parts store, Del, an old and passionate Jeep owner himself. Old Del always had a part and advice as to solving problems—often with bailing wire and duct tape. We spent hours keeping our machines running—the incentive being the freedom they afforded us.

We all had summer jobs, which on recollection were almost exclusively to earn enough cash to pay for parts and gas. Dad was gracious enough to pay for the insurance, but everything else was up to us. The smaller problems were neglected or overcome with ingenuity. I can't recall a single old Jeep ever that had a working gas gauge, but all Jeeps had a bracket on the side for a military shovel. Our Jeep had a hockey stick handle that Steve thinned and cut to length to fit into that slot. It was used as a dipstick. The gas tank was located under the driver's seat, and we didn't even have to get out of the Jeep to check how much gas we had. Our old Willy's was our ticket to ride. We maintained it, and we cherished it.

The choice of gear for our mountain endeavors evolved through trial and error. When we started out, the concept of actual climbing gear was never considered. We used our alpine ski racing gear and shouldered our skis to climb steep slopes and couloirs. When it became too steep for comfort, we held a ski in each hand and jammed them into the snow for stability and a rudimentary belay. With no concept of crampons or axes, we hiked in our unbuckled alpine ski boots and kicked steps in the snow to ascend ridiculous slopes. But trial became error, and gradually we started looking for alternatives. During the fall season, the winter snow would consolidate into extremely hard ice, and we were exposed to long falls as we progressed onto steeper terrain. We found that if we took the packs off our frame backpacks, we could bungie the skis to the aluminum frames and carry our skis on our backs, thereby freeing up our hands. We would grab our ski poles near the baskets and use them as picks. But as our enthusiasm for the new terrain grew, so did the exposure.

A point of no return on one steep gully left us high on a face, and we realized our blunt ski boot toes would not penetrate the hard ice, even the snow, on less steep slopes. We'd kick our boots so hard that often by the end of the day we had black and blue toes. We learned quickly. I remember one instance where we climbed a steep face well beyond where we should have and found ourselves in a difficult situation. The snow was too hard to allow us to climb to the top. Balancing on just millimeters of the rounded plastic toes of our boots, we were not remotely stable enough to contemplate transitioning to our skis, and we immediately learned that climbing was a heck of a lot easier than descending. Kicking madly at the ice, we found ourselves in a panic to get to the lower slopes. We avoided disaster that day, but we ran from the mountain with our tails between our legs, scared crazy at the prospects of what could have gone wrong.

On another adventure, we started late in the day under a cover of cloud. We climbed for a couple of hours in deteriorating weather and found ourselves on a high ridge in a windy downpour with no protection. Thunder and lightning started crashing down all around us. Steve gestured toward an outcropping with his ski pole—possibly a place where we could find some protection— and as he swung around, his ski pole left a wave of sparks that made a whirring sound. Our exposed hair stood crazily on end, and our cotton hoodies left us shivering in the cold. We threw our skis and ski poles down the steep snow slope and literally dove off the peak, grabbing and throwing our gear down the hill away from us. We scurried to the bottom of the peak and back to the Jeeps, shivering from the cold and shaking from an experience that left us speechless. The rain continued, and with no top to protect us, we buried our heads in crossed arms and bent-over bodies trying to preserve what little heat we had left in us. It was a cold, wet, and miserable ride home.

We learned as we went, and slowly we were forced to rely on common sense to accommodate our desire for more. I am not sure why some of these experiences didn't force us to give up on the sport, but probably dumb luck more than anything became an inspiration for improvement. At the time, there were no gondolas or high-speed lifts in Aspen, and we reasoned that if we could manage to stay warm riding a lift for forty-five minutes in subzero weather to get our fix in the middle of winter, we should be able to figure out how to stay warm and dry in August in the backcountry. We started to use our general ski clothing on our adventures as well as common sense. Our outdoor education programs taught us what we needed, as well as basic dos and don'ts. Cotton was out, replaced with military wool cargo pants we got from our uncle, Bud Marolt, who was a climbing instructor for the Tenth Mountain Division military unit. Gore-Tex had not even been invented at the time, but we learned basic layering systems and armed ourselves with gear that would allow us to survive. We took the time to read about what other people were using. We found old backpacks to carry our gear. And we saved our pennies to buy new gear.

Callahan's father was one of the first members in the local mountain rescue group. Back then, the rescuers were members of the community who were drummed into action by a phone call from the local sheriff. These men had knowledge of the local mountains and valleys through their passions for hiking, hunting, and just getting out, but they were not professionally trained rescuers. Except for a handful of ski patrollers, these men were just good guys that had massive respect for the dangers of the mountains and empathy for those that didn't. Callahan's old man was a ski patroller, and like the others he parlayed the basic first aid and mountain training he got through his job to mountain rescue. Over the years there were a few plane crashes and other events out of the realm of self-inflicted mountain mistakes, but those were rare. Even back then, a lot of people ventured into the mountains, often underexperienced and underprepared. It seemed that Callahan's dad was always being called late at night to help. For the closer rescues, he often brought his sons to teach them. That invitation was never offered to my brothers and me, but we got the full and often horrific reports. I have memories of John Callahan describing pulling a body out of a river with a grappling hook and having to help his dad put the bloated and mangled body in a body bag. Another nightmare story told of how his father had to pick up the pieces of a body, including an eyeball and a hand of a climber who fell down a mountainside in a rock avalanche. And yet another told of how Callahan's dad had to take a body out of a body bag high on the North Maroon Peak and get in it himself to survive the night. It was too dark to descend, so he had to wait for a helicopter that came the next morning to pluck the body. The stories were seemingly endless and served as a sort of driver's education reel of horrific incidents that happen when you don't take the great outdoors seriously.

As the rescues continued over the years, the local mountain rescue team evolved with training, gear, and organization. More and more people were headed out, and there was a need. Along with that, Callahan's father obtained a few simple pieces of gear— rope, crampons, axes, helmets, and so on—that he shared with us. We took notes and saved our pennies so that we could start collecting our own gear. Looking back to the steep couloir event I mentioned earlier, it wasn't long after that event that we realized crampons and axes were necessary gear. But along with it, we had developed a serious respect for the mountains, and a downright fear for what they could throw at us.

Accordingly, we became satisfied with moderate adventures. This was long before the days of Kodak courage, and having fun was more the objective than impressing people. Even what we were doing was considered stupidity by most people, who had little or no comprehension of how much fun we were having, so we kept our adventures a secret. It was not a matter of pushing ourselves to our absolute limits; instead, it was just finding other places to climb and ski that fell within our parameters of fun and safe. We certainly pushed ourselves to farther, steeper, and more technical places, but any kind of progression was not a goal at all. With no incentive to the contrary, we were happy just experiencing the backcountry at a pace that was doable. The epics did continue to happen from time to time, but they were a source of learning what not to do more than a source of learning anything about ourselves. At the time, we had no grand dreams to climb and ski any farther away than a tank of gas in an old Jeep would take us, but we were filling up that tank every chance we could. The humble seeds of a pastime were planted and would grow into our lives' passion.

Our years in high school advanced, and soon Roger, Jim, and Callahan were off to college. Callahan went off to become an alpine ski racer in the Pacific Northwest. Jim went off to chase his dream to play hockey. Steve, Roger, and I followed our dreams to play baseball in California. None of us had a clue as to what we wanted to do, and college was just the next part of our lives. But looking back, the enjoyment we found with our climbing and skiing would follow us. Without knowing it at the time, the climbing and skiing had taught us that the adage "you get out of life what you put into it" was true. That mentality was burned into our subconscious minds through all those adventures, and we applied it to other aspects of our lives.

Callahan didn't become a World Cup alpine ski racer, but he was in such good shape from all the climbing that when his college ski team needed a cross-country skier for one of its carnival races, he agreed to participate. He not only tried; he won. Success inspired him to do more cross-country races, and in no time, he found himself with the US cross-country team in the Olympic Games in Albertville, France. Jim used the same drive and became the first person in the history of Aspen High School to make a Division I hockey team. Roger, Steve, and I were the first people from Aspen High School to play Division I baseball. Again, at the time, I had no idea how the climbing and skiing work ethic would translate to other areas. But today, looking back at what we achieved in other sports, without question, a strong work ethic and our ability to practice literally until it hurt was the key to our success. We realized being successful was a lot more fun than being mediocre. Consequently, we became trainaholics.

Often on Friday nights when everyone was partying, Steve and I would find ourselves up in the nearby hills surrounding our college, looking down on campus and wondering why we were so odd. We didn't mean to be odd, but we were. For a young guy in a college environment, this presented a problem. We were young and lacked confidence. We didn't want to be square pegs in circular holes, but something made it clear that what we were doing was right. We spent our free time in the weight room or out running the local hills. Steve was influenced by friends at home who found a new form of entertainment, mountain biking, and soon we were riding the local fire trails in the hills of northern California every chance we got. We did manage to get to Squaw Valley on occasion, but without a car or money, the trips were mostly school-sponsored bus trips. We'd ride along with the St. Mary's College Ski Club on Saturday mornings, but as soon as the bus came to a stop, we'd be off on our own for the day. We were met long after the lifts closed by drunken students who'd racked their skis by lunch, started drinking, and were having to wait for the Marolt brothers. The keg would run dry, and they'd be pissed—in both senses of the word. But after a few trips, they acknowledged our passion and planned accordingly by bringing another keg for the wait. All was good. Over the years, people began to respect us for what we were. In any California school, there is an admiration for the small group of people that surf. In a similar manner, we found respect for being hard-core skiers despite being in a school where mountains were a long way away, and skiing was a purely social activity.

After the school year ended, Callahan and Roger and Steve and I would meet at Mammoth Mountain Ski Area, and we would start our summers. We'd stop there for a week, and then, on the drive through Utah, we'd stop for another few days at Snowbird. Skiing was becoming a way of life, but these trips excited us for more. As we grew older, we kept pushing our climbing and skiing to new places and new peaks. But the leisure days of college were fleeting, and soon we found ourselves in the real world.

Steve and I started working for one of the Big Eight accounting firms in Oakland; Roger was doing the same in Denver. Callahan was pursuing his career as a cross-country ski racer. Life was exciting; we were making our way. I have vivid memories of running to the bank with my paycheck every month to make a deposit, pay my car loan and the rent, and transfer a small bit to a savings account. I had no idea what I was saving for, but we all lived on a shoestring. Dad always said, "Save as much as you can." Soon enough, I would realize the importance of saving.

One day in 1988, I was sitting at my office cubicle in a rare instance of not having any work, and my phone rang. My buddy William Herndon, who was working in Seattle, told me grand stories of hiking the lower slopes of Mount Rainier, and to my disbelief, suggested that that peak dwarfed anything we had in the mountains back home. He was finding a passion for the mountains later in life, and on Rainier. His almost weekly phone calls became irritating, but after a month or so a letter arrived. It included photos and a description of his ascent of the peak. My mind flashed back to a book that Steve and I had taken to show-and-tell at grade school. Jim Whittaker had given a copy of the book *Americans on Everest* to my father. It described the first American ascent of Everest in 1963. Back in the late '50s, Jim's and Dad's mutual success in the mountains had brought them together via business, and they had become good friends. Even before Steve and I could read, we gazed at the photos in the book and knew that was what we wanted to do—climb mountains. The ice-covered slopes, the technical gear, and the excitement of it all were enough to plant seeds that would later allow us to experience those things for ourselves.

When William's letter arrived, the photos of massive ice cliffs and ropes and gear was accompanied with a single line on a piece of notebook paper: "We need to plan a trip together to climb this peak!" I immediately called Steve. He had received the same letter at the same time, and we knew we had to make it happen. Our savings accounts were finally big enough. We booked air tickets and cashed checks so we had enough money to head to Seattle. At the REI shop there, we rented crampons, axes, and all the gear we needed. We had Mom ship us our boots, and we were ready.

Our first trip to Seattle was met with massive rain and too much snow on the peak to climb. We settled for a miserable camping trip that completely squelched our desire to come back. "Never again" seemed to become our epigram. But as we took off to go home and the plane broke through the thick clouds, we were greeted with a sun-bathed Rainier. We gazed at the peak in utter amazement. Any inclination of "never again" was dashed. As soon as we got home, we called William and said we were coming back. We saved our money—forgoing decent food and living on PB&Js and ramen noodles for weeks—and a month later found ourselves crammed into William's small compact car headed back up. This time, the weather was perfect.

As we made the hike to the first camp, Muir, the massive ice cliffs in front of us were so foreign, so beyond anything we had ever imagined, that fear quickly tempered our enthusiasm. We reached the camp and listened to other inexperienced climbers tell stories of massive difficulties and scary crevasses and imagined perfect snow slopes opening with no warning, plunging them into the darkness never to be found. William laughed and tried to calm us down, but there was no calming us down. We thought the worst and feared for our lives, and it was no fun at all.

We prepared for bed by rolling out our sleeping bags in the dirty hut. We had to be careful of where we set our packs down, paying attention to avoid piles of human shit, which only added to our inclination that this sucked. This enhanced our misery in a powerful way, and when the alarm sounded at 11:00 p.m., we jumped at the opportunity to get up and get out. As soon as our crampons hit the snow, and we had roped up and started moving, all our fears were gone. We climbed quickly, passing all the guided groups to the chagrin of even the guides. They told their clients, "Don't worry; they will burn out—never make it—hold your pace." This only served to fire us up, and we nearly ran up the peak. We found ourselves on top, tired but full of an excitement we had never experienced. We walked the summit rim to see the vistas with an enthusiasm that negated the exhaustion of going from sea level to over fourteen thousand feet in thirty-six hours.

As we descended, visions of Americans on Everest came back, and Steve planted the seeds of climbing a peak I had heard about but knew nothing of: "Boys, we need to go to Denali!" William kind of scoffed; I had no clue, but Steve kept talking about it—a mountain he'd seen in a book that said it was one of the most difficult mountains in the world. I was content with Rainier and basked in the glory of a climb that at first scared me but later left me as excited as I had ever been. However, as we descended the final snow slope back to camp, a nearby ice cliff fell apart, letting loose a massive avalanche that slapped me back to reality. Although it was still hundreds of yards away, Steve and I began to run down the mountain, only to be met by laughing guides who explained we were totally safe. The guides then proceeded to slap us on the back for our speedy ascent, exclaiming we "had what it took," and that we "should keep climbing." The avalanche was etched in my mind, but those words of encouragement after being chastised earlier that morning were enough to make me realize that this was what I wanted to do.

As I settled back into life in the city, I started buying climbing magazines and making weekly stops at the library to check out mountaineering books. I even took the time to read *Americans on Everest*. Steve and I were hooked! We would get back home to Aspen as often as our savings accounts would allow, driving to save money. We did a couple more trips to Rainier, bringing Callahan and Roger out to share in the excitement. As expected, they too became hooked, and the far-fetched idea of Denali was something we thought seriously about.

I eventually transferred within the CPA firm I was working for to the Denver office to get closer to home and the mountains. Roger was working in the same office, and we found an apartment in Lakewood, Colorado, that gave us easy access to the mountains. Roger and I spent weekends climbing and skiing Front Range peaks. Steve was still working in California, which was the first time he and I had been split up in life, but he continued to work on getting transferred as well. Our salaries slowly increased; the cost of living in Colorado was a lot cheaper than the Bay Area, and along with saving a few bucks for trips, we obtained better gear for climbing and skiing. Life was good, mostly.

Steve was not as happy, and he spent his days dreaming of big mountains. He was insistent about a Denali trip. He did all the research, figured out all the costs, and called us with a plan. Roger was always the source of reason in our brotherhood trio, and when he proclaimed it a good idea, any doubt in my mind that we weren't ready and shouldn't go disappeared. The cost of a Denali trip was still a bit out of reach, so we gave ourselves a couple of years to earn the money as well as gain a bit more experience. In those years, Steve also managed to find a job with a CPA firm in Aspen, which created an envy of sorts and made Roger and me start to look for work closer to home. Roger pirated a successful client from his firm who happened to own property and some small businesses as well as a home in Aspen, which allowed him to move. I was alone in Denver and not terribly happy, but I made the best of things.

At the time, school, work, and distance all served to separate us from Jim, who was working as a computer programmer in Denver, and our friendship had cooled over the years. Then, one day when I was driving back from an adventure and filling up at a gas station in Leadville, I ran into him. He looked in the window of my truck, saw my gear displayed so it was obvious that "I am a climber," and he casually said, "What's up with all that?" One thing led to another, and Jim proclaimed he had let himself go over the past few years, had not even considered climbing, and had found himself with a hard-driving professional life during the week complemented by a hard-driving party life on the weekends. He told me the story of how the weekend before, he found himself on his couch one morning having a nip of the dog that bit him the night before, and a jogger ran by his front window. He walked outside, looked up at a crystal-clear blue sky, and decided he was pissing his life away. Out of shape and out of his mind, he went for a hike. At Leadville, he was coming back from a hike, and my gear piqued memories of the past, and Jim was all in. We exchanged numbers, and the next weekend, we headed off for a climb. That led to more weekend adventures, and soon he was committed to Denali.

Jim Gile is a short, stocky guy built for speed. In his youth, he was the fastest kid in the school and one of the fastest in the state. That he gravitated toward the slop endurance plod of climbing later in life flew contrary to his complete loathing of that sort of activity. But as we started to climb together again, his meticulous ability to plan, stemming from his math major in college, made the anticipation of putting together an adventure enticing for him. As we graduated to expeditions, Jim became the mountain planner. He researched places, routes, quantities for needed food, and fuel to a T. Jim always maintained a positive attitude on trips if he was moving, but when tent bound, he tended to dwell on home life. Jim is a man of few words who speaks only when he must, and inactivity made him so quiet in contemplation of everything other than climbing that often we worried about his mental state. But a blue sky and being on the trail brought out his sharp wit and enthusiasm, which Steve and I appreciated. Jim cemented his place in what would become known much later as "The Three Amigos": Steve, Jim, and myself.

In the year before Denali, I had changed jobs to one that had me traveling every week, and after the initial excitement of life on the road, I found I was not climbing nearly enough. I was getting fat and generally hated the city. My desire to get back to Aspen was amplified by an experience late one night in Baltimore when I was chased by a group of punks through a Holiday Inn parking lot, narrowly escaping a mugging. I lay in my hotel room scared to death to turn on my lights for fear that I would be found. The next morning, I went to my rental car to find the lights on, doors open, and battery dead; in my fight or flight condition that night I ran, totally forgetting to shut the doors of the rental car. Still shaking, I called in my resignation and hopped on the next flight back to Denver. I was done. I happened to have a copy of the *Aspen Times* in my bag, and immediately scanned the want ads: "Controller needed." I called the number to find that the boss was a former neighbor of my parents, and he offered me a job immediately. I left the city and never looked back.

After the horrific experience of nearly being mugged and then the excitement of quitting my job and immediately finding a new one, in Aspen no less, I slowly made my life change and settled into things at home. I resumed my training, rekindled my focus on the big Denali trip with Steve and Roger, and even found a girlfriend. Life was incredible! I had rekindled my effort to get my life pointed toward climbing and skiing, specifically Denali.

We ran the plan past Dad, and he thought it was a great idea. He suggested that we find a guide, as it was a big leap from anything we had done, so I took on the task of finding someone who could help. This was before the internet, so I went to the library and talked to other climbers in Aspen. After a bit of legwork, I was connected to a guide in Telluride, Colorado—Michael Covington.

Michael said he worked with a guy in Aspen who guided Denali for him every season, and he connected me with Bob Sloezen, a quintessential climbing bum with long hair, a pierced ear, and tattoo on his arm. He told us to call him Slowman, and his calm, slow nature made the nickname fit.

At our first face-to-face meeting with Slowman, the ice to be broken was a bit thick. Roger and I were eager, excited, squeaky clean young wannabes with enough experience locally to think we knew it all. Meeting with this hippie-dude climber, with a massive tobacco dip in his cheeks hidden behind a full-face beard, created an awkward moment on both sides with unsaid thoughts of *who the hell is this Covington setting me up with anyway?* But in what would become his main gleaming quality—charm—Slowman handled the situation as the mentor he would become. His ease of words and appreciation for our excitement, and his ability to let reality take its natural course, allowed us to realize we had the right guy. As crazy as our ambitions painted us to be, throughout the entire process of getting ready, Slowman let the vibrato of our excitement go, as only a guy like he could. When we told him we also wanted to ski the peak, he was taken aback but, again, let it roll. Tactfully, he went along with the plan, pointing us toward all the planning, training, and such, in a way that allowed us to slowly figure out just how big an objective we were taking on. He rolled with the punches, and then when he had to, especially when on the mountain, he reeled us in.

2

The Alaskan Years—1990–95

We spent three weeks on Denali. We experienced all the highs and lows one would expect, including the humbling psychological crescendo all new mountaineers experience when standing at the base of a massive peak. We flew in and landed at a strip on the Kahiltna Glacier, and standing there, gazing up thirteen thousand feet to the twenty-thousand-foot summit, our jaws dropped. Almost subconsciously but out loud, Roger proclaimed, "Boys, I got news for you. We ain't skiing that peak!" Standing behind us, Slowman heard the mumble, and in a way that only he could, pointed us toward the task at hand: setting up camp. He softly encouraged us with controlled enthusiasm and words of wisdom. "We have a lot of trip in front of us, guys," he said. "Don't get freaked out. I guarantee we will figure it out, and bit by bit you will get comfortable with all this. It's a big fucking peak, but we are going to do this." We soon found skiing the only method for glacier travel, and as the days rolled by, we learned how to set up camp, cook our food, and deal with the most horrific weather we had ever experienced.

Bit by bit, Slowman taught, and we listened. We learned how efficiency was the key. We learned how to read the mountain. We bit our tongues as Slowman held us back while people went up the mountain, warning us that "it's not right, guys; don't let the blue sky fool you." That was followed, of course, by teams retreating from high on the mountain after a weeklong storm, and utterances of "never, ever again will I do this shit" being proclaimed by the defeated climbers. Slowman's mountain wisdom—summed up with his mantra—"party down low; kick ass up high"—began to make sense. He taught us how to read the weather, how to "become one" with the mountain, and what it took to be a mountaineer, suddenly even experiencing the summit. In short, those twenty-one days were a crash course in how to survive and thrive in the largest mountains on the planet. We graduated from being guided clients to being novice mountaineers. Flying home, looking over the Denali range and then over the Wrangell Mountains and its massive ice fields, we saw Mount Logan. Then and there, we knew we would be coming back.

Denali had been a very difficult endeavor for us. The Alaska Range sits in the northernmost part of North America, and the peaks there rise to create the most relief, base to summit, of any peaks on earth. Their location is the perfect place for cold to meet massive amounts of moisture from the Pacific Ocean. The coastal parts of Alaska get huge amounts of snow. A visit to the region is more about survival than climbing.

After we successfully topped out on Denali, we had to descend in a storm that was dropping an inch of snow every fifteen minutes. Steve led the team down the upper slopes, and we found ourselves on a stretch of knife-edged ridge where visibility was down to a few inches. Later, in a tent at our midway camp, after literally swimming through waves of sloughing snow, we could hear the distant roars of unseen avalanches. Steve noted, "That was the scariest thing I have ever done! I had no idea if my next step would even be there. Why would anyone want to be famous for doing this shit? I am so out of here."

Just a week later we were at thirty-five thousand feet, flying over twenty-seven million acres of the Wrangell-St. Elias National Park with glaciated peaks in every direction. Looking down at Mount Logan on a rare, perfectly blue-sky day, any thought of not wanting more vanished. In what would become our modus operandi, before we were home from the expedition that we were on, we were already hatching plans for the next one. Logan, the highest peak in Canada, was next.

Our fearless leader, Slowman, looked at the peak from the comfort of his seat and calmly said, "You guys are ready. You don't need me." Then he promptly shut his eyes and dozed off. We failed to read between the lines. Slowman, a veteran of twenty-seven Denali summits, knew about Mount Logan, which sits on the Alaska-Canada border. Logan takes Arctic climbing to the ultimate level, exceeding even Denali with its ferocious storms and cold. Slowman had clearly been impressed with our enthusiasm. He could give you a list as long as both arms of people that climbed Denali only to say, "been there, done that" and promptly sell all their climbing gear. But he wasn't taking the bait in this instance.

On the other hand, the four of us experienced the delusional effects of rookie mountaineer's success. A summit, especially for young climbers, tends to eliminate the memory of the hardships. In that jet, we were not thinking about the time we almost blew up the tent with a gas leak, or the grim reality of going to the bathroom outside when it's twenty below zero. There was no thought of sitting in a tent for days waiting for a storm to pass while developing bedsores and bruises that come with lying endlessly on a thin sleeping pad. There was no thought of plodding one step for every three breaths at twenty thousand feet, gasping for each of those breaths while worrying about numb fingers and toes that were on the verge of freezing solid. No, there was no thought of that. Those were memories less than a week old, but they weren't remotely part of our thinking in the comfort of a jet flying high above the harsh reality of Arctic climbing. To us, everything was magnificent. What we saw was relatable only to the sheer joy we brought back with us—a summit experience on a mirror image, a single moment of the expedition where we could see what we were now seeing. We wouldn't acknowledge the moments of doubt that gnawed at our thoughts almost continuously for a month before the thirty minutes we spent on the top of North America. Those moments were the furthest things from our mind. Steve's comment after our summit was totally forgotten. We didn't have thoughts of being the greatest mountaineers in history, but we found ourselves dreaming of more. At that moment, we wanted more of what we just suffered through while failing to acknowledge the suffering itself.

Roger and John couldn't commit to Logan due to conflicts with their schedules. However, Bob Perlmutter, who was Slowman's assistant guide on Denali and who also lived in Aspen, was interested. Perl introduced us to a friend who had experienced the same delusional effects of a Denali summit followed by a Logan flyby. Penn Newhard was eager to join us as well as John's brother Pat. Pat was John's brother and cut from the same cloth. He was tough and came with a serious alpine ski background. He was not a question mark. Penn, however, was a different matter. He was a tall blond Scandinavian-looking guy with a degree from Brown. He was not a mountain kid but a transplant. This was a question mark given our inexperience and youth, especially for Steve, who was not keen on new faces; he often joked that new friends were a luxury he couldn't afford. But Penn had what few did back then—some experience. We needed another rope mate, and he got the job. Perl proved himself as a friend on Denali, and what he lacked in power compared to the rest, his experience and unfaultable enthusiasm for laughing at discomfort gave us confidence. He was a pleasure to be around.

I contacted our pilot from the Denali trip, and he gave me the telephone number of a guy he knew who could get us to Logan—Paul Clause. The Clauses owned a lodge in the lowlands of Wrangell-St. Elias National Park, and soon we had a plan in place. Almost a year to the date that we arrived in Alaska for Denali, we found ourselves in a fully loaded long-bed double cab Ford pickup driving to the small northern town of Chitna, Alaska. The driver dumped us out on a dirt runway and told us to set up camp. "Paul will pick you up when conditions allow," he said. Two days later the winds subsided, and an airplane landed. A second plane landed, and soon we were shaking hands with John and Paul Clause and making superficial small talk—just another day at the office for this two.

We loaded the plane, jumped in, and were off. An hour later we landed on a rough, flat patch of brown dirt on the edge of a massive river. There was a lodge in the trees nearby. We pried our fingers off whatever we had been clawing during the flight and stepped into a wilderness that was well beyond anything we had ever seen. Paul's wife assigned us to a cabin and, pointing, told us to "please pee in the same spot over there ... and the outhouse is over there."

The cabin was amazing, and the food was incredible, and after a week of waiting for the weather, we had formed a down-to-earth relationship with the Clauses that could only come from living in close quarters. The relationship would grow stronger over the next five years as we piled on additional trips. But our first taste of life in the Coastal Ranges was a waiting game; the weather dictates everything. We sneaked glimpses of the huge peaks far up the river valley when the clouds and glacier dust storms subsided, but it was a lesson in hurry up and wait.

Finally, one morning drew clear, and long before the sun was above the horizon, Paul knocked on the door and told us to get our glacier gear on and to get our gear out to the plane. "Hurry up," he said. "We have a window." Soon, we found ourselves flying low above endless peaks and valleys en route to the Sella Quintella Icefield on the Alaska-Canada border. We looked down to see a single military tent in the middle. Paul angled the plane down for a "touch-and-go," a maneuver in which the plane doesn't land but rather allows the pilot to test the snow. After a couple of these precarious and nerve-racking maneuvers, Paul softly landed the airplane and taxied up to the tent. He turned the plane off and explained that he didn't have clearance to land in Canada and that we would have to ski to Logan, which was a long way up the glacier. "Just head up this glacier and ... well, you can see the peak," he said.

Logan is the largest mountain on the face of earth in terms of volume. Its base is nearly two hundred miles in circumference, and it has a summit plateau that is thirty-five square miles—all of which is above seventeen thousand feet. Sure, we could see it, but we reckoned it would take all day to get to it. As Paul hopped into the plane, he said, "Good luck. I will check back in five days. That should give you enough time to get to base camp." We immediately thought he was out of his mind, but when we got the map out, we found we were nearly forty miles from the peak. This was our first realization of the magnitude of the region. We roped up and set off, trying to grasp the scale of this wild place.

The glaciers in Southeastern Alaska butt up against the Yukon Territory of Canada. The glacier we were on ran eighty miles down to the Pacific Ocean and was consistently twenty-five miles wide. The ice we traveled across was nearly a mile thick. We roped up, but crevasses were not a big issue. The cracks in the ice were as big as golf courses, and who knows how deep; they were hard to miss. We plodded along in nearly perfect, still weather, and as Paul predicted, found ourselves at the base of Mount Logan five days later. We heard the buzz of an airplane, and we broke out our two-way radio. Paul asked how we were and proclaimed that we were experiencing an unusually good weather pattern and that it didn't look to be going anywhere over the next week, possibly two. The long ski tour was a large piece of humble pie compared to the confidence we had gained with our success on Denali. But as we settled into life on the glacier, and the weather stayed unusually calm, we slowly gained back our confidence.

We spent the next two weeks establishing a long slog route up the King's Trench. The King's Trench is a massive valley that bifurcates Mount Logan and is the first part of the easiest route up the mountain—easiest, of course, being a relative term. Between our numerous hauls up the mountain, we enjoyed skiing. At one point, late in the day, we stopped on a knoll above our camp to have a snack. The glacier rolled out before us, and the enormous pyramid of Mount Saint Elias—rising eighteen thousand feet out of the Pacific Ocean eighty miles away—became obvious as a focal point for a photograph, but impossible to explain. What we were experiencing would be a complete secret despite our best effort to share it back home with anyone who'd never been there. It was nearly 10:00 p.m., but at that time of year that far north, the sun never fully sets. The sky was blue-gray, and it contrasted sharply with the endless white snow below. The silence of the moment was broken only by one comment from Jim: "Damn, I knew it was going to be just like this." We laughed and headed down to base camp to get out of the cold.

Once we had a fully established camp on a col at fourteen thousand feet, we began to work on the upper and steeper part of the route to the summit. We were caught up in the joy of three consecutive weeks of nearly perfect and extraordinarily calm weather, which allowed us to establish our high camp at just over seventeen thousand feet. Our confidence was high, but our guard was down. As we reached our tents at the col, the wind picked up.

A half hour later, we were engulfed in ninety-mile-per-hour winds and a total whiteout. The temperature plummeted. Yet another half hour later, the snow had accumulated so drastically that we had to institute shifts to shovel it off the sides of the tents so we wouldn't be buried, depleting our oxygen and threatening us with suffocation.

The roar was deafening. When I stepped out of the tent, I was terrified. On Denali, Slowman had taught us that in those peaks, walls made of snow and ice and a tent pit were critical to survival. We learned well; however, the shovel was just outside the tent walls, and when I stepped beyond our fortress, the wind caught me and blew me face forward onto my stomach. I grabbed the shovel, thankfully jammed well into the snow to prevent it from blowing away, and slithered back to cover. I shoveled two feet of blown snow from all sides of the tent, being extremely careful not to touch the nylon wall; a rip would have destroyed our tent. The wind did offer one benefit, however. As soon as I lifted the spade of the shovel above the wall, it was blown clean. I crawled back into the tent, dragging a pile of snow with me, and quickly Steve zipped the tent closed, preventing loads of spindrift from entering. We cleaned out the snow as best we could before our body heat created puddles. I sat in a huff, recovering, and was terrified at the thought that all that separated us from the harshest environment I had ever experienced were two thin pieces of nylon supported by quarter-inch aluminum poles.

We took shifts keeping the tent pit clean for five days. The storm was relentless. The thought process in a situation like that is unpredictable. We approached Mount Logan with a great deal of respect learned from our Denali success. We realized that storms in the Alaska Range—where Denali sits—generally last for a few days. In the Wrangell Mountains, they last at least five, so we were not in a state of panic. Nonetheless, as a storm like that screams on, you do realize that experience has no bearing on the laws of nature. You can guess, but you have no idea if the situation will end in five days or five weeks. Your mind plays games. You calm yourself with conversation. You count your supplies. We had two weeks' worth of food and gas, so we were in good shape, but to suggest that we did not discuss rationing on the fourth or fifth day would be lying. We did. While we maintained healthy levels of hydration, lying on your back for that many days, not able to get up and go for even a short walk, doesn't burn a lot of calories.

Keeping the snow clean around the tent was at first a dreaded activity, but after a couple days it became something you looked forward to just to move, but it was a twenty-minute job at most. Likewise, the desire to eat was enhanced only by the stimulation it brought to another part of your sensory system. We were not even slightly hungry. It was easy to justify not eating, which created a form of rationing. We passed the time playing cards, reading, and listening to our Walkmans, which did create a bit of stress in that our batteries were running out of energy. And then we prayed.

Expeditions obviously entail a great deal of tent time in dangerous environments, and for me, it's always been a time for spiritual retreat. On Logan, I prayed often. I prayed for the tent to not blow away; I prayed that we didn't go crazy; I prayed that the storm would break; I prayed that we all stayed healthy. In short, I prayed for everything. As miserable as it was, I even prayed in thanks. I was asking God for a lot that week and didn't want him to think I was getting greedy. But the reality is, when you're in a situation like that, the contrasts to life at home become extremely evident. At home, we take the simplest things for granted, never giving them a second thought. Those tiny things become monumental tasks when you are confined to a tent with two other guys during a long storm. It's an extraordinary experience.

But there's another effect of sitting through a storm like that: an otherwise comfortable tent designed for three people shrinks. Despite our best efforts to keep the tent clear of blowing snow, the snow walls we built surrounding the tent created a space that quickly filled in. After just a few days, the snow filling up that space began pressing against the walls, slowly compacting the tent and drastically reducing the space inside. Instead of having a few inches between us, we were soon jammed together like sardines. It happened slowly, and with other things to worry about, we were soon in a bind.

The other miserable aspect of riding out a storm like this is the art of relieving yourself. Everyone brings a pee bottle, which takes care of one side of the equation, but the second—that's a different matter. Normally, you dig a hole in the glacier away from camp and line it with a trash bag. When it's full, you toss it into a deep crevasse. But as noted, with a ninety-mile-per-hour wind, that was impossible. Beyond the fact that you can't stand or squat in wind that severe, two seconds after you drop your trousers, they are full of snow. We were forced to squat in the vestibule of the tent, to zip the main nylon door closed, and to do our business there. Nylon is not a great barrier for smell, and, suffice to say, number twos created a shitty experience for everyone.

The sixth day dawned, and we were awakened by the drone of an airplane. For five days, as the storm raged, we'd gotten very little sleep. At some point that night, the wind stopped, and instead of celebrating, we all fell into a deep sleep. The plane droned, and we reached for the radio. Paul was doing a flyby to check on us. He had deep concern in his voice and made it clear we had just survived a major storm. When we described our plan to get organized and head up, we thought the radio went dead until Paul, incredulous, said, "You are going up?!"

Apparently, this was not the first time a storm had rolled through those peaks and pinned climbers below, but it was obviously not normal for them to want to do much climbing after such a storm. "Well, boys, you guys are hard men!" Paul said. "Way to go, and I will keep an eye on you." Given Paul's reputation—not only as a pilot in those peaks but also as someone who'd climbed as much as anyone in the area—we had no incentive to try and keep up with him. But we had no intention of getting off the mountain. Rather, while we had a reinforced respect for the raw power of this environment, properly and successfully suffering like we did became a point of pride. Guardedly, we had to continue. Paul's affirmation that we were "hard men" only added to our confidence.

Over the next few days we proceeded to establish our high camp. The weather deteriorated a bit, and it got much colder. We soon found ourselves comfortably situated at over seventeen thousand feet, sipping tea and slurping soup. One night, Pat was out in the midnight sun taking care of business. I noticed that he was taking an awful lot of time. It was twenty below zero, and he stood out there fidgeting and fidgeting with something. I tried to go back to sleep and not think about it.

The next morning, however, we all realized we had a big problem. Pat woke up and pulled his aching hands out of his sleeping bag. His fingers looked like golf balls; they had frozen.

Perl, who was also our certified mountain medicine expert, set to wrapping his fingers in protective gauze and proclaimed that we had to get him down immediately. We dressed Pat and told him to not use his hands. We told him to get his mittens out. He said that was the problem. The weeks of great and relatively warm weather had given him the impression that he didn't and wouldn't need them. With only a short climb to camp and then an immediate return to a lower camp before a summit bid, he thought he could save weight by not carrying his mittens, which to that point had remained in the bottom of his pack. The climb had destroyed his ability to use his fingers, and while taking a crap the night before, he couldn't use them to do anything. Pat had not been with us on Denali and was totally new to the Arctic. We were green but not too green to establish a rule, then and there: look out for one another. Pat was in a bind.

Steve had good gloves and gave Pat his mittens, and we headed down. The descent was complicated by the fact that we were on skis—the snow was too deep to walk on. We used a rope to secure Pat and belayed him as he descended. Pat was a fantastically talented ski racer, which really helped with the rescue effort, but it was extremely difficult work. We reached our camp at the col, and we were exhausted from the effort. We settled in for rest and recovery, but we knew we had to get Pat out. By this stage, after the storm and now a rescue, we knew the trip was over.

To our relief, the next morning broke without a cloud in the sky and no wind. It was very early, and we were eager to get going. To say that there was not a bit of disappointment would be to lie; however, our buddy needed help, and that superseded any disappointment. We had our hands full getting Pat all the way down the long glacier to base camp, and disappointment faded quickly with the task. We also realized that base camp was a long way from where Paul could pick us up. With the good weather, we hoped that Paul would miraculously fly by so we could get Pat out quicker, knowing a rescue would trump border laws, but one never came. By midday, we had Pat stabilized at base camp. The next discussion was getting Pat all the way back to the airstrip.

Gravity helped us in our evacuation, but while we would be going down the glacier, there was very little pitch over the forty-mile stretch to aid us in the effort. Combined with the reality that time was of the essence and that Pat needed serious medical attention, Steve, Jim, and I decided that we needed to keep going to get back to the strip's radio telephone. That would allow us to call Paul and get him to the strip two days later. We spent an hour or so brewing up and filling our water bottles, and under the midnight sun, we set out leaving Penn and Pearl to take care of Pat. We carried a tent and survival gear but kept our loads as small as possible, knowing we had to go a long way and as quickly as possible. We vowed not to stop until we reached the line of communication. We decided that we would take the two-way radio with us in case Paul happened to fly by. The glacier was also the line of flight, and if we were able to contact Paul, we would tell him to pick up the others and then come back for us.

As we set off, the anticipation of the effort, as well as the debilitating and depressing nature of Pat's condition, dissipated. We concentrated only on the task at hand; worrying about anything else was a waste of energy. Steve led out on the front of the rope; I was in the middle, and Jim was on the end. As the day ended, we found ourselves in a precarious spot. It was still light enough to travel, but it was just dark enough so that the massive crevasses that we had to cross were nearly hidden. Steve watched for the slight uplifting that preceded these canyons, but in a couple of instances found himself literally hitting the brakes with his ski tips hanging over an edge. The snow was hard, and the slight downward angle of the glacier allowed us to free-heel on our ski gear. We endured a pretty slow and monotonous descent, which was necessary to avoid the crevasses but also to scan the darkening glacier ahead so that we didn't have to deviate too far from where we needed to get; the glacier was very wide.

We glided across the ice, mesmerized by the rhythmic movement. It was bitterly cold, but the constant action increased circulation and, oddly, the process was extremely pleasant. Hours ticked off like minutes, and slowly we moved closer and closer. Twelve hours after we left base camp, and nearly a day since we started, we found ourselves at the airstrip. It was too early to expect Paul or anyone at the lodge to be around the phone, so we crawled into the large tent. There was no floor, and the size of the tent did not offer much resistance to the cold or capture what heat our bodies produced, but there was a stove. We fired it up and managed to warm the tent slightly. We pulled out our sleeping mats and sleeping bags and shivered in the cold until the sun came up.

When we woke up, we fired up the radio phone. Paul's wife, Donna, answered. We explained the situation and were assured that help was on the way. The sun warmed the air throughout the early morning, and we soon found ourselves outside the tent, enjoying the perfectly calm weather in our camp chairs. The disappointment of a perfect day and the ability to see the entire route, knowing full well that this day would have been our summit day, was a bitter pill at the time. Frustration made us cranky.

We were not so much mad at Pat as we were at ourselves, and we harshly critiqued our inability to recognize when a friend was in need—albeit a friend that had no experience. But we were also baffled that a grown man could make such a basic mistake. Alaska or Colorado, how in the hell could he not have his warm mittens on a carry, and how was it that a few ounces of weight outweighed common mountain sense? This was the first instance of something that would follow us on all the expeditions to come. We became extremely leery of bringing along anyone that had not already experienced similar situations or been on expeditions. This stuff was real, and it was serious. This discriminating feeling was not borne of superiority but rather pure outright respect and humility for the environment and the game we were playing.

Soon we heard the buzz of the airplane, and I reached for the radio to update Paul. He flew up the glacier and went through the touch-and-go process of landing to pick up Pat. Pat was flown out to the lodge, where a doctor happened to be visiting. The rest of the team showed up later that day. We found Pat soaking his hands in a solution and grimaced at his swollen and black fingers. The following day we were all flown out. Pat was flown directly to a hospital in Anchorage, but the experience was not soon forgotten. We learned a lot on that trip, both obvious and not so obvious. We perceived the mistake as our own, and it cemented the seriousness of what we were doing. We failed to make the summit, but we worked together to perform a successful rescue. Pat would lose the tips of two fingers and never return to the high, cold peaks, but for the rest of us, it created a guarded but optimistic approach we would carry with us forever.

Ironically, Logan paved the way for more. We accepted our mistakes, and the situation spawned a mantra that would follow us: never lose the lesson. We found ourselves back at the lodge every spring for the next several years. And time after time, we found ourselves back at the base of some beastly looking peaks. John and Roger accompanied us back to Logan the next year.

We met John Callahan at age six while sledding on the golf course greens adjacent to our homes in Aspen. After a territorial war with him and his brother, Pat, we formed a relationship that even today makes him and Pat brothers from a different mother. We were continuously outside climbing anything from trees to the nearby mountains, or tubing the rivers flowing from the Elk Range through Aspen. John, more than Pat, became a confidant in action. We all gravitated toward endurance sports primarily because we were good at it. From the get-go, John was our climbing and skiing partner. In college, we found ourselves heading out before heading back to school doing ridiculously long two-hundred-mile treks around the state, where our "pure" approach took roots; we would not think of resupply and subsequently carried everything we needed on our backs. Later, John capitalized on his endurance and ability to sustain pain to the point of thriving on it as an Olympic cross-country skier. John is probably the most levelheaded guy we have ever climbed with, knowing the potential hazards in the mountains on the fly. Steve describes John as Spock from the TV show *Star Trek*. "John is levelheaded," he says. "No matter how bad it gets on a peak, he thinks things through; never freaks out. He's a good man to have on your rope." John is also a complete smart-ass, never missing an opportunity to needle a guy on his misstep or weakness, but he has thick skin and can take it as well.

Roger was a mentor to Steve and me and was the voice of reason in the beginning of our mountain adventures. He is three years our senior and is built like a model—handsome and with a ripped physique. He also is one of the overall greatest skiers on the planet. He can ski anything at any time. Roger, like Jim, was the fastest kid in his class, but he also had an ability to go out for long days at a superfast clip, unusual considering his fast-twitch anatomy. He never quite took to the discomforts of climbing, but when he was out, he was a source of inspiration to the rest of us, noting all the time that no matter how miserable it was out there, it was only for a week or two: "Make the most of it." Despite his Mensa-level IQ and a soft-spoken approach, he didn't hold back on contradictions in theory, especially in the mountains. Roger and John were the "big brothers," being the same age, and we looked up to them.

At one point, where we watched a massive avalanche cross the King's Trench and then experienced the power of the slide when crossing the gouged path of destruction that it left behind. Thinking it to be an astronomical event—that is, one that rarely happened—the following day we crossed the debris path only to find another avalanche bearing down on us. I vividly remember not panicking but looking at Roger asking, "What do we do?!" His response? "Run!" And run we did! Fortunately, the huge serac slide found its way into an enormous crevasse field and was swallowed up, but afterward we recognized that this was how things were going to be. We had no sense of fear but rather a calm feeling of simply knowing that there were places we could never be.

That was Roger's last expedition. The mental misery of Logan pushed him to his limit. He reached Prospector's Col at nineteen thousand feet on Mount Logan and unveiled a flag he'd made during a storm identical to the storm we'd sat through the year before. "Mike, get a photo of this," he said. The flag, made of athletic tape and a bandana, simply read, "Marry me Susan." John, on the other hand, took the stress and misery in stride as only he could. He would become a staple on future expeditions.

On another trip, we found ourselves standing in the midnight sun at the base of Mount Saint Elias. Saint Elias was a pretty big leap in terms of mountaineering substance over anything we had ever experienced, including Logan and Denali. Legendary Alaskan mountaineer Charlie Sassara was with us on that trip. We'd just spent a week of playing grab ass at the lodge, waiting to fly up, and basking in accolades from less-ambitious adventure seekers who were planning to fly around the park and not actually climb anything. While we were transfixed by the view of the mountain, Charlie slowly came up behind us, put his arms around our shoulders, and, proclaimed, "Boys, aren't so cocky now, are ya!"

Soon we would find ourselves at twelve thousand feet on those lofty slopes, too scared to climb, and finally abandoning the peak altogether. We were simply biting off more than we could fit in our mouths, let alone chew. One story, in particular, haunted us. The previous year a team of climbers had set up base camp and then been hit with more than thirty feet of snow in three days. It stopped them from getting on the peak, certainly, but they also found themselves in a life or death race to shovel snow in order just to survive. The tale haunted us throughout our attempt with thoughts of "what-if?"

Looking through our journals, we calculated that on several expeditions we spent 70 percent of our time in the tent, and only 30 percent out climbing. In the rare instance where we did stand on top of a small, subsidiary no-name peak, or in the case of a significant peak, Mount Bona, it was never as planned and was always after a severe modification of expectations.

On Bona, we planned on ten days to reach the top. On the second day, we found ourselves at Camp 1 in perfect weather, only to realize a colossal wall of clouds was approaching from the west. After little success over the previous few years, summit fever kicked in. We dumped all our gear and ran to the top. We headed back down, retrieved our camp, and soon found ourselves at the base of the peak. With no ability to contact Paul for an early pick-up, we had to wait and wait—and wait. For three days the storm kept us pinned in the tent. We had no books, no music, no nothing, so we read the labels of all our supplies and passed Callahan's watch around, trying to start and stop the stopwatch in as short a period as possible. It was excruciating waiting, but this time at least we had the satisfaction of a summit; excitement trumped misery.

The next year we found ourselves high on the north ridge of Mount Blackburn in another big storm. The light of the midnight sun went black when an avalanche sloughed off the slopes above, burying us completely. We survived, but the tent was flattened and destroyed, and we retreated to our midmountain camp. Paul happened to be doing a flyby the next day in perfect weather. He managed to land his Super Cub beside us, but because we were still so high and a Super Cub was so small, he could not pull us off the peak. He told us he would go back to get the Beaver, a large airplane that could haul everything, and meet us at base camp. We knew we had plenty of fuel at the base of the peak, so we took survival gear, sleeping bags, and a tent. We thought we'd be able to fly immediately back to the lodge, fix the broken tent, and then head back to finish the climb. We made it safely down; the weather came in, and while we had survival gear, we failed to bring down a food bag. Water is the main ingredient in survival, and while we had plenty of fuel to melt snow for water, lack of food was a painful misery. We rationed a single granola bar for three and a half days before we were awakened by the debilitating whir of a De Havilland Beaver, five feet from our tent. Paul screamed, "Come on, guys, get in the plane. Forget the gear. We have one or two minutes to get back out through this sucker hole!"

In underwear, we hurled ourselves into the plane and then bounced around until we could find seatbelts. Paul gunned the engine, and the plane rumbled down the glacier into a ferocious wind. We barely got out. The weather closed in behind us, and seven days later, we found ourselves back in the plane, heading for more. When we got there, we found not a single trace of any of our camps. All our gear was somewhere under fifteen feet of newly fallen snow. We lost everything we had acquired. The expedition was over. When we got home, we threw a dart at an amazed and totally sympathetic insurance agent (Steve and I lived together), and he told us to take our list to a single store, and he'd work out payment for total replacement. We were back in business.

The next year, Charlie Sassara had convinced us to take our enthusiasm to a lesser peak in the same area and do what we could on our own. Paul Claus and famed Swiss mountaineer Rudi Homburger attained a first ascent on a fourteen-thousand-foot peak, which they later named at the Bureau of Alaskan Land Management after Paul's wife, Donna. There are so many unnamed peaks in Alaska that you can do that—climb a peak and name it whatever you want. The climb was on very steep ice (sixty to seventy degrees) broken by a few benches between pitches, which would allow for us to collect our wits. Paul flew us in and proceeded to do flybys as we climbed. We set our systems in place utilizing ice screws for running and static belays. The ice was typical glacier ice, and the flat spots did come as a relief between, but they were massively crevassed, adding to the experience. But the weather stayed cold, and the snow stayed firm, allowing for relatively easy travel albeit with a zig zag for finding a route over snow bridges. We set up a camp at midmountain below a near-vertical headwall, and after that the route steeply meandered in a ridged buttress to the summit.

Paul had suggested a few days, but by 10:00 a.m. on the second day, we were on top. He and Rudi flew over and dipped the wings back and forth in congratulations. But the fine day continued to warm. At the top, there was no wind, and we found ourselves stripping layers; the day blew in hot. Too hot. We were glad for the early summit and realized that the deposition zones below the steeps would be avalanche prone and that the snow bridges would be soft. We set off immediately. At the top of the headwall above camp, I added an extra screw to the anchor, as I knew at the cup below that face, the snow would be bottomless slush, and we feared it might avalanche. As I reached the curve below, sure enough, the snow settled, and I felt a floating sensation. I held tight to my belay device and merely let the snow slide beneath me. No problem!

But after the snow left, and I untied from the rope to head to camp, I heard Jim and Steve's screams coming from above. Later they would tell me they wholeheartedly expected to see my bright yellow snowsuit rolling away in a massive avalanche. I hadn't even noticed the slide, which went all the way to the bottom of the mountain leaving a six-foot crown on both sides. I made my way to camp and yelled that I was okay, to their great relief—they had written me off for good reason. The slide was massive!

We arrived at camp shaking from fear of the obvious and decided that we had to wait until the next morning to let the night freeze the now sloppy slopes. We woke up to find only slightly colder temperatures, but with the delay the day before, expecting to meet our ride back to the lodge midmorning. We set out slowly. The steep sections were not a problem and, in fact, the ice retained a rubber-like consistency that made down climbing and belaying excellent; however, as I led below the first rappel and crossed the first snow bridge, I fell through up to my chest, with Jim catching my fall, as we had roped up for the descent. I probed the next one, and it was pure slush beneath an inch of crust. I told Jim and Steve to watch me, and I slithered on my stomach across to spread my weight. With success, I kept going, stopping to belay from the bottom as Steve and Jim swam the same way. In all, we slithered across a dozen or so slots in this fashion with relief coming only from the steep rappels. Six hours of incredibly slow going found us safely at the bottom. Paul flew in and taxied the ski plane to our loads.

As we took off, however, another problem arose. The friction from the plane's skis sliding in to stop immediately froze the plane to the glacier. We got out and kicked with our boots as Paul gunned the engine, the whir of the props blaring our eardrums out of our heads and spiking our faces with fragments of ice. Soon we were off and back at the lodge. After a huge meal midafternoon, we were all out, totally racked in sleep. Thirty-six hours later, Paul woke us up.

Donna was epic to say the least. But the experience left us with a new drastically needed skill, and combined with our rapid success on Bona, things began to fall into place. We honed our alpine rope systems and ice-climbing technique into what would lay the foundation for all that was to come. For ski mountaineering, 90 percent of the adventure is the climb to get to the skiing. All the Alaskan trips had netted a lot of frustration, but in the process, we learned not only how to survive but how to push ourselves to new places with new skills. Donna was icing on the cake. It was a second ascent to add a bit of sweetness on top of that.

Looking back at what we refer to as our "Alaska years," I find it amazing that our passion was not diminished. While on the surface there was a lot of failure, inside we found instances of personal and mountaineering growth. If anything, success was redefined, and we found a great deal of satisfaction in the reality that we could, if nothing else, survive in conditions that were impossible for family and friends to comprehend. Steve's words on Denali—"Why would anyone want to be famous doing this shit?"—echoed through our thoughts repeatedly, but we found a deep appreciation for throwing ourselves into perilous situations and figuring them out. We achieved a huge sense of satisfaction. We were also beginning to realize that, as the old saying goes, a climber quickly forgets the misery of his last game when a new one is upon him. Moreover, that misery was superseded by the sheer beauty of the environment and appreciation for being able to experience what can hardly be explained to anyone who has never been there. Our egos were brought well into check with the humbling situations, which gave us experiences that became intoxicating. We couldn't get enough. We were addicted. Having seen our own brother and friends come to the realization that they had been there, done that, and had no desire to go again became a source of pride in that we had been there, survived, and we most definitely wanted more.

In the years that passed, we didn't find much use in telling our stories to many people. Our summit ratio was so dismal that when we did share our experiences with would-be mountaineers at home—people who were bagging fourteeners in Colorado—we found ourselves to be the brunt of jokes rather than having any cache in the mountaineering world. We were the guys who did a lot of trips but didn't have what it took to get to the top of anything.

Again, you can't explain the magnitude of the major ranges to anyone who has not been there, and at times, the lack of recognition played into our basic human desires to be appreciated for our passions. Humbly, we proceeded to not discuss our trips with anyone. Years later it never ceased to amaze me when otherwise interested mountaineers—with zero to little knowledge of everything we had done—would criticize us as posers with a single successful expedition to Denali. It was easier to just live out our dreams and forget about accolades from the climbing community. The rare sources of pride we carried came from our mentor, Slowman, who fully realized who and what we were, and from guys like Paul Claus who admired our ability to keep coming back. That was enough to fuel us on our path. Climbing partners fell by the wayside as we carried on, but the core group of Steve, Jim, John, and me gave us enough synergy to keep planning and going on trips. Every spring we found ourselves in Alaska. We were still totally in the dark in terms of what was available in the world and the multitude of places we could go. Then it happened.

3

South America, Altitude and Attitude

One night in 1995, I was out having a beer and ran into one of Slowman's old guiding friends from Denali, Steve Gall, who also lived in Aspen. At the time, Steve was a well-respected mountaineer and guide who fit the description of a climbing bum to a T. He wore his hair long, pierced his ear, lived in a van, and supplemented his life between guide jobs with whatever he could find. His personality was inviting and open, and he didn't hold back on giving us his opinion. He belonged to a small circle of Alaskan climbers that knew we were regularly playing the game up there and that we understood just how difficult it was. Simply the fact that he came up to talk shop was a source of pride. He had just come back from guiding in Bolivia. Under the influence of a few beers, he proceeded to explain how delusional we were, and how heading to Alaska—with all its commensurate difficulties— was a surefire way to learn to hate the sport. "South America is tits, guys," he told us. "The weather is awesome, and the peaks are superhigh. You guys need to go. Fuck Alaska. That place sucks!"

I had been introduced to the climbing in South America through our former teachers. These were the same guys who had created the outdoor education program we all went through in middle school, which really cemented the basic skills we needed to climb. Griff Smith, especially, had followed much the same path we did with summer trips to Alaska, and I credit him with firing us up. Steve and I had been to his house and watched his slideshows and listened to his stories. I called him to find out more about his recent trips to Bolivia. He reinforced what Steve Gall had said and put me in touch with his liaison in Bolivia. The liaison, in turn, could pick us up at the airport, get us to the peaks, and provide us with a base camp cook, a concept of "expeditioneering" that was as foreign to us as warm beer.

None of us even had a passport at the time, and a family vacation to Hawaii was the only exotic travel we had experienced. True, we had been to Canada, but not in any formal sense outside our climbing trips to Alaska. With the exceptions of Colorado and Alaska, where we had been, we had little or no knowledge of big mountains. To us, South America was a hot, dry, desert place where the food consisted of tacos, and there was a coup every few months, and Wild West outlaws fled there from the law, at least in the movies. We were beyond ignorant. This was long before the internet, and we had simply never been exposed to the developing countries of South America. Outside of history lessons of the conquistadors and Spanish migration to the region, we had little to go on when it came to the continent, and mountains never tracked across our radars. Looking at Griff's slides, combined with Gall's blatant disregard of Alaska in favor of such, it became a tantalizing curiosity. We had to go!

The Cordillera Real (Royal Range) of Bolivia sits above the edge of the Puna de Atacama Desert, which is the driest place in the world. In May and June, the heat rises from the desert and generates no moisture that would otherwise produce storms. Consequently, you can go on expeditions there and at that time of year experience few if any storms. Griff had done a dozen trips to the region over as many years and had a single bad-weather day. There are glaciated summits from sixteen thousand to over twenty-one thousand feet. To our Arctic-numbed climbing minds, we found the concept hard to fathom.

We set off with overloaded haul bags bulging with the massive gear pile we had become accustomed to carrying as well as a fair dose of skepticism about the stories from our contemporaries. Our logistics liaison met us at the airport in La Paz and in broken English supplemented his disbelief with a "mui fuente!"—a term that sneaked through the language barrier on both sides. He rolled his eyes and loaded the gear onto a bus.

La Paz's airport sits at over fourteen thousand feet, forcing the airlines to allocate specially outfitted jets with larger than normal engines and flaps that allow for landing and taking off at such high altitudes. As we alighted the craft, the tarmac was lined with ambulances that were there to accommodate passengers who'd flown from sea level to fourteen thousand feet and experienced altitude sickness as soon as the cabin was depressurized.

The city of La Paz is a metropolitan area of several million and sits in a valley that starts at the airport and descends below to twelve thousand feet; it's high. Although we had been climbing and skiing at these altitudes back home, we realized we needed to spend a few days acclimating in the city before heading out. The culture was a complete shock. It was our first taste of an exotic international (i.e., non-US) city as well as our first Third World experience.

Along with us were two high-school buddies as well as a gear shop owner who was a customer of my father's ski distribution company. The former were childhood friends that wanted to give mountaineering a go. They were good guys. We had done a few local adventures, and they considered us experts. They knew enough to take care of themselves, and everything was fine.

The other guy was an owner of a ski shop in Wyoming. I'll call him Joe Shnook for our purposes here. My father did business with Shnook, and he was prominent in the direction of a local mountain rescue outfit in his hometown. We had visited his house and gone ice climbing with him. It was clear that Shnook knew little about climbing high peaks, and he was nowhere near fit enough to do any significant mountaineering.

But he was interesting. He had opened his home to us—Cody, Wyoming— and a few beers into dinner, we suddenly realized that apparently we had invited him to go to Bolivia.

Later, we didn't have the heart to say otherwise, so we prodded Shnook with training questions while overinflating what we were up to. Our disingenuous goal was to get him to train and get into reasonable shape so he wouldn't become a burden. He was an EMT, too, and we reasoned that that was not a bad thing to have on a trip. Now, in La Paz, walking around the streets at thirteen thousand feet, even despite our hypoxia, we realized Shnook was going to be a problem. On the walk back to the hotel after a little sightseeing, Shnook was huffing and puffing. At one point we found him sitting on the steps of a building trying to make sense of what he was doing but never admitting that a complete lack of training was the culprit for his miserable state. "I ate something bad down there," Shnook said at one point. We got him to his room and didn't see him the next day. But we were satisfied by the sounds coming from his room when we tried to figure out if he was still alive. The trail would have to sort this out. The trail sorts everyone out.

A few days later, we found ourselves at a base camp at fourteen thousand feet, gawking at a cirque of glaciated peaks as we luxuriated on soft green grass beside a lake—thus far the camping had been on glaciers. It was all we knew. Sipping coffee and tea served to us in comfortable foldup camp chairs, any whiff of problems disappeared. The next morning, however, we were taught another lesson that would stick with us: problems in the high mountains tend to not go away until you make them go away. On a simple and short acclimation hike, Shnook again succumbed to the dreaded combination of being drastically undertrained and attempting to climb to an altitude his body had never experienced. A hundred yards out and slightly up, Shnook toppled over, dizzy, and started drooling. He was completely unaware of our efforts to hold him up as we quickly descended back to camp so we could put him back in bed. The only sound that eclipsed our heavy breathing while carrying him (he weighed 210 pounds) was his constant blabbering to "leave me here and just get me on the way back if I don't catch up."

I was the trip leader, and after consulting the others, I told Shnook he was in no condition to climb. When he argued, I reminded him of all our phone conversations in which we discussed training. Grudgingly, he admitted he had not trained, and in a tearful haste departed for his tent. This was our first experience with a grown man crying over something—climbing. It was awkward, to say the least.

The next day, we set off for another peak, full team minus our fallen comrade. We reached a beautiful summit, but on the way down, one of the other newcomers was slowed down by a big, fat headache and altitude sickness. We managed to slowly get back to camp, but the situation deteriorated. It was obvious he had a fairly severe case of edema. We didn't have to tell him his trip was over. The next morning, with little recovery, he and his partner headed down. Seeing a chance to get out, Shnook licked his wounds and agreed to go out as well. We would not see our friends until three weeks later in Aspen. As for Shnook, time healed his wounds, and in the small world of mountaineering, word got around: "We had had a difference, and those assholes had left me to climb alone." We were, apparently, "bad guys." We took the high road and let this one go, more than happy with the knowledge that he didn't die on us, and in fact was healthy enough, if not delusional, to berate us. For his part, Shnook continued to be a big customer to our father, who understood the situation based on many years of working with him. "Yes, boys," Dad said at one point, "he's a bit of a blowhard."

The point being, with our group reduced to just Steve, Jim, and myself, we had only ourselves to blame for some unfortunate situations—the one we'd just experienced as well as the situation with Pat, the new guy, on Logan. Now, in Bolivia, not only had we experienced a full-blown life-and-death case of edema, we had witnessed an otherwise nice guy, successful-as-they-come businessman, brought to tears—all in the name of climbing. It's not that we made any mistakes directly, but what the previous five or so years had taught us wasn't quite getting hammered home. Namely, while we were figuring out how to take care of ourselves, we weren't figuring out how to take care of others, people we liked but who had no business being there.

The limited experience we had gained was always together, and it was enough to contemplate trips to large mountains, but we were by no means guides. Sitting at that camp in the Cordillera Real, we understood that we had mostly dodged a few figurative bullets by sheer luck. One of those bullets took the tips of a couple of Pat's fingers, something that we would never forget or take lightly. It was a point of reflection and realization that would follow us on every trip despite the intoxicating ability to have plenty of would-be mountaineers inflate our growing egos with requests to "come along and help haul gear." We realized that was a tough no to hand out, and with that, we mandated a new rule: we all must agree on if and who when it came to adding new faces to the mix. Simply put, people are wonderful, but they're also weird and unpredictable in the high peaks; we didn't have the experience to accommodate much beyond ourselves.

We managed to climb a handful of peaks ranging from seventeen thousand to twenty-one thousand feet in Bolivia, all in perfect weather. We were able to climb significantly more difficult routes without the anxiety of outrunning storms or the stress that comes with cold weather. We proved we could handle the altitude very well, and enjoyed the euphoria that comes with hypoxia. We worked on our ice and snow protection skills and improved our rope work efficiency. Bolivia was, as everyone had suggested, a mecca of sorts for fueling our passion. Unlike climbing in Alaska, all the training we put forth in the months leading to the trip was put into obtaining summits, and not endless and excruciating tent-sitting—waiting on storms, waiting on snow conditions, and waiting for airplanes. We had chewed on international mountaineering, and we were hooked. Nothing could put a damper on our enthusiasm.

This was June 1996, and on the way back home, the pictures and headlines of the disaster that had unfolded on Everest during May 10–11 barely registered. *Time* magazine had the story on its cover, and while the event did create a knot in my stomach, even then, we correlated it with the evils of commercial mountaineering and totally inexperienced oxygen-sucking clients getting into trouble. Our feelings were enhanced by the photos, which depicted exactly that. Only later would it fully register. For the time being, we were international mountaineers, and we most certainly did not experience tragedy.

By 1996, when we had happily suffered through a half dozen expeditions to Alaska and Canada, another aspect of our development—of which we were unaware—was taking root. The more we climbed, the more we wanted, but the reality of what we were doing gradually snuffed out any childhood fantasies of climbing Mount Everest. It was not a case of losing the desire but rather a brooding sense of what we could realistically take on. Certainly finances prohibited any inclination toward Everest, and we had found that for a fraction of what the tragedy suggested (i.e., climbing Everest cost around $60,000), we could try a zillion other mountains that offered everything the Big E had with the exception of the highest point.

Our performance in Bolivia was beyond positive; it was one of the most fun things we had ever done. We proved that we could take the lessons taught in Alaska and apply them to other large peaks. At that stage, we did not have the money to hire guides, but our success so far had taught us that we could do this stuff. The surreal events that unfolded on Everest, combined with the ego-pumping success we'd had to that point, gave us a healthy disdain for commercial climbing and all the evils that in our young minds it brought. We viewed commercial clients as wealthy adventure seekers who had little experience and were totally incapable of understanding the notion that mountaineering was not just a test of human endurance; rather, it was an activity that required a process. The typical scenario that played out for commercial climbers was set in stone; hire a guide to get you up Rainier, then Denali, then maybe Aconcagua, then Everest! Write a check, head to the gym, maybe take a trip to Colorado and climb Mount Elbert, get into shape, and go for it. This contrasted greatly with our developing method. Training was just our way of life. We hit the local peaks in our backyard as often as possible not for training per se but because it was fun. After a few trips to South America we realized we had approached the sport backward. We should have started in South America before going to Alaska, but a logical progression was becoming clear.

Bluntly, mountaineering is not a matter of ability; it is a matter of time. While we read the stories of people with a fraction of our experience taking on Everest, and some even attaining its summit, we had gained enough experience to know we were not even remotely ready to take on Everest. We knew that we'd never use any methods outside of those we would use to climb in our backyard, which stood in great contrast to the manufactured summits with fixed lines set by others, Sherpas, and supplemental oxygen. But regardless, Everest was to us the ultimate mountaineering challenge. We could not comprehend what it would be like at twenty-nine thousand feet and had no desire to try. Twenty-thousand feet was a great experience for us, and we would take our time getting higher. Point being, we were humbled by the great Andes and the massive peaks of North America. Our expeditions were enormous fun, and we accepted the sport for what we knew. We never set goals beyond the next expedition.

We did look at the sport with eagerness to push ourselves, and "higher" became the overriding objective. We felt the altitude when we were there. We embraced it. We loved it. The more we went, the better we felt. But along the way, we also saw the debilitating effects. We watched other climbers struggle where we seemed to float. We saw the dark side of altitude with rescues, during some of which we became rescuers. We learned from those events, but we also realized we were different. We excelled at altitude and were good at it. At the time, we didn't correlate our ability to some genetic disposition; we would learn that years later. Rather, we thought it was our unwavering ability to train combined with taking the time to properly acclimate.

We inherited the mantra "party down low and kick 'er in the guts up high" from our mentor Bob Sloezen, and we paid attention. We took our time down low, fighting the urge to compete with other climbers who whizzed past us up the mountain. We carried the extra weight of real food—real meat and potatoes—to energize us low on the mountain. Acclimation hikes became a source of fun, not an uncomfortable hassle as many other climbers viewed them. Then, when we felt great and knew we were adjusted to the altitude, we kicked ass up high, taking enormous delight in passing the climbers that had scorned us below.

Our methods were no doubt critical to our success and well-being up high, and they helped cement our passion to climb tall peaks. Our confidence grew not over an idea but over time. The 1996 Everest tragedy was a loud and clear signal to the world that "you can do this; it's possible," and served to spark an explosion of interest in climbing Everest and other high Himalayan peaks. We weren't listening. Instead, we delighted in our steadfast ability to maintain total discipline with regard to our climbing and to not look past the next expedition. Bluntly, we had enough experience to be arrogant and were young enough to not care about tactfulness in spewing our opinion about Himalayan climbing. When asked, we answered. We were old enough—and in our minds good enough—to understand what was going on in those high peaks, but we didn't have enough life experience to recognize that our opinions didn't matter. We blasted away.

At this point in our careers, we weren't remotely known for accomplishing anything special in mountaineering. After we climbed Denali, a local paper ran a story on our trip, and that climb almost came to define us. At that point in time, there was no such thing as social media, and all our trips to Alaska and Canada, as well as South America, were known only by a few friends and coworkers. Success after Denali was met with very few summits in that region, and while we did have great success in South America, telling people about those trips and the magnificence of the Cordillera Blanca was like telling them about flying frogs. Most people associated the Andes with more cosmopolitan countries like Argentina and Chile. Bolivia was perceived no differently than it was at first for us. Climbing, let alone skiing, in Bolivia never registered with most. So, our experience went unnoticed.

Our cocky attitude was not without reason, but even in the local climbing community, we were considered cock-dog ski racers that never ventured much past the ski area boundary, and the only success we claimed, Denali, was an anomaly, and it came about under the tutelage of Slowman, a well-respected guide. Given that three of the survivors of the 1996 Everest tragedy lived in Aspen, our opinions of the situation were not received well, even though on our own we had accomplished enough to speak with at least a bit of experience on the subject. While our opinions paralleled those of well-known mountaineers who were contributing to the discussion, the aggressive, in-your-face maelstrom that comes after a disaster like Everest 1996—combining testosterone-filled young men and naive writers—added up to us not being credible commentators. Looking back, I realize we would have been better served to just shut up.

And we did get caught up in it, unfortunately. At a gala event in Aspen, I found myself with one of the unfortunate-but-fortunate survivors. Over a beer, he cried—real tears that can come only from someone who has witnessed something terrible, on top of my well-known, at least locally, opinion on the matter. The errors in our ways were clear, I felt terrible, and while I reconciled my actions, the damage was done. Thereafter, in the local climbing community, we were neither respected nor genuinely even liked. We continued to climb but never really recovered from that damage. We learned the hard way that when you point the gun of critique, especially for situations when people were killed, people don't soon forget. Our successes were often scoffed at as a result. Inherent in this scenario, unfortunately, success is often met with the inevitable door of envy that screwing up like we did opens a bit wider.

Climbing envy is the dark side of mountaineering. We would figure that out with time, but it needs to be understood because it's a significant aspect of the game. We were used to envy in the world of ski racing and in skiing in general. I remember listening to my father talk about how success often came at a cost. The psychology of the issue is that when someone achieves something, unless it is clearly and without debate a case of ultimate success, issues will arise. If a skier wins every ski race, a critic can't do much to belittle that success. But in the process of reaching that level, which few ever will, disparity opens the door to debate. In effect, there is an opportunity for another racer to bring himself up by belittling a skier who is experiencing a fleeting high point in his career. In the belittler's mind, he somehow feels like an expert when he denounces the success of another. You've heard the comments: "Yeah, he did achieve this or that, but ..."

The list of belittlements can be wide and varied, but they stem from a general idea that the skier doing well got lucky. The pedestal in elite ski racing shines the light on whoever is in it, and everyone else that so desires it becomes simply jealous. In one story, Dad was skiing very well one season, beating all his mates, and they came to the infamous downhill in Kitzbuhel, Austria— the Hahnenkamm. The most difficult track, the Streif (streak, or stripe), was particularly difficult that year due to low snow. For a variety of reasons, including flat-out fear, everyone on the US Ski Team that day bowed out of the race except for dear old Dad. He went through his normal routine, headed to the start, and had no one to prep his skis or offer any coaching whatsoever. (Granted, Dad was a rebel of sorts taking his disdain for "the man," the system, and showed up for the Olympic team photo in street clothes—not a stitch of team logos or garb—and made matters worse by lowering his head. The coaches and the organization did something I can't recall that pissed him off, but I know Dad was a man of extreme principles and didn't take shit from anyone—he had a good reason and the balls to stand up for himself.) Anyway, there at the start of the greatest event a world-class downhiller will ever experience outside of an Olympics or World Championship, the US Ski Team ignored the only racer—my father—to make the start. Fortunately, the only people disgusted by the lack of respect for a human being—let alone the prestigious race—were the Austrians. They prepped Dad's skis, and the coaches and racers took him under their wings. The stories are endless not just for Dad but for all racers that achieve moments of glory.

In mountaineering this effect is even worse. At least in ski racing, you compete. There is a clock, and the clock never lies. A derided skier can always point to it. In mountaineering, the same pedestal exists for climbers that find themselves on top, no pun intended. But the door to bring one's self up is as vast as the mountains themselves.

Laura Bakos, the first woman to climb and ski from an eight-thousand-meter peak, told me that before she even reached Cho Oyu base camp, climbers had cranked up the rumor mill, which would later call her out as a liar and a cheat, and broadcast that she didn't climb the peak let alone ski it. Laura was a complete no-name on her first eight-thousand-meter peak—no résumé of skiing, whatsoever—and the crowd was not going to let this one go. While there is no clock in mountaineering, there are cameras, and only long after the fact, once the film was developed and printed, did the naysayers shut up. And, of course, that was with the nasty old caveat: "She got lucky."

Jim Gile coined a phrase for such antics: "tea house fodder." We experienced similar treatment when the spring before Laura's historic achievement we became the first Americans to ski from an eight-thousand-meter peak. More on that later, but suffice to say, until the photos were developed, we experienced the same thing.

But one instance stands out for me. Again, it relates to becoming the first American to ski from an eight-thousand-meter peak, a major North American ski mountaineering milestone. I was back for a week or so after that expedition, lending time for the accomplishment to get around in the circle of mountaineers.

I found myself at a wedding. One lady, who was married to an accomplished mountaineer, approached me. There were no congratulations or salutations, but rather a rant: "That's an easy one, yes. I think my girlfriends and I are going to plan a trip to that peak and ski it."

Suffice to say, as I have mentioned, we started our careers—at least locally—on the left foot, and it was clear that in our home climbing community, we were not going to be given credit for anything. Wherever we went, there was a passive-aggressive vibe, and there seemed to be no way the climbing community was going to give us credit. It didn't help that we got along with our parents, didn't smoke dope, and had never lived out of a VW Eurovan while rock climbing in Yosemite Valley or anywhere else. On top of all that, we made our livings as accountants and computer geeks. The narrative was far-fetched at best, and our successes were down to dumb luck. Again, the photos didn't lie. While these instances inspired us to let our actions speak for themselves, I'd be lying if I didn't admit that it made me sad. Our enjoyment of the high mountains made us want to share our experiences, but that door, locally, was shut.

In a weird way, it humbled us and quashed our cockiness. We took advantage of media opportunities outside of the Aspen area, which exacerbated the degradation at home, but we clammed up about it all. We took advantage of new sponsorship opportunities, but the animosity grew. We accepted it and quietly kept it all to ourselves. A decade later with social media available, we missed the boat on the professionalism of adventure sports. A major magazine ran a story on us twenty years later titled "The Most Accomplished Ski Mountaineers You've Never Heard of." Looking back, however, it wasn't all bad. Our careers outside ski mountaineering were a blessing. They allowed us to keep our passion separate from otherwise normal lives. Ironically, this has created a local belief that the only reasons we've been successful is because we are wealthy businesspeople. There are hordes of young people that simply barely survive life financially let alone head to the greater ranges, so going pro seems the only viable option. We were lucky; being a pro wasn't even a thing when we started. I must admit that having a job did allow me to pursue my passion, but that wasn't without saving every penny from my meager accountant salary. The irony is that without the option to be a pro, I have a living outside the sport, and have not had to pay for gear or trips for most of my avocation. But enough already.

After Bolivia, our anticipation was huge. The lack of perceived success in all the years in Alaska was superseded by the contrast of total summit success in South America, and we wanted more. We loved altitude, and while we feared and respected it, we set out to explore the high peaks of Asia. Slowman had become a rare foundation of support locally, and we looked to him for guidance. He had been on a couple of successful expeditions to Everest and Cho Oyu, but also to the Gasherbrum peaks in the Karakorum range of Pakistan. He claimed the Karakorum to be the ultimate mountaineering and cultural experience of his life. He suggested we try the twelfth highest peak in the world—Broad Peak.

4

The Himalaya and Transformation to High-Altitude Skier

Broad Peak rises to 8,051 meters (26,414 feet) and its regular route offers a relatively straightforward and safe climb. I read everything I could on the subject. We balked at taking on an eight-thousand-meter peak at this stage in our careers, but Slowman explained that if we were to take the time and spend the money to take on any peak in Asia, an eight-thousand-meter peak was advisable. "You may never get to Asia again," he said. "Get the most bang for your buck. You can climb six-thousand-meter peaks easily and cheaply in South America, and the cost is about the same for a seven-thousand-meter peak, so just bite the bullet." Added to this was: first, we didn't have to climb to the summit, and second, we needed to explore altitude and figure out how much we really did like it and how good we were at it.

There is a drastic difference between the altitude we had experienced at that point (just over twenty thousand feet) and, say seven thousand meters (twenty-three thousand feet), but again, Slowman advised, "you don't have to stand on the summit." He also knew from his guiding career that most people that reach twenty thousand feet are proud of their accomplishment and leave the sport satisfied but with little or no desire for more. We were not just satisfied with our experience at altitude; we craved more. The argument to go was sound. We set out to make it happen and soon found that the preparations were to be as difficult as the climbing.

On Slowman's advice, I reached out to a guiding logistics company that ran treks in Pakistan and had an office in Aspen. I arranged to have coffee with the owner, expecting raised eyebrows and to be talked out of Broad Peak for another, more reasonable, peak. To my surprise, my contact was more than supportive and said he could arrange everything. He didn't have any mountaineering experience but ran many treks up the Baltoro Glacier, which was an eighty-mile trek that ended at the base of K2. Broad Peak rose sharply out of the glacier on the way to K2, and he was eager to get involved. The first step was getting a permit. Then we would need full expedition services, which for the Baltoro are extensive.

Expeditions to Broad Peak entail getting to Islamabad, Pakistan, then a short flight to a small mountain village, Skardu, followed by a day drive to Askole, a small agricultural village at the start of the trade routes up and over the Karakorum. Travelers and traders have been using these routes for hundreds of years. Our journey would include a several-day trek eighty miles along the Indus River to the toe of the Baltoro glacier. Because so much of the trek was on glacier, animals were out of the question. Instead, we needed about fifty local Balti porters to carry our expedition equipment and food for more than two months—compounded by the requirement for additional porters to carry food for our primary porters. This was so extensive and beyond our experience that we had no clue what we were getting into. We reached out to Slowman, who was more than happy to assist us in the process and logistics and to assure us that our logistics agent knew what he was doing. He did, in fact, and quite well. And while he had little mountaineering experience himself, he most certainly knew what it took to get a massive team of people and the support into the area.

A week or so later, our logistics guy got back to us with the first hurdle. The permit alone was $8,000. We didn't have anything close to that amount of money. We started to contact gear companies and didn't find much luck. Locally, businesses that knew us threw a little bit of money at the project, but we were well short. We fully anticipated that each of us would have to cover the $800 airfare, as well as another $3,000 apiece for the logistics and support. Even after all was deposited into an expedition bank account, we were still short the $8,000 for the permit.

The permit also had a deadline, and before we had the total funds needed, we decided to take the risk and secure it with funds we did have. We figured we could sell old skis, take on night work, whatever it took. A copy of the receipt for the permit came weeks later, but by February we were still short. Our departure date was at the end of June. In the weeks that passed, we worked hard to cover the necessary funds, but, as the months dragged on, it was clear we were about to eat $3,000 each.

Then in late March, the phone rang. Ed Viesturs was on the line. Ed was not well known outside of climbing circles in 1997, but within, he was a legend. I sat up at my desk, bewildered. He said he had been trying to get a permit to climb Broad Peak but had missed the deadline and that he "really need to make it happen this summer." He had heard from one of the gear companies we were pitching the trip. To that, we had room. Our permit was for six people, and we had three signed up. I explained our situation: we didn't have enough funds, and we were working on it. He explained that this expedition was extremely important, and he had support from his sponsors to do whatever it took. I told him I had to put pencil to paper and to see if Steve and Jim agreed to have him and his partner, Veikka Guffstason, join us. I also approached Slowman to get his take on the situation. Slowman took it all in and smiled. He said that in the process of helping us, he had started to wonder if he might be able to join us, but he didn't have the money. Now, knowing that we had a gear manufacturer involved, we had an opportunity to make the trip happen and bring him along. So, the permit had already been paid for. But if we could get Ed to pay what we needed, that would allow for Slowman to afford the trip as well. Slowman warned us that we would need a few grand to cover unforeseen costs over and above the budget we had in place from our logistics guy. I called Ed back the next day, gave him a dollar figure number, and he asked where to send the check. Game on!

I called Steve and Jim to tell them the good news. Steve was beyond excited, but Jim, not so much. In the aftermath of believing we had pissed away nearly $3,000 each, he had resolved himself to the fact that Broad Peak was not happening. Added to that the fact that his wife was due to have their first child in the months before we departed, he was a resounding *maybe*. This *maybe* aspect was something that Jim would throw at us for most of the trips to come and became a running joke. But again, as soon as Jim was signed up, as soon as we hit the trail, he was a tiger. "I have to run this up the flagpole at home," he said. I didn't hear from Jim for over a month, but Steve and I figured that with Slowman now on our team, we had enough people to haul the gear up the peak to establish camps. Slowman's experience would add considerable value to the endeavor. Added to the mix was the fact that Slowman had much of the equipment needed— fixed lines, anchors, supplies—in a storage shack in Askole, which would save us a ton of money. We carried on with our plans.

We were nervous and disappointed by Jim's absence, but we resolved to continue. A month later, the phone rang once again with good news. Jim was on board. He said his wife was not at all happy, but out of the blue she had told him he had to go. Apparently, Jim, who had stayed interested in how things were progressing, had become a bit of a beast at home. We were more than elated to know our team was intact, and with everything in place, we prepared for the climb of our lives. That is, of course, without a full realization of what we had gotten ourselves into.

Over the last months of the winter of 1997 and through spring, we climbed and trained with intensity. Mentally, what we were headed for was significantly beyond our experience. Slowman told stories of the vast cultural differences between Pakistan and what we had experienced in Bolivia and spoke of the difference between life philosophy between the East and the West. First, we would be experiencing severe jet lag, something none of us had thought about. Also, the third world nature of rural Pakistan would, he warned, make Bolivia look modern. But over and over and over, he explained we had to be calm and patient. "Nothing ever goes as planned in Pakistan," he said. He explained how we would be "wealthy Americans" even when dealing with local agents who were by Pakistani standards at the top of the economic food chain; they would try everything to rip us off. Two trips had taught Slowman what to expect, and we were more than happy he was on the team. "Make sure you bring a briefcase with every piece of documentation, all your receipts, notes with dates when you spoke to whom and what you spoke about," he said. He explained that the key to success once in-country was to have everything documented "like an attorney planning for a case." I was the trip leader, and I paid attention.

In the meantime, we concentrated on our climbing technique. Broad would be our first eight-thousand-meter peak, and taking a page from our book on Denali ("Boys, we ain't skiing that"), as well as Slowman's insistence that we leave the skis behind, we concentrated our efforts on climbing and only climbing. The route descriptions told of steep ice climbing and sustained steep rock and snow slopes, so we prepared accordingly. We climbed ice three days a week and spent the weekends climbing various fourteen-thousand-foot peaks between Aspen and Denver so that we could train with Jim, who was then living and working in Denver. We lifted weights, ate healthy, and lived well. Any notion of sharing our next trip with locals was snuffed out with humbleness and a desire to avoid conflict with naysayers. We knew we were biting off a large chunk with Broad Peak, and we didn't need the stress of so-called experts telling us we were crazy.

Once we knew the trip was a definite go, the next mountain to climb was getting the time off. At this point, Steve was working for himself, and the timing—given that his clients' tax deadlines would have passed—was perfect. Jim simply told his employer he needed the time off, and somehow, he managed. I don't recall the details, but I suspect his employer never knew; he chalked it up to his first kid being on the way. I, on the other hand, had my hands full. At the time, I was working on a shift from private accounting to public accounting. However, well over half my income was derived from one client with whom I worked a deal to do their full business and personal accounting at a reduced rate in return for them letting me do my other client work from a private office within their office. This created a big problem in that I didn't have the money or work to just rent a single office elsewhere, which was compounded by the fact that their business was a property management rental company, and July was a busy month. After a solid no from my client, I took a gamble and explained that if they lost me, it would end up costing them twice to replace me. I promised to write a manual on what to do and train a woman that

I was close to who worked in the office and whom I fully trusted to keep the train on the tracks. I pleaded almost to the point of tears and eventually won. I was relieved but realized that sooner or later I needed to start my own practice so that I didn't have to go through that again. While I had won that battle, it was a small part of a war I knew I could never win. Steve had set an example, and I needed to follow it.

We continued to climb with the skis as the spring backcountry snow turned into corn, and by the time the snow melted and took the ski season with it, we were running and riding our mountain bikes to stay in shape before departure. We felt ready, and following Slowman's advice, tapered our training to avoid getting sick or depleted before the trip. The end of June arrived, and with tearful goodbyes to family and friends, we found ourselves on an airplane headed to Pakistan.

This was 1997, before excess baggage fees, airport security, and strict agent procedures. We had a layover in Los Angeles and got friendly with the gate agent. We explained where we were headed and spoke with a $100 bill on the counter in front of her. We wanted an upgrade to business class. It was important for this USA expedition; we had to rest on the flight. She laughed and told us to "work this out with the flight attendant inside." With little more than a query as to availability, she snickered and welcomed us to the glorious life of first class—all the way to Islamabad. She refused the $100 bill, but we made sure it made it into the pocket of her apron and noticed a wink of her eye.

In Islamabad, the capital of Pakistan, we met Ed and Veikka in the hotel lobby along with our first taste of what travel in Pakistan is like. They told us scornfully that they had been to the Pakistan Ministry of Tourism check-in and were told they had no record of our permit or anything whatsoever. They were not happy. I calmly showed them the fax I received and all my paperwork. Immediately, we crammed into a few tiny taxicabs and headed off to visit the government. Once there, we were told of the situation. "There is nothing we can do," we were told. I produced my paperwork, including the receipt, and suddenly they found our file, literally in the front of a drawer in a file cabinet. Had I not been able to produce the paperwork, I am certain we would have been able to sort things out, but not without what we would learn is standard procedure in Pakistan: a bribe. With proof, they had no choice.

We sat in a small hot room and were lectured about the wonders of Pakistan, the dos and don'ts of a system set up to demand much but follow through with very little. An actual permit was produced and notarized, and we were introduced to our liaison officer, a corporal in Pakistan's army, dressed to the nines in a uniform. He was all business. He introduced himself as Waqas Bin Siddique but told us to call him Vicki. From that point, he would go everywhere with us.

Back at the hotel, Vicki made it clear that the first point of business was his outfit. We were required to provide him with full climbing gear. We set him up head to foot, and he warmed up a bit. We were also required to get him two sets of street clothing. He took Slowman to a shopping center and returned in crisp blue jeans and a Chicago Bulls T-shirt and cap. Vicki warmed greatly, and we formed a solid relationship that has lasted to this day. He, like many Pakistanis, was extremely proud of his country and his culture. Being very Muslim, he followed the religion to a T, but being from the modern generation, as well as a career officer in the military, he had a liberal perspective on the world. He blended his culture as a devout Muslim with a remarkable world view. He didn't care that we weren't Muslim and respected our belief in God. With mutual respect, Vicki would become a friend and valuable member of the expedition, resolving many situations in which locals would require bribes or give us a hard time. We loved him.

The next hurdle was dealing with our logistics man, a member of a sort of local mafia that included well-off Pakistanis in Islamabad. Iqbual was a towering figure who had made—by Pakistan standards—a tremendous amount of money through his businesses, one of which was a tour company. Even Vicki cowered gently around him. At the time, I had no idea of this man's position, and when he started the process of screwing us over issues I had fully documented, Vicki and Slowman calmed me down and said to just pay what he wanted. But it was not without first going toe to toe with him, literally screaming and cussing him out. Only later did I realize how exposed I was, and to this day I shiver at the thought of treating a man that could have "offed" me at any point the way I did. He was a serious character, going so far as to make us pay a restoration fee for a village that was wiped out by a landslide. The donation went straight into his pocket. We resolved our issues with a handshake, and I believe we both enjoyed mutual respect for standing up to each other.

We flew from Islamabad a week later than scheduled due to the blowup with Iqbal but were relieved to soon find ourselves in Skardu, ready for the expedition. We stayed at the famous K2 Hotel on a bluff above the Indus River at the gateway to the Karakorum. Slowman located his supply cache at the hotel where he'd left it, and we were off. The drive to the drop-off at the village of Askole is beautiful but harrowing. The road is often wiped out, and problems that would normally take a few hours to deal with often take as much as a day. We made many road repairs in order to simply proceed. It was hard work, often requiring a solo driver to take the risk of driving over washed-out roads through rough, deep side rivers. We were relieved to reach Askole and set up camp on a beautiful grassy field above the now-roaring Indus.

The first morning brought a beautiful but extremely hot day. Balti porters had assembled in the field next to our equipment, and the process of dividing the loads began. Slowman and Vicki played an integral role in the process, policing every item loaded and making a detailed list with a number on the load and the porter's name and number on a list. This ensured that the porter would not take off on his own with gear he could use or sell down the road. Having Slowman on the trip became a huge bonus we had not fully anticipated, and his experience was invaluable. Although he made it clear he was not interested in being the guide, we saw that this type of work was his forte, and he in effect ran the logistics with military precision. He was in his element as the expert, and he loved the responsibility. Meanwhile, the rest of the team formed bonds, and the two newcomers to the group, Ed and Veikka, fell confidently into stride with the oodles of shit we were accustomed to handing out to each other. Ed is somewhat quiet and reserved in general, but his shell was quickly cracked, and he followed the ass grabbing step for step. Veikka never missed a beat and was as comfortable at dishing it out as receiving it. We all knew it was going to be an entertaining trek to Broad Peak.

The journey to Broad Peak requires nearly eighty miles of walking. The schedule included a week to get to base camp, and although our team was fit and willing to meet that schedule, the porters dictated the pace. They were extremely fit as well, but they were paid by the kilo and made every penny they could. They carried all our gear, and others carried their gear, while others carried their food. All told, we had nearly seventy-five porters to get us all to base camp. That number shrank as we proceeded and supplies were used, but we had an army of people trailing us the entire time. We were required to provide a pair of sunglasses to each porter. They took great care to not remove the stickers on the lenses, yet still wore them for the protection. They were no doubt preserving them as brand new for sale after the expedition. The porters did not speak any English, and they kept to themselves. They were pleasant and cheerful, and seemed to have an experience like ours. They gave each other shit and were happy.

About a third of the trek was on long-established trade trails that had existed for hundreds of years. The trails connected Askole to other remote villages and formed an ancient trade network throughout the Karakorum. The development of more modern roads had seen the trails long since abandoned for trade, but they were now used for the growing trekking industry. We followed the Braldu River to the toe of the Baltoro Glacier. The trail was, for the most part, very good, but it often deviated when the course of the river had changed and wiped it out.

Being near the edge of the river was scary. The Braldu River flows out of the largest glaciated region outside of the poles, and it boils and bounces with a force we'd never seen. We could hear a constant gulunking of massive boulders rolling into its torrent. We ran into an expedition of Grand Canyon kayakers scouting the never-before-run river and were astonished by their opinions. For them, this river was not possible to float. They compared it to the Colorado River in the Grand Canyon, explaining, "This river makes the Grand Canyon look like a ditch."

In many places, the trail deviations led us above the river on ledges cantilevered with flat stones and logs. It was stressful and harrowing. At one point, the trail took off up the side of a near vertical cliff where we followed load-laden porters who never missed a step, up and then down. We followed, but not without thoughts of protecting the fifth class climbing and descending. One of our porters dislodged a large boulder that fell to the river but not before completely smashing his toes. Slowman took on his second passion, mountain medicine, and we triaged the gentleman enough to then send him home with a couple more porters. He was lucky. We were met with further grief when we found out that a couple of porters from another expedition fell to their deaths the day after we negotiated the same spot. The fun and games were subdued by the seriousness of what we were doing and where we were. We continued, crossing rickety bridges and resting in dilapidated cable buckets from time to time, until we found ourselves at the toe of the glacier. From there, the river was behind us, but so was the trail.

For the remainder of the trek, we followed an undulating moraine of slick ice covered with precarious house-sized boulders. The boulders sat on pedestals of ice where the heat of the sun could not penetrate below, a bit like huge clenched fists raised in the air. It was serious, but we were in an environment that we could do little about. The towering and vertical Karakorum had been called "The Throne Room of the Mountain Gods," and it was easy to see why. We gaped at enormous mountains like the Trango Towers, rising straight up for six thousand feet—the longest sustained vertical faces in the world. Mustagh Tower, Masherbrum, and the Gasherbrum peaks were all towers we had read about, but here we were gazing at their horrendous ridges and faces. It was beyond comprehension. It was incredible but humbling. A sense of fear was becoming a constant companion, and we wondered what the end of the glacier would hold. We couldn't see Broad Peak or K2. What we could see was in our minds. It wasn't the beastly peak we were seeking, but much greater than that, in a valley with countless sheer peaks lining the sides, we shuddered at the thought of it, making us question what we were doing.

Stories from Ed and Slowman of their first trips up the Baltoro comforted us; they had felt the same way that we did. Schedule limitations and permit requirements prompted us to continue the journey with a semblance of normalcy, but at night, alone in our tents, we trembled at the reality of what we were doing. Thoughts from Denali seeped into our minds: "I don't want to be famous for mountaineering."

Base camp at Broad Peak sits exactly at the foot of the mountain and offers a view nearly straight up to the summit. As soon as we established camp, Ed and Veikka were on the route. They had spent the spring on Everest and were fully acclimated, and we watched them run up Broad Peak. We quickly learned that Anatoli Boukreev, a powerful Russian climber and guide, was climbing Broad Peak with a team next to us. With no real reason for it and probably without realizing it, the competition was on. We had met Anatoli on Denali. He lived in Colorado, and we had bumped into him from time to time. He was a gracious and gentle giant. He was a massive hulk of a guy, chiseled from a life in the mountains, and weathered to match. But he was a great companion and comfortable with the social life that develops at a base camp.

There were only a few teams at the base, but with friendship kindled from Denali, and mutual respect for Ed and Veikka, we found ourselves sipping coffee and talking with Anatoli about climbing, life, and his horrific experience in the 1996 Everest disaster. It pained me to see arguably the greatest alpine climber of our generation brought literally to tears over the tragedy. Worse still was the devastating berating he had endured in the press. We had never heard of Anatoli before Denali, but after watching him flash that peak in two days, we knew he was different—a talent rarely seen in the high peaks. To have the opportunity to hang out with him—and not only hear his side of the tragic story but to get to know him as a man—was a moving experience.

He was a deeply caring human being despite his larger than life ability in the mountains. The contrast of how he impacted the climbing world against the obvious pain and anguish he'd experienced told a sad and convoluted story. He was a simple man who shared our passion, but despite his great ability, he still had to battle all the trials and tribulations of the human experience. He was humble. In the days that passed, it was fantastic to see him almost float up Broad Peak with a power and grace that surpassed even Ed and Veikka's. Anatoli was clearly a great man and superior mountaineer. For Steve, Jim, and I, the whole setting was inspiring.

After acclimating a few days at base camp, it was our turn. The route was extremely steep and included ice and rock climbing to Camp 1. We had to fix numerous spots, and we used old ropes left from previous expeditions to aid in the process. Slowman was the ultimate route engineer and excelled at the task. After we established the first two camps, Slowman proceeded to put in a near vertical solo route to Camp 1 that was probably a first. He was not the power climber that the other three stallions were, but Slowman was a technician, and his climbing was clinical. It was as amazing to witness him as any. Since we didn't have any porters, Steve, Jim, and I continued to haul loads, and over the weeks, we enjoyed the effort and responsibility of working the mountain, gaining experience and a level of comfort as we slowly made our way up the peak.

The camp of superstars was complemented by the arrival of Andrew Lock, an Australian climber that we knew was also special, and who would later earn acclaim for his own difficult climbs in the Himalaya. Andrew fit in well with our group. He had an ability to laugh hard, and he appreciated the bond only found among climbers competing separately but working together on an eight-thousand-meter peak. From our perspective, we gained an understanding of what was possible in those peaks. A handful of incredible mountaineers were showing us a road map of how it was done. We supplemented our lack of experience with a firsthand lesson in how these men talked, how they planned, and how they set out to climb an eight-thousand-meter peak. Thor Kieser, another Colorado climber who had been on K2 with Ed and had a ridiculously deep mountaineering résumé and who would become a good friend, cemented the academy of high altitude climbing and education for us. We did our best to emulate them. We found that what we lacked in know-how, we made up for with an ability to enjoy altitude, and with that, we found ourselves close behind these guys, always taking in how they did everything. For first time "eight-thousanders," it was a perfect storm of knowledge, action, and experience.

Life in the mountains proceeded in normal fashion, and although ours was a sparse and meager camp compared to the commercial high-dollar camps other Broad Peak aspirants enjoyed, we fell into a routine. The conversation varied from politics to religion to sex to everything imaginable. In the mix was a common complaint between Steve, Jim, and me that revolved around our decision to not bring skis. As we climbed the higher steep and smooth slopes, we regretted the decision. Apparently, this part of the discussion became tiresome for Ed and Veikka, and over coffee we experienced something I doubt few if any have: a pissed-off Ed Viesturs. The guy just rarely goes there, but that morning, he had had enough. He slammed his coffee down, threw his arms up and wailed, "I can't take this anymore! I am sick and tired of hearing you guys complain about not having skis!"

We sat stunned and looking at the frustration on a face that rarely sees this emotion. We started laughing, hard. After dishing him oodles of shit to chill out, even he began to laugh at himself, but we realized he was right. He suggested that "with your ability to ski and now obvious ability to climb high peaks, you guys need to go to Shishapangma and take your f'ing skis. It's a perfect ski peak, and you guys will never be happy in these peaks unless you try." He was right, and from that moment on, none of us ever spoke out loud of skiing on Broad Peak, but everything we did, on Broad Peak and after that, became training. Secretly, Steve and I were constantly whispering back and forth: "Do you think you could be carrying skis right now?" or "Can you imagine what that would be like to ski?" and on and on. One way or another, we knew we were going to find ourselves on Shishapangma with skis, and we vowed to never ever again go on an expedition without skis.

When we finally established the first two camps—the second at just under twenty-two thousand feet—our next task was to put in a high camp at about twenty-three thousand feet. We were moving into new territory—going higher than we had ever been. We slowly gained our high camp, established it, and spent a night there, gazing out at the Karakorum. We could see the mass of Nanga Parbat, the last major peak of the Himalaya on the horizon, and it towered above most of the horrible peaks that were a source of fear on the trek in. To the left, we could see the walls of the Gasherbrum peaks and Chogolisa, and to the right, the tower of K2. K2 was like a billboard depicting the ultimate nature of where we were. The vista fueled a bit of pride and accomplishment. We were higher than we had ever been, which exposed and diluted a primal fear of mountaineering and the question of what it was going to be like up there.

The experience was pure ecstasy. The toil of the trek, the load carrying, and above all the agonizing and stressful torment of simply not knowing what we were capable of or how we could possibly climb peaks like this vanished as we sat in our tent brewing our coffee and preparing a meal. The sun set, darkness descended, and we felt the cold creep through the tent walls. We zipped the tent up tight. We were doing it! This was a precious moment for us. While we appreciated the effort we had put in and knew there would be many more mountains in our future, this was the kind of moment that a mountaineer experiences only once: the first night at a high camp on an eight-thousand-meter peak. Somehow, even if subconsciously, we knew we would never experience this moment again. Mountaineering success was redefined in our young minds. Trite as the expression may sound, it really is about the journey.

The next morning, after we'd secured our camp, summit fever set in. We had accomplished much, and the entire route was set. We needed to get back to base camp for a few days of rest and recovery so we could then make one final push to the summit. The weather was perfect. The route was sustained and steep; caution was advised. We had repaired and reset old fixed lines for most of the route, which we would use to carefully and safely descend. As I stepped from the flat tent platform and tied into the fixed line, I realized this was no place to let your guard down. I picked up the rope and ran it through my belay device. As I leaned back, the friction from the rope running through the metal device created heat that melted the light dusting of snow that had accumulated; it was a familiar scent, and with it came a sense of comfort. Soon I found myself in a rhythm and rapidly descended the line, stopping at the anchor points along the way. I carefully unhitched myself from the rope—which left me precariously free to fall—and grabbed the line below the anchor, threaded it through my rappel device, double-checked what I'd done, and then resumed my downward plunge.

After weeks of going through this process, you become accustomed to the way the system works, and it becomes familiar. What took nearly a day to ascend was thus descended in a matter of hours. We unclipped from the rope for the last section of the route and walked the trail we had marked with bamboo wands across the moraine back to base camp. We spent the next few days in total relaxation, eating and drinking as much as possible. We were preparing ourselves for a marathon of sorts. The weather turned on the day of our planned summit bid, but we welcomed the two days that it lingered, and spent an additional day letting the new snow slough off. Our day of reckoning broke, perfectly windless but very cold.

On the way back across the glacier, we found ourselves a team of four with heads down in serious and quiet contemplation. We clipped into the fixed lines and slowly and deliberately headed up the route. We climbed past our first camp and then to our second camp with ease, our bodies rested and fully acclimated. We spent the night at Camp 2, and the excitement of the following morning had us back on the line earlier than anticipated. We were on the shady side of Broad Peak, and it was cold. With movement our cold limbs and faces soon warmed, and although the climb to our high camp took about three hours, we were in a serious climber's trance and had no weight in our packs.

Soon, we found ourselves in the sunshine at high camp. We stocked our snow supply for boiling water, filled our water bottles, and sipped the day away hydrating our bodies. We were preparing for our biggest adventure yet, into what for us was a total unknown—the dreaded "Death Zone" and the summit of our first eight-thousand-meter peak. Later in the day, another team arrived, and while we realized we were no longer alone on the mountain, it was only a few climbers. There is a comfort in numbers on those peaks, and this being our first such summit, we welcomed their presence. We were all on the same schedule, with the same goal; we were like-minded on many levels, and mutual respect was unstated. Camp went deadly silent at about 3:00 p.m., with everyone snuggling down for a bit of sleep. Of course, slumber lost out to the time of day, the anticipation of a summit bid, and the discomfort that comes with being at high altitude.

The beeps of our watch alarms welcomed the new day at midnight. We had slept in our down suits under a common down blanket that let much of the cold seep into our bodies. We turned on the stove for a cup of coffee and bit of oatmeal. We slept with our boot liners on to keep them warm, but the cold of plastic shells quickly absorbed the effort as soon as we put our feet into the gear. It was very cold. The thin air hampered the little stove's ability to melt snow in the pot let alone to boil the water produced by the melting snow. We sipped coffee and gulped down a bit of mush. Drinking and eating were not for enjoyment at this stage but rather a necessary step to get as many calories and as much moisture into us as we could. We plugged our noses and choked it all down, knowing it was fuel for the difficult task ahead.

As we staggered out of the tents, we made sure everyone had the gear they needed: extra mittens, water bottles, a bit of food, and extra batteries for headlamps. That was it. With numb fingers we put our harnesses on. When we were ready, we stood together in a circle and brought our hands into the middle, one on top of the other, and—as we did on all our days in the mountains—thanked the good Lord for allowing us the chance to be climbing and asked for safety and a good day. At this point, there were no more fixed lines, but the slopes in the cirque above were crevassed, so we would be tethered to each other. We set out.

Once our crampons bit into the frozen snow, familiarity set in once again, and with only the beam of our headlamps to light the few feet in front of us, we were once again in a climber's trance, slowly ascending. My feet were incredibly cold and numb. I wiggled my toes constantly. After a couple hours, we reached another higher camp to find another team sleeping. I stopped on one of the tent platforms—I had to. I swung my legs one at a time to flush blood into my toes. To my delight, it worked. My toes warmed rapidly, and we continued. We had started climbing after another team that had camped next to us, but we caught up to them. They were not climbing on a rope, and one member was not comfortable with that. He asked if he could tie in with us, and we agreed. Little did we know that not only would we share a rope for the day, but Roger Gocking would, from that moment on, become a friend for life.

Roger was one of the only African American climbers I have ever met, and we would learn only later that he had more mountaineering experience than just about anyone we had met before or since. We would find ourselves hard-pressed to talk about a mountain range—let alone a specific peak—that

Roger had never been to. He was a university professor, highly calculating, and on that rope, his assessment fit in with ours in a manner that for that moment was welcomed; he understood the game of mountaineering. We had no idea that morning of his vast experience, but the way he approached what we were doing struck a chord with us; this guy was going to be an asset. He was extraordinarily strong, and we passed his team and proceeded onward without missing a step.

As we got higher, a glance at the altimeter showed we were at about 25,500 feet, higher than we had ever been, with a mere six hundred feet to go. By this time, the shadow of Broad Peak's three high summits graced the entire glacier below us, and although we were still in the shade, the appearance of the sun below was a welcome sight. The view was magnificent, and none of the oft-mentioned problems associated with being that high were materializing. Although we were moving very slowly and breathing extraordinarily hard, we were truly enjoying the experience. As Steve commented at one point, "I feel bionic!" We could see the route ahead. It led to a small col that then led to a ridge and the summit. The snow from the previous storm, however, became deep in the amphitheater cirque. The wind had blown snow off the summit ridge, compounding the accumulation. We took turns breaking trail, and the team following caught up to us.

I took the lead, and suddenly the snow in front of me fractured. The crack ran across the entire face. Calmly I pointed it out to the others. There was very little discussion. Roger was on the end of the rope, and he came up to the front to look. In a deep island drawl we would come to love he said, "This gawd-damned slope is about to avalanche! We need to get the hell out of here naoooow!" The situation was dire, and both teams turned around. There was not a panic or any rush—altitude prevented that, and on recollection there was not even any disappointment. It was just something that happened, and we had to deal with it the only way you could deal with it—leave. Looking back, I shudder with the thought of that black line and will never forget how it broke at my knees and shot off in both directions like a lightning bolt. At the time, we just turned around and went down.

We left the route intact, the hope being that we could make another attempt. Back at camp, Roger joined our team to discuss the situation. We had been on the expedition for about two months, and time was running out. Jim was anxious to get home to his wife and new baby, and another expedition from K2 was heading out, and he asked if he could join them. Steve and Roger and I pondered the situation and agreed we would make another attempt, but that night the weather turned. For two days it raged on and—coupled with the reality that it was yet more snow on top of a slope that had already threatened to slide—our eagerness to continue the climb fizzled. The trip was over. But there was no regret. The entire experience was incredibly powerful. Sure, we had missed the summit, but we had pushed ourselves significantly further and harder than we ever had, and the experience was magnificent. We found ourselves with Roger sipping coffee and discussing another expedition to an eight-thousand-meter peak: Shishapangma.

We were excited that we had something to look forward to, and we headed back up to clean the mountain. Slowman agreed to take down Camp 1, and Steve and I cleaned the high camps. We packed up base camp, and our porters arrived the next day. They suggested heading out of the mountains by going south, over the Gondogoro La—a high pass that required a bit of technical climbing—instead of heading west, along the Baltoro Glacier, the way we had come in. Apparently, the summer runoff had washed out a significant part of the trail we had trekked in on. We didn't mind, and the change of venue brought us back to civilization with a final view from the La that showed the entire range—from K2 to Broad Peak and the Gasherbrums—that left us in awe. We stood there for a few minutes. We didn't have thoughts of being famous mountaineers, but as we pondered Broad Peak and viewed how far we had climbed, and how close the summit really was, a bit of regret entered our thoughts. More importantly, though, we knew we'd graduated into a whole new league in mountaineering. We turned our backs, knowing it would probably be the last time we would see the Karakorum, but our passion to become mountaineers was fueled to a level that left no doubt: this was what we were supposed to do with our lives, but even more so, we knew we'd never forgo bringing skis on our expeditions.

After Broad Peak, our appetite to climb and ski from eight thousand meters was huge. We came back and went through the often-depressing reentry process that happens after an expedition. Living minimally with bare essentials for survival seemed so much cleaner and more straightforward than the rat race of normal life. This was enhanced by the fact that we were gone for more than two months (expeditions to the Karakorum involve extraordinarily long treks compared to other parts of the Himalaya). Work had piled up into its own mountain of sorts, with clients lining up for various things as the knowledge of our return spread.

Living in Aspen only served to increase the contrast with where we'd been. In one instance, I was walking home one afternoon, and as I passed a Lamborghini parked along the sidewalk, I was startled by a voice coming from nowhere suggesting that I, "Back off; you are too close to this car." I walked by, but it took a serious effort to not spit on the shiny red door.

We returned from the mountains without pomp, circumstance, or much else. Although the expedition allowed us to climb to an altitude that we never imagined we'd attain, we didn't have a summit, and our young egos barred us from explaining that we didn't make the summit, despite the valid reasoning behind it. We also kept it to ourselves. We didn't want to arm our perceived belittlers. But we knew we had accomplished a lot, and the experience of extreme altitude and our newfound ability to not only enjoy it but to thrive in it fueled excitement for the future. This is not to say that we didn't respect the altitude. We did. If anything, the difficulty of being at altitude made us want to explore it more. At this juncture, however, a bit needs to be made known about high-altitude climbing. The following is a short essay I wrote that does as good a job as anything.

Thoughts on High Altitude

I had just started my travel home. I was returning from a road trip where I was screening a film I wrote, called *Skiing Everest*. After about a hundred of these public screenings over the past couple years, I was pondering a question that is almost always asked after these screenings: "Why do you choose to climb and ski the greater ranges around the world's five-thousand-meter to eight-thousand-meter peaks?"

The film paints a skier-bleak picture; the air is thin and at these altitudes you are literally surviving while skiing as the altitude slowly deteriorates your body; without eventual descent, you will perish. The snow conditions are generally poor at best, and the effort to climb let alone carry the extra weight of ski gear—an almost guaranteed scenario for not reaching the summit—not to mention the time and money involved in that all these peaks are on different continents from my secure and comfortable home in Colorado. I pondered the question on the flight home and came across this bit from a web site for a climbing and training guru, Mark Twight, who I have used for years as a source of inspiration and guidance:

> Michael Gilbert and Scott Backes got soaked to the bone climbing The Waterfall Pitch on the north face of the Eiger. When they stopped for the night at the Brittle Ledges, they discovered their sleeping bags had been drenched as well, Michael asked, "What are we going to do now?" Scott replied, "We're going to suffer."

At first I chuckled, but upon recollection, I realized this verse of a situation played out thousands of times in the midst of thousands of adventures since man first set foot on a mountain, is the basis for why people since the beginning of time have chosen to venture across the globe's mountains, rivers, deserts, oceans, and even space. Fundamentally, it is not the adventure itself but rather the ensuing challenges that force people to take on adventure. Ironically, fear and suffering are the primary magnets that draw people to adventure and is why people are interested in hearing about it.

My mind began to wonder, and I looked back at my own adventures during my life in an attempt to see myself as I saw these two climbers on the Eiger. Invariably, this started with a comparison to various conditions I found myself in over all my trips spanning three decades and expeditions to some fifty of these major peaks and trying to look back at situations that allowed me to relate to a simple phrase, "We're going to suffer." I was not looking for the stupidity of this situation but rather scenarios that allowed me to feel what these men were feeling. Adventuring for these guys, as well as for anyone who takes on adventure, entails self-manifested suffering that is totally expected and even planned for. At age fifty-two, with a wife and kids, and a profession as a CPA with my own firm, I set out to understand why I would choose to place myself in these absurd situations that on paper appeared not only appealing but romantic and to answer the question why my immediate reaction was to try to relate to this line: "We're going to suffer." It also became crystal clear that the trips that held the most suffering and problems, regardless of outcome, were the trips that burned in my mind's eye the most. For some of the trips where everything went as planned, anticipated success generated, I found them hard to remember, rendering an overall feeling of fun but nothing outstanding regardless of the plot. It also made me realize that success turns out to be not necessarily what you start out searching for, but also how large a role suffering is for success, and why.

On paper, adventure often sounds appealing and even romantic, or to put it another way, tea house fodder is the stuff that dreams are made of. It never ceases to amaze me how bold I am in the planning stages and how much that contrasts to when I get to the foot of a major mountain. I can recall a trip to St. Elias in the Wrangell Mountains in southeast Alaska. We had been tied down due to weather for about a week, and the pilot could not get us up and out. We were held up with the comforts of a fully stocked Alaskan wilderness lodge with all the comforts of home and staff to serve us. The other guests were typical nature seekers and recreationalists, and we were the macho mountaineers heading to one of the greatest mountaineering objectives on the planet—a peak with eighteen thousand feet of relief from the Pacific Ocean to the summit in the largest glaciated region outside of the poles, where the weather is as severe as it gets. We had heard stories of storms dumping thirty feet of snow in a few days, experienced similar situations on several trips to the area already and realized temperatures could plummet to minus forty in minutes. Just talking about it with the guests was enough to put us in the limelight. In the ensuing time off, we laughed and joked and soaked in the oos and ahs. A week later, the weather cleared, and our pilot dumped us out on the glacier at the foot of the peak. The three of us stood in complete awe, totally speechless, and positively on the verge of shitting our pants. The pilot came up behind us, put his arms around us, and chuckled, saying, "Boys, ain't so cocky now, are ya ..."

There is a reality when you stand at the base of Everest, or any major world peak, and a process that takes you from the joys and excitement of a dream to the reality of exactly what you are intending to do. This is where the fear and suffering begin. Because suffering is not just physical agony involved with actually hauling heavy packs, the long cold days on the trail, the incredibly unsatisfying food, ah, er, make that the crap you eat on these trips, the lack of a toilet, or even the endless days, weeks, or even months of foregoing something as simple as a hot shower, let alone a change of clean underwear, it takes time to understand. The suffering I am talking about is the mental suffering that forms the initial and unavoidable basis of fear such as these men on the Eiger experienced. One would think that years of experience would diminish this fear, but in fact, if anything, it only enhances it. It enhances it to the point of experiencing it long before the cockiness of pretrip grab ass and clowning around and takes root at the start of the process. To put it in terms many can understand, it's like the kid who comes out for the baseball team for the first time and steps into the batter's box and gets a hit. For the time being and until he is plunked square in the back by a bad pitch, or worse, fields a ground ball with his jewels, the game is the greatest thing he has ever done. Then the next time he steps up to hit, the first pitch blows by him as he bails out of the way only to hear the ump call, "strike"! He will learn only through time and experience how to appreciate what he is doing. Mountaineering is similar; however, a wild pitch can come in the form of something that will not only hit you square in the back but also can take your life away. It is through experience alone that this reality takes root, and if you play the game long enough, you begin to realize just how little you really know, or in other words, how many variables God's green earth can throw at the center of your back. A mountaineer learns over time that the conquest of the mountain is really the conquest of himself, and if you try to compete against the natural environment, you are doomed to fail. Failure takes on a wide variety of forms from not obtaining your goal to losing your fingers or, worse, your life. It's serious business no matter how blue the sky is.

So, let's go climbing; it all sounds like so much fun. But trust me, it gets worse. For the hard-core climbers, they must take it to another level. The mountain has to be climbed in "pure style," whatever that means, but amounts to in my mind as climbing the mountain without the perks that writing a five- or six-figure check to any number of commercial guide companies will afford you. For this rare breed, using any "crutches" such as supplemental oxygen, fixed lines, porters, and a medical bag of altitude drugs, among many other varying available scenarios and tools to aid in the objective of reaching a peak's summit, are shunned. But again, this mentality only adds to this concept of fear. To climb without the infrastructure available from the many certified guide companies for any mountain on the face of the earth exposes a climber to thin air, steep slopes, and exhaustion entailed in experiencing the peak on as close to its terms as mother earth created it. But this is also where the controversy begins.

Take Everest as a great example. It's the highest and arguably most famous peak on the planet. For decades, it was the penultimate feather for a mountaineer's résumé. To climb it entails pushing yourself into an atmosphere that airliners cruise in. Books, articles, and films have depicted massive ice falls, countless deaths, and an objective that sets itself apart. However, over the years, through technology and infrastructure, the peak has been engineered to allow people from all over the globe and all walks of life to stand on its summit. People from thirteen to eighty, men and women, blind and deaf, you name it, have climbed Everest. The mountain has not changed, but the way it has been engineered to be climbed has made the mountain a molehill. However, by looking at the culture of modern climbers and how they relate their experiences climbing the mountain, you can see that despite the reality that the peak is significantly easier to climb today compared to climbing it by, as Messner coined, "fair means" or in other words without the infrastructure available, it becomes obvious how important the fear and suffering aspect is.

The first premise one must learn in order to understand what I am talking about is that virtually all skiers and climbers think they are better than they are. Even with modern helmet cams, it is a rare occasion for a skier or climber to see how he or she performs. Today, the popularity of helmet cams attempts to bring reality to the situation, but if anything, because they are often mounted on the skier/climber, only serve to make the skier/climber feel even more "rad" than they actually are. Unless people are being shot by a photographer, they will never have the disappointing experience of seeing just how good they are. Notice I shoot films and am rarely in them.

One also must understand what the infrastructure amounts to. Fixed lines are lines that are permanently attached to the mountain for an expedition. Generally, as is the case on say Everest, the guiding companies will meet at the beginning of a season, agree to terms, price, and logistics of where the lines will be placed, and then they send an army of high-altitude Sherpa up the mountain with spools of rope to set the lines. The clients then can use a device that slides up the rope but not back and is tied to them to follow up a rope that prevents them from falling off the mountain. But it also allows them to draw on the rope to hoist them to the top of the mountain. Without a fixed line, climbers have to tie into a rope that moves up the hill with their climbing partners, and along the way, they set protection, which they run the rope through; if someone falls, the protection along with the other climbers can prevent the fall. But this running belay, as it is called, is not a bread crumb trail to the top, and it forces the team to not only utilize energy to carry the protection (ice screws, pickets, and flukes, all driven into the slope with a hammer, which takes time and is extremely tiring), but to find the route. These mountains are huge, and the easiest route is not always obvious as it is if you are on a fixed line. That takes mental and physical energy to create, but more importantly, time. You can't pull on the rope because it will pull the climber ahead of you off his feet.

Porters are another crutch. Based on my experience, guide companies have adopted around a 3-1 ratio (three porters to one climber). The need for this is to establish camps on the mountain. The porters carry all tents, stoves, food, fuel, sleeping bags, mats, and bottles of oxygen, you name it, up the mountain. All climbers must do is carry their personal gear, clothing, and a bit of food and water for the day climb to the next camp. To put this in context, when you climb one of these peaks without porters, instead of carrying fifty- or as much as seventy-pound packs, you carry ten- or twenty-pound packs. It typically takes two to three separate days to set up each camp, a day or two to acclimate and return to the previous camp, and then another to climb to the camp to sleep. On an eight-thousand-meter peak, you generally have three to four camps. So, by doing the math, you can see that there is a ton of running up and down to be done. The difference of climbing with porters compared to without has exponentially drastic effects on a climber's body by the end of the weeks that this process entails. For ski mountaineers, you can add a day to each camp to the process in that you also have to get the ski gear up the peak. Porters are a huge—make that monumental— perk. Having climbed with and without them, it is the difference between night and day. As you will see below, at these altitudes, the body begins a slow debilitating deterioration in that recovery above seven thousand meters is impossible. You only have so much energy and time to climb the mountain before you simply run out of gas and can climb no more. The fear of running out of energy is a fear that is constantly on the mind of a climber. If you run out of gas on the mountain, getting off becomes a major ordeal and is a huge source of fear.

The whole concept of oxygen is another topic, which is probably the most controversial issue. Dr. Charles Houston did studies in the '40s and again in the '80s to study the obvious effects of supplemental oxygen for use in mountaineering. I have heard that he coined the phrase "the death zone," a technical term where the body starts to deteriorate and without descent will perish. Contrary to what most climbers believe—that the death zone is eight thousand meters (26,300 feet)—this starts at seven thousand meters (about twenty-three thousand feet), according to Dr. Houston. The oxygen at these altitudes is approximately ⅓ of what it is at sea level, and the combination of lack of air pressure and obvious impact of the gas for the human body to survive goes without saying; we are breathing, eating beasts. Supplemental oxygen allows the body to breathe, decreasing the amount of effort needed to climb, which in turn allows it to eat and utilize the nutrients the body then processes to thrive. Using the analogy of a burning candle, Dr. Houston describes how without oxygen, the flame can't consume the wax, which is the food that it burns. But oxygen as it relates to climbing has another impact—to help the body stay warm. At altitude, the body goes into survival mode, and it forces the blood to flow to the vital organs, forgoing the areas of the body that it can survive without. Toes and fingers, noses, and ears all suffer from this process. It is amazing how cold twenty degrees is above seven thousand meters. By supplementing the expedition with oxygen, this process, per Dr. Houston, brings the altitude down significantly:

> In the 1996 tragedy on Everest, most of those who went for the summit on Everest were using supplementary oxygen during the final climb; for many, their oxygen supplies ran out at various times during the ascent. For them, the altitude had a greater impact than on those who had not used oxygen. With oxygen they had been at an altitude equivalent to about 22,000 feet, but when the supply suddenly ran out, they were breathing the much thinner air near Everest's top at 29,000 feet.

There is a physical aspect, but there is also a mental aspect. Just knowing you have supplemental oxygen is a massive mental crutch. From my experience, when I was climbing Everest without oxygen, it was a massive crutch just knowing that there were other climbers and Sherpa on route with oxygen, so that if shit totally hit the fan for me personally, I more than likely could have found supplemental oxygen had I needed it. To know you have Sherpa carrying canisters of oxygen just for you completely takes the issue out of your mind, leaving you to never question where you are or how vital oxygen really is.

Supplemental oxygen also brings up another rarely discussed aspect that is rare at best but extremely important when talking about high-altitude climbing. At altitude, the thin air and lack of oxygen creates an environment where even moderate activity forces the body at times to require more oxygen than it can obtain, forcing the climber to go anaerobic at times. This allows the body to build up large quantities of acid that can inhibit the muscles from firing. I have heard it referred to as high-altitude paralysis. Oxygen allows the body to function at far less levels, preventing the condition from manifesting itself. I personally experienced the beginnings of this on a ski descent of Shishapangma in 2000 where I suddenly lost the ability to hang on to my ski pole after pushing through a few ski turns beyond what I should have. It was only after sitting down and forcing myself to hyperventilate to obtain more oxygen and to recover that I regained my power, but I had to really concentrate on going much easier. For climbers not using supplemental oxygen to begin with, and also for ski mountaineers who exacerbate the situation by doing an anaerobic activity—skiing—in an environment where you absolutely can't let yourself to get anaerobic, the condition is something to be aware of at all times and is a huge source of fear.

Along the same lines as using supplemental oxygen, many climbers make a practice of using altitude drugs. The most widely used drug is diamox, a pill that in effect helps the body to artificially acclimate. I have witnessed the drug in use, and it generates amazing results for those that choose to use it, and in my view is on par with a bike racer using EPO. It allows a person to get to altitude and to acclimate without having to endure the long, tiring, and uncomfortable process of acclimating, allowing for recovery at rates that are simply not natural. It is a wonder drug that eliminates a lot of fear.

That said, as a climber once put it to me, mountaineering would be a pretty good game if not for the boots and the people doing it (me included). Take that for what it is; mountaineering, let alone ski mountaineering, is a made-up recreation that at best has been made out to be a sport. As I see it, you can't compete against anyone but yourself, so I don't see much sport in that. But to the point; it's a by and large made-up activity that it's players often use to generate extreme accolades when they return to home to hang prayer flags and schedule public slideshows (or films) where they can and do embellish the realities of what they were up to on their vacation to people and friends who soak it in not knowing or wanting to know why or how but just what; the door for greatness and accolades can be engineered to be as large as the ego that is sure to walk through it. I speak from experience, trust me. Anyone who would go to the lengths to climb and ski and shoot and then go through the hours of writing and editing a film on himself and his best friends, all totally on spec with virtually no possible return on investment, is truly an expert. But in the process of how people relay their stories, it becomes extremely clear that the concept of fear is an important factor in the process. Look at any bookstore adventure section, and it is filled with epic stories but rarely with accounts of when everything went perfectly as planned. Or when was the last time you read a climbing article other than an epic. The characters in these accounts are the climbers that I am referring to here.

I recently came across an article penned by an Everest guide who tells a story that is a good example of how mountaineers tell their stories and how often things are embellished in order to manufacture as much out of a situation as is possible in the name of this fear and suffering I am talking about. It is in the wording and context that this becomes clear. A major point in the story is for the guide to put to rest his feelings that guiding Everest without supplemental oxygen is wrong. His article goes on to explain how on one of his Everest expeditions his oxygen mask failed, and how he climbed for the morning to the summit with "none of the oxygen reaching my lungs."

He says,

> To truly experience another's dilemma, we must wear the same boots, or in this case, breathe the same thin air.

And also,

> Until you experience your brain with no supplemental oxygen—oxygen up there—you can't fully comprehend what the real limitations are on your faculties and physical abilities and the hallucinatory effects it causes. It was one of those serendipitous experiences where an unexpected bad had become the gift of understanding.

The text is woven to clearly lead the reader to now understand that this man has just accomplished something that places him in the "same boots" as someone facing the "dilemma" of climbing (and guiding) Everest without oxygen, a rarely accomplished feat. His description of climbing to the summit sans oxygen is harrowing and extreme, which I don't doubt. What he failed to explain are the facts and circumstances that would greatly influence the reader's conclusions. Namely, because he was using oxygen to begin with, his description of hypoxic hallucinations and limitations cannot be compared to what many of those that have climbed without oxygen would attest to. In my own experience at being at over twenty-eight thousand feet on Everest without supplemental oxygen, it was not even remotely like his description. Climbing Everest without supplemental oxygen is definitely significantly more difficult than climbing with oxygen, which is what leads this guide to embellish toward it, but when you slowly acclimate and adjust to extreme altitude, you won't experience what his story portrays—a severe case of hypoxia. As I have already mentioned, per Dr. Houston, there is a drastic difference between a climber not using supplemental oxygen, compared to a climber using it, and it fails, and when the facts behind the story are pointed out, it is clear that this guide has neither climbed Everest without supplemental oxygen, nor is he really in position to use his experience as an example to prove his philosophy that guiding without supplemental oxygen is wrong. One could argue that without even realizing it, he proves the exact opposite.

This guide, however, is not alone in his desires. In my own experience, of all the people I know that have summited Everest with supplemental oxygen, no less than eight have similar stories of alleged oxygen failures on summit bids, actually claiming they climbed Everest without oxygen but fail to explain that while their oxygen may have failed for a few hours, they did have it on many other days and, more importantly, slept on oxygen. The true dilemma of climbing Everest without supplemental oxygen is the cumulative effect it has on your body, not just from a summit day, but for an entire expedition. Ironically, I never heard of any climber's oxygen failing on any day other than a summit day, and of those eight, only two understood the real severity of their situation when it failed, enhanced by the fact that both of them nearly died. I am not going to pretend that climbing Everest with supplemental oxygen is not a difficult and dangerous endeavor, but it is ironic that despite this, there are so many people that are not satisfied with standing on top without manufacturing even more suffering and fear than their actual experience.

There is a need to explain, "It was there, but not really. It was way more difficult, superserious and hairball shit, I'm telling you ..." There is a need to make our experiences as harrowing as it was for the guy that climbed without oxygen, or didn't use any porters, or fixed lines, or whatever, because these benchmark situations represent the ultimate level of fear and suffering. Or in other words, had Messner not climbed Everest without supplemental oxygen, there would be no need to embellish this aspect. In the world of the Messners and the Boukreevs, the superelite, they have created their own monsters. To put it bluntly, they are significantly more experienced and talented than the other 99 percent of the hardcore alpinists I am referring to, leaving us with an opportunity to compare, but rarely if ever, equal, despite our desire to do so. Back to my premise, all climbers and skiers think they are better than they are.

My point is that climbers have a need to make climbing more difficult, more significant, and the basis of this insistence is that danger and a fear factor all relate back to this concept that fear and suffering are an extremely important aspect to why mountaineers head to the mountains or why people go to slideshows or movies on the subject. The phrase, "we're going to suffer" made me instantly search for the suffering I had endured in my own experiences over the years, and the tug of this simple story became clear. It is obvious that mountaineering is a manifestation of suffering and endurance, but it is the suffering of fear that is what mountaineers thrive on to the extent that beyond reality, almost always after the fact, it is often manufactured to be, even if only slightly, more than what it actually was. But the irony of this manufacturing that happens is where the topic gets interesting and only proves my point that fear is not only a desirable suffering, but almost necessary.

When was the last time you went to a slideshow of a golfer returning from a two-week golf trip, or heard a tennis player recant his exploits from a tournament outside of a great result, and how often do we dread the infamous summer vacation slideshow (unless it is our own)? The reality is that mountaineers are involved in an activity that fully supports their ability to come back and allow people not involved in the activity to live vicariously, not having to take on the hardships and suffering. There are simply not that many people stupid enough to take on the world's greatest mountains, and the very nature of limited people doing it creates an environment where a mountaineer can get away with saying anything that if he tells himself enough times, he actually believes. As I mentioned I have toured my film *Skiing Everest* around the country and have been the focal point of endless q&a sessions, and I have come to the realization that I could say just about anything I want, and people would believe me. I must respect that and use honesty as my guide. In the thousands of people who have come to my screenings, I have yet to come across a single person who has skied from above seven thousand or eight thousand meters, thus providing me with virtually no one to doubt anything I could say and, to the contrary, leave them in awe. And even on the rare occasion that I have come across someone who has been climbing these high peaks, I get the feeling that there is almost an unwritten rule or slap on the back that my harrowing accounts only serve to make that guy look more impressive to his friends. With this environment, however, and also the fact that I am in the golden years of my ski mountaineering career, (i.e., with age comes wisdom) and witnessing as well as creating the picture I have portrayed, not to mention the motivation to even write this article, what I have learned is that the reality is always enough to paint the picture that this stuff is extreme, or more to the point, beyond what most people would like to do outside of living it vicariously. Anything beyond this only serves to feed the notion that if not for the boots and the people doing it …

I was sitting in a café in Alaska about fifteen years ago having a cup of coffee with a buddy and a renowned high-altitude doctor who had just come back from summiting Everest with supplemental oxygen, and I will never forget his description of what it was like. This doctor was a highly educated and experienced MD specializing in high-altitude medicine and had logged months over the years at the Denali medical station at fourteen thousand feet, and I was a young gun climber, primed for his performance, the ultimate captive audience. For the next fifteen years until I was able to actually make it to Everest, his description of "hypoxic euphoria," and "feeling like I could jump off the side of Everest and fly, and having to tell myself that this was not possible in an effort to talk myself out of jumping" stuck firmly in my mind, and generated a great deal of anxiety and fear. For the dozens of high-altitude expeditions I would go on, I kept waiting for this feeling, chalking up lack of it to the magnitude that Everest must have held over all the other six-thousand-, seven-thousand-, and eight-thousand-meter peaks that I had actually been on only adding to my anxiety. The reality is that I can honestly say it was never remotely like that. Along these same lines, I have had to endure endless recants of actual Everest epics and exaggerations that simply have not materialized in any way shape or form like the anxiety that I endured over the years until I actually set foot on the peak. But don't think that I am belittling the fear I am talking about.

Climbing Everest or any of the seven-thousand- or eight-thousand-meter peaks is superscary business, but not for the reasons you might be led to believe. Ironically, in my mind, the scariest aspect to climbing in the death zone, especially without supplemental oxygen, is the harrowing activity of … sleeping. Until you lie in a sleeping bag at twenty-seven thousand feet or any altitude above twenty-three thousand feet without oxygen, you have no idea how dangerous these peaks really are. You feel like you have a combination of a hangover with a superbad case of the flu, and with each and every unavoidable chain stoke, a process where the brain forces your respiration to stop in an effort to utilize every last bit of what oxygen you can obtain in a single breath, leaving you gasping in a pant to catch up with your next breaths only to start the process over, you feel as if your heart will just stop at any moment, and it could. Over time for more than a few unfortunate mountaineers, it has. Also, lack of sleep leads to fatigue, which obviously leads to accidents; however, as soon as you start climbing, when all the harrowing stuff is supposed to happen, if you have taken time to acclimate and slowly adjust to altitude, you actually feel good. Circulation increases, and although you are moving a lot slower, it is extremely enjoyable and exciting! I will admit it is amazing to see people at altitude puking sick and clearly not in condition to walk to the store let alone to the summit of Everest pushing forward, in which cases I understand the epic nature of Everest; however, in my experience this is fairly limited and outstanding as pure stubbornness, which is generally thwarted by the obvious, and not the norm for the climbers I am referring to. And mentally, if anything, what I have found is that while hypoxia definitely eliminates one's ability to do calculus or any technical thought processes, it eliminates most emotions, and enhances your ability to analyze exactly and only what you are doing—climbing. My awareness of danger and how to prevent it becomes acute at altitude—a good thing. I believe that when you climb without oxygen the magnitude of what you are doing may scare you into thinking about things a bit more than without, but regardless, at those altitudes, you are going to be hypoxic.

But in my experience, that simply doesn't lead to hallucinations, and these, in my view, exaggerations one might hear about. On Broad Peak at 25,500 feet, we came across a big fracture line in the snow. We didn't freak at all. There wasn't a huge discussion of what to do. We didn't have to figure out if it was or wasn't there. We simply turned around. On Everest at over twenty-eight thousand feet, my feet started to freeze. I didn't start calling for mommy or start looking for my hallucinatory set of wings to fly back down; I walked down. On Shishapangma, when Jim lost his crampon in a hundred-foot fifty-degree ice couloir at 25,800 feet, it is remarkable how, on camera, he simply recanted the event with little or no emotion at all. "I told myself you are a climber; climb your way out of this." End of story. Also on Shish, we reached the central peak at over 26,300 feet in a raging blizzard, and there was no celebration but rather an obvious and unspoken desire to get back to the tent for a hot cup of coffee. The only reason we skied was because we had the gear. On all my expeditions over the years, when out climbing, it didn't matter one bit if we reached a summit or not, or even what was going on. There was nothing too exciting about it, and we simply made decisions that neither left us happy nor sad. Unfortunately, sleeping doesn't make for very exciting slideshows or stories, and if you dare say this stuff is fun, you run the risk of losing your audience. If not your audience, you run the risk of upsetting the small community of mountaineers that satisfy themselves with harrowing accounts of what most people dare think of doing—accounts such as "we are going to suffer" that in effect derive a sense of purpose.

I was at the gym recently and a buddy was pitching me shit about how hard I train, and how much I sacrifice for these trips. "I can't imagine what it is like to have an ego so big that it would drive you to do this." What is difficult to explain and even admit, is that it's not the obvious goals of the summits and ski descents or getting major plug in a major magazine that drives me. Not even remotely. Experience drives me to understand better the reality of what I am doing, and this forms the basis of why I behave the way I do. At this stage, I am experienced enough to understand by and large that summits and skiing are either going to happen or not despite my intentions. The mountain, the conditions, the weather, all the environmental factors come into play that will dictate success of a goal. So, this success is relegated to a large amount of luck. It goes without saying that being prepared enables a climber to take advantage of this luck, but the reality is that none of that drives me as much as fear. I train and prepare to give myself every possible advantage to handle the fear factors for when I am facing them. I train harder than I think I need to; I train in conditions at home that no one would think of training in to simulate as best as possible what the big mountains will throw at me. I eat the right foods and limit my vices in the months before a trip. I run around town in as little as possible during the winter to acclimate to colder temperatures. I research the peak, the route, all I can to understand what I am taking on. I go through worst-case scenarios based on my research. In short, I do all I can to prepare physically and mentally. Not because I must ski from a summit; that's a byproduct. I do all this because success in my mind is dictated by being able to go to a major mountain and to survive what I fear. I have enough experience to literally fear what I am setting out to do. I choose to suffer fear and therefore do all I can to not only handle that fear but to thrive. I eliminate all the crutches because crutches eliminate fear, and that is not desirable for me. I train hard to handle altitude without supplemental oxygen to the best of my ability. I carry my gear to see what it is like to be a Sherpa, to know what I can carry and for how long and how high. I don't mask my fear with drugs. I want to know if my body is hurting so I can make good decisions based on my ability. My fear is so strong that I don't want to let anything mask what I am doing; I want to be able to handle it or know that I can't. So, no, my ego doesn't drive me. The driving force that keeps me coming back to ski the five-thousand- to eight-thousand-meter peaks is the reward I get from willing myself to suffer fear, and the process I go through from planning an expedition, to when I am safely off the mountain, emphasis on safely.

In that same article by Mark Twight, he put it in simple terms:

> The mind and body adapt to both comfort and deprivation. The difficult experiences of mountaineering may appear irrational and risky from the comfort of the armchair, but learning to deal with them is essential. Relish the challenge of overcoming difficulties that would crush ordinary men. A strong will grows from suffering successfully and being rewarded for it.

Our new objective, Shishapangma, helped get our lives back into a routine. We trained like we were training to save our lives and took enormous pride in pushing ourselves as hard as we could. Our businesses began to grow, which—given the great cost of our newfound passion for Himalayan giants—was a good thing. We used the same drive we were developing to climb high peaks in our day-to-day lives. As soon as I returned home, I was welcomed with the news that I had finally passed the CPA examination. Although Steve had easily attained that credential, the process was endless for me. I was terrible at taking tests, and I could not seem to pass the exam. With the incredible news that I had finally completed it, I was able to further my growth as a professional and started my own practice in earnest. Steve found himself in and out of relationships, but I had found longevity with a woman that brought me confidence as a young adult, and life was good. Jim continued his life as a computer programmer with a pharmaceutical company and was enjoying his dive into being a parent.

We set our sights on the spring of 2000 for the attempt and hatched a plan that we thought would allow us to save the money needed. I had had my share of being the trip leader on Broad Peak and gladly handed the responsibility to Steve, who set out to figure out the process of obtaining permits and organizing the logistics. Steve is my identical twin brother, and growing up, we were inseparable. We did everything together. We were twin brothers and didn't have a need or ability to understand we were different people. As young adults, however, our personalities as well as physical differences were manifesting themselves, and those differences became apparent. Steve developed to be a full inch taller than me and was just larger in general. He weighed twenty pounds more. This physical difference translated to a stronger version of me as well. Whether it be a long bike race or long day in the mountains, I would not say Steve was in a different league, but without question he always seemed to be stronger than me. This didn't encourage competition; it was just how things were. In addition to the physical differences, our personalities manifested in different ways as we got older as well. I was the easier-going twin and didn't let things disrupt my mellow approach to life. Steve, on the other hand, was known as the "cranky" twin. Bluntly, Steve didn't easily suffer fools. He had also been forced to set up his own CPA practice earlier than I did, and with that, he developed a keen sense of details and procedure for all aspects of his life. Organizing the next expedition was a perfect fit for Steve, who embraced the opportunity. He would go on to lead all our Asian expeditions, leaving me to handle the by-comparison easier South American trips.

But two years is a long time. We needed more climbing. While we continued to climb and ski locally as much as possible, we decided we needed to go on another expedition. Jim had had a different experience on Broad Peak compared to what Steve and I encountered, and he was not so eager. Cooped up for weeks during the expedition, Jim had been stressed beyond imagination knowing that his wife was all alone at home with an infant. While he appreciated the experience for what it was, his desire post-Broad for another expedition under basically the same scenario, to Asia, was pretty thin. Steve and I, on the other hand, were basically free from the enormous responsibility that comes with having a family. But also for Jim, his sense of what climbing was all about was different. Jim was very quiet and tended to be very introspective. When he was not outside actually climbing, the stress of young children and leaving his wife alone to deal with it infected his ability to be alone in contemplation of where he was and what he was doing. Bluntly, he hated camp life and dreaded down time. His idle mind literally drove him crazy. Steve and I, on the other hand, relished tent life as an opportunity to not only recover and rest, but to listen to music, catch up on reading, and generally contemplate where we were and how being in those majestic mountains was what we were supposed to do. In a sense, while down time let Steve and I pump our desire to be full-on mountaineers, the same down time gave Jim an opportunity to think about what he was missing at home, and his mathematical mind to calculate constantly how much longer the trip would be. Added to this, Jim's definition of success was in my mind depicted by his life experience; Jim was a goal-oriented person and through his life of incredible athletic achievement in literally everything he took on, the result, winning, defined his success. With climbing, it boiled down to the summit. Steve and I were never remotely near Jim's athletic level, and we savored the process. Summits were desirable, but we grew to just love being in the mountains. On Broad Peak, when the summit was forgone, Jim had to get home. No summit meant the game was over. Steve and I, on the other hand, relished the thought of cleaning the mountain and leisurely walking out, and we dreaded the end of the trip. Ironically, over time as Jim's kids grew older and more independent, he relaxed and began to savor the process more. At the same time, Steve and I found ourselves with young kids as his got older, and the tables were reversed. As a trio we found balance in enjoying the experience but also appreciated the need to not waste time while our families were fatherless during the expeditions.

Jim bowed out for another quickie expedition but remained fully committed to Shishapangma. Steve and I weren't happy with his decision, but we understood. We also reasoned that the last weeks on Broad—after Jim had departed—showed us that we could enjoy expedition life without Jim, although it was not ideal or as fun to go without him. We decided to plan a trip to a seven-thousand-meter peak in Kyrgyzstan—Peak Lenin.

At the time, our cousin Jeremy Oates was a US Army Special Forces lieutenant. He'd served as a mountain division leader in Alaska and found himself home on several months leave. Although J. O. was several years younger than we were, we had climbed and skied with him often in Colorado, and his previous adventures with Alaska climbing piqued his interest; he wanted to join us for Lenin. J. O. was hard-headed and stubborn and marched to his own beat, or at least what he thought was the correct way to approach life. These qualities went with him into the peaks, and, fortunately, the combination of his intense military background and training generally made his way the right way. He was possessed with toughness that when coupled with a very strong level of intelligence made J. O. a no-brainer for the team. All this combined for a sharp wit, and his uncanny memory and storytelling ability were appreciated around base camp. He and I often butted heads in that his strict military approach was often in contrast to my laid-back approach, but the end results were the same, so with a bit of humor, we got along well. He's one of the funniest guys I've ever been around. Humor is critical on an expedition.

Bobby Williams, who had come with us on a past trip to Bolivia, was also welcomed on the trip. Bobby was a mellow version of J. O., and with very little mountain experience despite his Special Forces credential, he humbly took his place to listen and learn. He also possessed a massive sense of humor, leading me to believe that for both he and J. O., the military created an intense scenario where humor was critical for survival. Both had extensive combat experience, and on the mountain, they were as calm and cool as John Wayne on the shores of Iwo Jima. We trained together over the winter, found a logistics guy based in Almaty, Kazakhstan, who would take care of the permits and logistics, and put together a plan. Climbing in the region was a fraction of the price of the Himalaya proper, which allowed us to quickly accumulate the necessary funds.

We arrived in Almaty, and promptly drove to the airport and flew to Bishkek, the capital of Kyrgyzstan. We then took a Russian Eurol troop carrier across the barren and roadless landscape to base camp. Another Aspenite, Charlie Hopton, who was our initial contact for the logistics company, was a tour operator for the area, and he joined us as well. From the get-go, the atmosphere at base camp was very pleasant, but hints of the misgivings we'd experienced in Bolivia arose, making Steve and me realize this expedition was going to be difficult. Although J. O. was family, and we had no issue with him, Bobby was a bit of a question mark in our minds; we were not certain how he would react to a seven-thousand-meter peak. Added to the mix, the logistics company—led by a local Kazakh legend, Vadim Khaibullin, of the national mountaineering club—had assembled a team of young, talented climbers who would be climbing the peak to get camps ready for a commercial group that would arrive later. Hailing from the same camp, the new faces brought out the competitive nature that comes with young bulls. The testosterone was flowing.

We started the process of carrying loads, and from the first step, the race was on. Our Kazakh campmates wanted to show us up and outperform each other. Normal loads were increased, and on the trail, we pushed each other to the tops of ridges, down the back sides of ridges, across rivers, and so forth. There was one equalizing factor: we had skis, and the Kazakhs didn't. The race was soon over. We found ourselves gliding smoothly over the glacier, snickering as we watched the competition posthole well behind. In our minds, the weight of the ski gear and ski boots was the equalizer; we won the race. This only served to heighten tension around camp, but then a miraculous event occurred.

Lenin was not to be climbed. We found ourselves at advance base camp confined to a small mess tent, shoulder to shoulder with our foes, in the middle of a massive storm that dumped huge amounts of snow for the better part of two and a half weeks. When a storm like that hits, conversation soon wanes, and with all food product labels in Russian, the need for stimulation becomes apparent. With nothing to discuss, nothing to read, and cassette tapes that were becoming irritatingly repetitive, we were forced to get to know our foes. Competition was thrown out the door, language barriers were brought down, and cultural differences were dismissed; we were all climbers, tent-bound at sixteen thousand feet, trying to survive the mental anguish that comes with these types of situations. J.O., who had to learn basic Russian in the military, taught basic English to a few aiding in the transition. Tent time allowed our relationship with the Kazakhs to grow, and before we would depart, we realized that these men needed to come to Shishapangma with us.

If you are a mountaineer in Kazakhstan, you are a member of their national mountaineering club. In modern times, the club has produced some of the greatest alpinists in history. Anatoli Boukreev was at the forefront of a long list of great alpinists hailing from the country. The guys we were now befriending were the next generation, and they were looking for a break. They were enormously strong and climbed with antiquated gear, which we laughed at. But they were proof that mountaineering is not about the gear but about the person. These guys were not at a level to compete for the limited funding available for international expeditions. Yet in their own region, as guides and expedition hands, they had gained extensive experience that—while unnoticed in most climbing circles—put them at the forefront of the game. They had unlimited six-thousand- and seven-thousand-meter peaks to their credit, and in any other more advanced system would have been fully sponsored mountaineers. We pledged to them we would raise the money to get them to Shishapangma. This further cemented our relationship, making us mountaineering brothers with Vadim Khaibullin, their coach, and Maxut Zhumayev, who since then has gone on to reach acclaim on par with his mentor, Anatoli Boukreev. It is yet one more example of mountaineering's ability to create friendships for life.

Peak Lenin was an enormous exercise in patience. It snowed and snowed, and then when it let up, it would snow some more. We did make trips back and forth to base camp and advance base camp, but it was more for a change of environment than any specific climbing-related purpose. Our initial hesitation with regard to Bobby was manifested after a week of the waiting. We had descended back to base camp after watching the entire north face of Lenin avalanche with nearly five feet of freshly fallen snow, the roar and resultant pile of debris leaving us in freaked-out awe. This was followed by an electric storm that left us gazing at smoking holes along the same moraine we were camped on, worrying us that the next hole burned would be in one of our tents. Frightful is an understatement. Now, safely and comfortably back at base camp, it was frustratingly rainy. But at least we were at a lower elevation where it was easier to sleep the drudgery of time away, with the added benefit of a cushy base camp mess tent and very good food.

But for Bobby, the stress was too much. In the middle of the night, there was a stirring and the sound of a Jeep. Some of us heard it but went back to sleep. In the morning, we awoke to find that Bobby was gone. He left a note. "Can't take it anymore. Divide my gear up between you guys and thanks, but no thanks." We laughed it off, but the reality given Bobby's background and ability to deal with stress in general brought us all down to reality; what we had become used to over the years was extremely serious and scary stuff.

The event further cemented in our minds the need to be significantly more selective in our decision of with whom we would climb. A psychology is depicted in one of the first mountaineering books we ever read—*Surviving Denali*—that says, in short, you never break up the group. When you do—even if you do so with completely valid reasoning—the game is over. You go down. In Bolivia, and now at Peak Lenin, when members departed, it messed with our psychology. For me, I think these situations leave a mental hole. While life in the mountains on an expedition is fun, it's also enormously stressful. The mountains of the greater ranges are beyond comprehension, the living conditions are difficult, and stability is one key to success.

When stability is disrupted, it takes time and energy to repair it, although it never really can be repaired. That exposes a team to, for lack of better description, mental turmoil. It's not pleasant, it's not healthy, and it makes you think about leaving yourself. This situation on Lenin was a lesson that eventually registered in our minds. "Never again" became a mantra. We would only climb with tried and true friends, guys that we had spent significant time in the mountains with, guys that we knew had the experience and ability to take care of themselves and, more importantly, accepted the way that Steve, Jim, and myself operated.

Peak Lenin never saw anyone climb past ABC that season. It was a total bust, but time heals all wounds in mountaineering. The experience was reminiscent of our experiences in Alaska but took the waiting game to an unprecedented and oddly valuable level. In Alaska, we often didn't find summits, but despite the tent-bound nature of those expeditions, we always managed to find weather holes where we could get close. Lenin completely shut us down. This would not be the last time we would be shut down, so it was a lesson in yet one more aspect of life in the greater ranges: sometimes the mountain won't let you do your thing. The experience was thus another test in our development as mountaineers. All adventurers find themselves at such crossroads in the field. In mountaineering, the ones that persevere and take the right turn toward the mountains are climbers. The others, as Bobby did, sell their gear and never look back. For us, the experience fueled our desire to want more. The misery of Lenin—and it was miserable—only served to blend with the successes we had had and whet our appetites for more. There was an unsaid desire to take on the mountains, to persevere, to embrace the hardship that comes with it. By this point we had enough experience to know that when everything worked out, if everything worked out, the misery served to make the successes that much sweeter. We looked forward to more. We became obsessed with Shishapangma.

5

Shishapangma, the Defining Expedition

Back at home, we eagerly started planning the Shish trip. Steve took the role of trip leader and made all the contacts to get a permit. I started to figure out how we could generate sponsorships to cover the $9,000 per-person cost. We realized we would have to pay out of pocket for at least half. And the rest? We had no clue. I had accumulated airline miles to get us to Nepal, but by the time the bill was due for the initial payment required by our liaison in Kathmandu, we were still $12,000 short. We had no clue how we were going to fund this. We had no hope of figuring out how to bring our friends from Kazakhstan with us.

At the time, outside the world of guiding, there were not a lot of people planning private expeditions to the Himalaya. The people out there were generally sponsored climbers who had connections with companies that could write the big checks. While our climbing résumé was growing, we were still perceived in that world as novices. Our first few pitches to gear companies were met with marketing people reaching out to athletes they had already worked with to inquire as to our ability—we were still totally unknown. The fact that we were pitching it as a ski expedition served to make our pitch outlandish at best, foolhardy in fact, and the polite rejection letters were round-filed by the day. The competitive nature of ego-driven mountaineers created an environment that presented itself as a good ol' boys' network that was difficult to tap into. Sponsored athletes went out of their way to protect the limited money that was available. From what I could tell, this increased the negative feedback we'd been getting locally as well as the feedback from mountaineering circles in general. Word got back, and we found mountaineers we had never even met scoffing at our plans and requests for funding. We were perceived as not having a clue about what we were setting out to do. Some went as far as to suggest to gear manufacturers that we would be killed if we attempted to ski an eight-thousand-meter peak, leaving gear company executives wanting nothing to do with us. This left us short funds, but just as importantly, gear.

We reached out to Ed Viesturs, who was a fully sponsored athlete with Mountain Hardwear, at least to see if he could help with gear. He gave us an expedition's worth of tents, down suits, and clothing. It was desperately needed and appreciated, and the donation addressed some major issues on the gear front. We would be a ragtag crew with used equipment, but we had what we needed. By comparison to what our Kazakh buddies used for climbing, the gear was infinitely fantastic; if they could climb those peaks with the antiquated gear available to them, we would be better than good.

We also developed a disdain for commercial and professional climbing as a result and used the tarnished inventory as a source of pride. Rejection formed a mental toughness in our minds, and contrary to the initial depression and lack of validation we had experienced in the mountaineering community, it fueled our desire to make Shish happen, regardless. We developed a collective chip on our shoulders, and our message to the rest of the climbing world was basically, "Fuck you all." That was tempered by our more subtle public mantra: "Just watch me." We understood that ours was a long shot, but at least we were out there trying—trying a project that few if any were considering.

We spent the winter climbing and skiing as much as we could. This was around the time that the internet was just becoming available, and there was really no way to research skiing an eight-thousand-meter peak yet. Although we had been planning the expedition for more than a year, it became evident that no one from North America had skied from above eight thousand meters, and the only attempt we could find information on ended in tragedy the previous fall. This revelation and the magnitude of what we were attempting was a source of pervasive and unnerving fear. This was serious business with only a dozen attempts at skiing from eight thousand meters and none with names less than the greatest alpinists to strap on crampons—and all Europeans. Names like Kukuczka, Kammerlander, Afanassieff, Saudan, Tardivel, and Karničar were on the list—all total legends. Clearly, it was a long shot at best. We would simply go and see for ourselves if it was possible. So, we prepared and trained like never before. People told us we were delusional, crazy, reckless, and even stupid. One experienced mountaineer was signed up to join us, but with our insistence on taking the skis, he bowed out for another eight-thousand-meter peak, not hesitating to let us know that what we were attempting was "well beyond your experience and ability. You guys are being arrogant fools." So, we kept the project hush to limit the backlash of negative comments and kept things so that only a handful of people knew what we were attempting. We looked at the expedition as part of a logical process to learn something about ourselves. We were not delusional about the prospects for success, and we let the process flow organically as we had for the previous decade. The naysayers didn't have the perspective of working up to an eight-thousand-meter peak as we had on Broad Peak, coming to the conclusion that we should probably have taken our skis and that we could probably ski the highest peaks on the planet. The process was lost on our foes, and only now looking back do I see the hole we left in our pitch. Skiing Shish was not an outlandish, foolhardy decision but rather a well-thought-out plan that was a natural extension based on our experience to that point. What we soon found out, however, is that timing is everything.

As ridiculous as our ambitions were perceived, the reality of the grassroots coverage of the attempt the fall season before exposed the sport of high-altitude skiing. What was foolish, risky, and outlandish to equipment executives was a unique opportunity for film companies to tap into a never-before-told story. Steve had a business relationship with a local film company based in Aspen that was in dire need of a segment topic for a series they were producing for OLN (Outdoor Life Network). A discussion ensued, and before we knew it, an offer was made to sponsor the expedition if we allowed a film team to join us. Still completely short on funds for our Kazakh friends, we pitched the executive on their situation, and it was received as a bonus for the content. The team was complete, and we had ample funds to ensure the expedition was a go. Given our recent bad luck with new faces on the team, we were not terribly excited about having a film crew of unknown people along on our trip, but we needed the money. Only later would we realize how important this deal was for all future expeditions. (John Wilcox, the owner of the film company, American Adventure Productions, had a massive influence on our entire careers.)

In 2000, the craze in alpine touring (AT) ski gear—equipment that allows a skier to free his foot from the heel piece—was not even a distant proposition for the ski industry, and with the exception of the first generation of AT boots and bindings, skis were basically lighter-than-normal narrow intermediate skis with top skins and simple graphics like "Rondonée," complete with the quintessential hole drilled into the tips. The term alpine touring was not even coined. A company called Fritschi in Switzerland had developed a rudimentary touring binding; the DIN rating had not been invented. Skis could be twisted off with a swift kick in midair. Prereleasing was almost expected. Scarpa had engineered climbing boots to resemble ski boots. They were made from soft rubber-like plastic that allowed for moderately decent climbing and skiing that was better than the alternative—modified climbing boots with straps and plastic to allow skiing. The gear was better than anything to date, but it was heavy, and the main question was could it be used to ski steep, hard snow? Not considering skiing boilerplate ice at altitude, the gear left question marks in our minds, and we literally justified the project based on our ability to ski big bumps down the Ridge of Bell, a double black run on Aspen Mountain. We reasoned if we could do that, we'd be okay.

Point being, in 2000, gear was a massive concern, and not even considering Shishapangma, I often wonder today how we didn't kill ourselves just skiing some of the stuff we did "testing." The weight alone was an issue even for climbing and skiing fourteeners in Colorado. It took all you were worth to carry skis up local peaks, with no discussion of the line you skied. Skiing anything was noteworthy back then. Hauling that gear up an eight-thousand-meter peak was one of the most ridiculous things imaginable.

By the end of April, we were ready! We used my father's van to haul all our gear to the local airport, and the excitement of what we were up to was enough for the local bag handlers to load the gear without a single extra baggage charge. They checked the gear all the way to Kathmandu, and we boarded the plane. We arrived at LAX bound for Nepal, and again, hyped the expedition to the ticket agent who without even a slight hesitation bumped us up to business class for the fifteen-hour flight. Try that today, and you will get laughed out of the airport.

We met the film crew in Kathmandu and were introduced to Aspenite Cherie Silvera, whom we all immediately loved. Cherie was a Harvard grad who had dedicated her life to her passion: adventure film production. It was odd that we had never bumped into each other around Aspen or that we had no idea of her abilities. Beyond a great sense of humor and obvious skill for shooting films, she was a hard-core climber and a fantastic skier. This would not be the last trip with Cherie, and despite our growing ability to use skepticism with regard to picking teammates, Cherie broke the mold. She was on the trip as a hired photographer, but she earned an open door for any future expeditions. Pat Marrow, the first Canadian to summit Everest, was the lead photographer. He had a film résumé that was remarkable. Pat was soft-spoken and our senior by fifteen or so years, and it was clear he was on assignment; he worked hard on the trip and communicated well, but at the end of the day, he was on his time. We never gelled with Pat past the professional relationship that developed in creating the film. We respected his time, and given his background in the peaks, fished him for advice, and we respected his wisdom on a variety of issues. He was respectful of us, and while we never really got to know him, we liked him. We settled into the hotel to wait for our Kazakh buddies, who were driving from Almaty to Nepal, as we didn't have the funds to fly them. They arrived two days and two flat tires later, and we bused our way over the Himalaya into Tibet with acclimation stays at Zhangmu (seventy-five hundred feet) on the Chinese border, and the next day at twelve thousand feet in Nyalam. We spent a couple of days climbing local peaks and then set off to base camp at the base of Shishapangma on the Tibetan Plateau.

Shishapangma is the only eight-thousand-meter peak that sits entirely in Tibet. The view of the peak from base camp is spectacular. On a clear day, the golden plateau meets the white Jugal Himal region of the Himalaya, which touches hard blue sky. We did acclimation hikes on nearby hills, and the view of Shishapangma's northeast ridge was humbling. We knew that there would be fifth-class climbing, and the thought of the climbing—let alone hauling the skis—was enough to make us question the goal. Steve, however, was a source of great confidence. "I am going to stand on skis up there, or I won't stand on top at all," he announced at one point.

After a couple days at base camp, yaks were wrangled and loaded, and we started the hike to advance base camp (ABC). The trail was gentle, the views spectacular, and in a slow meander—with our Walkman headphones blaring rock and roll—we headed out. ABC was at eighteen thousand feet, and our heads were spinning from altitude. We spent the next several days just hanging out, acclimating, and getting ready. The descent back to base camp didn't offer a lot of relief, and we realized that we had to be fully acclimated at ABC to proceed higher. If one of us got high altitude edema, we were a full day's trek away from base camp, and that trek dropped the altitude by only a couple thousand feet. A more substantial decrease in altitude would require a Jeep ride up and over an eighteen-thousand-foot pass, a day's drive away, before any substantial altitude could be lost. It was an often-overlooked aspect to climbing Shishapangma that we respected.

When everyone was feeling good, we hiked to a pilot camp a few hours up the glacier at the foot of Shishapangma. This involved rough moraine walking with no Sherpa support. Our initial loads were massive. After a couple of hauls, we rested a day and then geared up to haul to Camp 1 in a single push.

The trip from Pilot Camp to Camp 1 at about twenty thousand feet started with a ski tour across a rough glacier before we attained the lower slopes of the mountain. Once on the lower slopes, we had to race under a massive serac that was far enough away to be safe but close enough to make us nervous. Once on the steeper slopes, we zigzagged our way on skis up to Camp 1. Just below camp, we had to negotiate a large crevasse field, through which we marked the route with wands.

At Camp 1 a storm blew in. We struggled to set up in the snow and wind, and after a couple of hours, we managed to make it livable. The storm raged on, so we waited things out. Other than the immediate storm, there were no signs of a major front, and we guessed it was an afternoon squall blowing through. We passed the time napping and woke to perfectly calm blue skies, but the storm had left almost a foot of snow. We clicked into our skis, negotiated the crevasses, and had our first experience skiing in the Himalaya—powder skiing on the perfectly smooth slopes back to Pilot Camp in the late afternoon sun. We headed back to ABC for much-needed rest with the satisfaction of having our first camp in place, and excited with our first turns—in powder no less—behind us.

We woke up the next day to a commotion. A Taiwanese climber sat limp on a horse nearby, and I knew he was in trouble. Almost unconscious, he fell from the horse, and we immediately rushed to help. His team had no altitude drugs or oxygen, so we got our medical kit and Gamow (pronounced "gamoff") bag from our cache. A Swedish team doctor immediately started working on the guy, and another team provided oxygen. As we deployed our Gamow bag (a flexible pressure chamber that effectively increases the air pressure in the bag for people suffering from altitude), the doctor injected the patient with various medications. Steve was taking the guy's pulse, and when he had it, he let the doctor know. We put the guy in the bag, pumped it up, and held the pressure. There was initial relief in the guy's face, but soon he lost color and closed his eyes. The doctor pulled the victim from the bag, and he had no heartbeat. CPR was administered, and Steve yelled, "I have a pulse!" Then he noted "no pulse." This went on for a few minutes until we realized he was gone.

The mood at camp was morose. Death is a part of the game in the Himalaya, but to have a guy die literally in your arms … sobering, to say the least. The reality of what we were doing, what we were attempting, became as real as it gets. The post-first-ski excitement was all but gone, and the question marks of what the hell we were there for were scrutinized and discussed. Mentally, the Taiwanese climber's death was overwhelming. The quiet of camp was uncomfortable, but later in the day, we vowed to continue. Justification came in the normal dissection of all the mistakes that the Taiwanese had made, and there were many, and we fought the fear and tried to concentrate on what we came to do. We had an intense focus on doing everything right and checked and double-checked gear, the plan, and everything to not make any mistakes. This helped eliminate the tragedy mentally, and we put it out of our minds as best we could, almost getting angry at a dead man for subjecting us to that. In retrospect, I think often of that guy, whom he left behind, the pain and loss of it all. But at the time, we did what we had to in order to not let it happen to us and to carry on.

In time, we settled into the normal routine of life in the high mountains and slowly moved onward up the mountain. We established a high camp at just under twenty-two thousand feet, stocked food and fuel there, and slowly acclimated to the thin air. We were climbing pure style with no Sherpa, oxygen, drugs, or fixed lines. We found old fixed ropes on the steeper sections, which we did use. The lower slopes had no such old gear lying about. They were, by and large, smooth and moderately steep, and not only were our skis a great tool, the skiing was incredible.

Our Kazakh brothers were not skiers, and we were able to cover carries in half the time. Eventually this took its toll on them, and as we experienced summit fever, all but one of the Kazakhs experienced actual fever; except for Maxut Zhumayev, their youngest climber at twenty-one, they were done. Maxut would climb behind us. His strength was a hint as to who we were climbing with. Maxut would later go on to become the youngest climber ever to summit all the fourteen highest peaks in the world. He would go on to gain legendary status in the mountaineering community and in a country that produced some of the sport's greatest alpinists. And he would later join the ranks of the true elite. He maintained a happy disposition the entire climb despite postholing in deep snow while we glided along on skis.

Pat also succumbed to the illness going around, and thus our lead photographer was out. I had financed a lot of the expedition by selling photos from previous expeditions, and he gave me a crash course in the use of shooting video. Cherie and I would become the photographers on summit day. I was not excited about the prospects of having to haul all my ski gear as well as a video camera and batteries, but in retrospect, my film career was born; I have not shot anything other than video since.

After establishing the route, we rested for about five days at ABC to be as ready as possible. We had opted to not use the normal high camp at about twenty-four thousand feet, reasoning that without Sherpa support, we didn't have the power to haul an entire camp to that altitude and then also climb the peak. Also, the thought of having to remove an additional camp from the mountain after the climb was too much. Point being, we had to be rested because our summit day from high camp would include a push to over twenty-six thousand feet and nearly five thousand feet of climbing. With only one trip to that altitude in our past and knowing it was beyond the normal window of how those peaks were climbed, it was daunting.

After resting, we set off with no loads to Camp 1. We climbed in silence, preserving strength with a reasonable pace. The day was beautiful—clear, calm, and warm. The next day we ascended to high camp. The sky was filled with wispy clouds, and we feared that a storm was coming in. We arrived at high camp, and the sky was gray. We brewed up and crawled into our sleeping bags at about 3:00 p.m. The plan was to wake up at midnight and get on the trail as quickly as possible.

At midnight, Steve poked his head out of the tent and woke us up with excitement in his voice. "Boys, we have a perfect night! We are going to bag an eight-thousand-meter peak!" We roused ourselves, got into our climbing suits, brewed up, and hit the trail with a full moon and calm sky.

We skinned to the northeast ridge headwall, and the route steepened. We put on our crampons and started to strap our skis to our packs. Cherie never had intentions to carry skis past this point and vowed to climb with Max who, on foot, was well behind us. Jim was not certain about his ability to haul skis up the ridge at this point either and decided to leave them as well. This left a massive question mark in my mind and threw me for a mental loop. Although earlier in the trip Jim had discussed the possibility, for some reason it caught me off guard; I was rattled. Steve, however, continued unphased to strap his skis onto his pack.

Again, he muttered "If I can't stand on top with skis, I don't want to climb this peak. I am taking them." He stopped momentarily and grabbed me by my shoulders and looked at me with the assertiveness of being the trip leader and as only an identical twin brother could. He made it perfectly clear to me: "We have three thousand feet, Mike. That's less than Aspen Mountain. You are moving well. Get your skis on your pack, and let's fucking do this!" I was, in fact, feeling great, and his words inspired me to do what I knew I had to. The terrain now was steep and more technical. We traversed steep snow slopes to a col, which marked the start of the ridge. There we stopped for a brief drink, and as I filmed the team, noted, "It's about 4:00 a.m., and we are at about twenty-four thousand feet."

The route up the ridge was spectacular! The horizon took on a magenta hue as the sun started to brighten the sky, and we could see Cho Oyu and the Everest–Lhotse massif in the distance. We negotiated steep snow slopes through granite ledges and spires. I remember thinking to myself, *This is what this sport is all about; this is what I came for*. The climbing was steep, and route-finding was exciting. There were no other people on the route above ABC. The snow between the rocks was deep, and Steve, who was feeling energized, took the lead. Even with the deep snow, he was climbing ahead and breaking trail, an activity that would consume his entire day. It was one of the most amazing physical performances I have witnessed in all our expeditions. He was hell-bent to get up this peak and was enjoying every step!

We attained the notable spire marking seventy-nine hundred meters, and in an instant, clouds blew in. Wind came in massive gusts, and only the rough nature of the ridge allowed us to understand where we were supposed be in the complete whiteout. I looked at Steve and said, "I think we can make the summit, but should we drop the skis to give us a better chance?" He looked at me in total disgust and, shaking his head without a word, continued. I radioed back to ABC, "The weather has set in, and this is a total bitch! We are about an hour and a half from the summit; over and out."

Steve and I forged ahead and negotiated the final vertical rock band to the top. The thin air seared our lungs, and we slowly staggered on. While we were able to get up the steep and exposed rock step, we quickly thought it wasn't the route, and we yelled down to Jim to go around. Jim proceeded to wade through waist-deep powder, obviously taking what we realized later was bad advice. He found a rock ledge that offered him protection and climbed up to vertical ice. He was clearly off route, but he proceeded, thinking his climbing ability was up to the challenge. Halfway up a vertical thirty-foot section of ice his crampon fell off. After a brief panic, he thought to himself, *What would you tell your kids? You are a climber, and you need to climb your way out of this.* He miraculously found an old fixed line blowing in the wind slightly above him but had no idea what it was anchored to. Without much of a choice, he grabbed it and tied in but didn't remotely rely on it. He climbed to the ridge, where the snow slopes led to the Central Summit, and he put on his crampon. Disaster avoided. A fall would have netted a three-thousand-foot tumble. Later he would recount that it was the only time in the mountains that he felt like he "wasn't going to make it home." Jim's training and incredible athleticism and ability to remain calm paid off. Lesson learned; never get split up so far you can't discuss things like the route finding face-to-face. I shudder at the recollection of that bad advice.

Meanwhile, Steve and I continued up not aware of Jim's situation. We arrived at the prayer flags on the Central Summit and proceeded along the steep and icy ridge leading to the main summit in a whiteout. The ridge traverse to the main summit had not been climbed for the previous three years by any party, and we quickly realized why. The knife-edged and double-corniced ridge was not navigable. We didn't have the gear to attempt it, we were totally gassed, and the storm was raging around us. We settled for the Central Summit, a couple of meters lower, and half an hour from the main summit, when passable.

The top of the Central Summit of Shishapangma is a small perch large enough for two people to precariously stand upon. I helped Steve step into his skis and watched him descend, with the knife-edged ridge between his legs, to a small ledge a short way down the ridge. I followed by foot and then clicked into my skis on the flatter ridge to meet him at the top of a rock step. By this time, Steve met Jim as he topped to the ridge, and I soon arrived. Jim dropped his pack and headed to the central summit alone.

Steve and I stopped to figure out the descent off the rocky cliff we now knew was in fact the route. This was a class-five climb on the ascent but had solid holds that didn't require a belay, but here looking down it, we knew it would be tricky to down climb. There was an old fixed line that we uncovered. We retied it to an old anchor and then checked it twice to ensure it would hold our weight. Then we carefully used it to rappel the short thirty-foot cliff. We considered ski descending the route Jim had climbed, but the deep snow was too dangerous, and we feared setting it off. Below the rock step, we waited for Cherie and Maxut, who were still climbing up though well behind us. They continued on foot to the Central Summit while we rehydrated and had a bite to eat.

We then descended the ridge in a whiteout as a group. Steve made a few turns, and I waited behind while the rest descended by foot. We needed to stay close due to the whiteout. The skiing between the rocks was now deep powder, and while the skiing was excruciatingly difficult due to the altitude, we progressed, skiing and then resting while the others down climbed all the way to the col. While waiting, I had to fight off sleep. I was exhausted! From the col, we traversed out onto the face above the tents. Here, below the harrowing wind on the ridge, the light was better, and we skied smooth slopes with soft powder snow, despite our tired legs. We reached the tents and collapsed. It was midday, and we settled in to hydrate and recover for the effort needed to clean the mountain. Without Sherpa, we still had a massive job ahead of us.

The next day, the sky was blue and calm, and we packed up. We reached Camp 1, and a team from Saudi Arabia requested the use of our tent. We gladly let them use the tent, which meant they would have to clean that camp. We packed up our personal bags and gear and headed down. The skiing was incredible, but the weight of all our gear didn't leave much room for effortless turns. Our cook and his helper met us at pilot camp to help carry gear, and at the end of the day, we were off the mountain and back at ABC.

I lay in my base camp tent alone, and it dawned on me what we had accomplished. We were the first Americans, North or South, to ski from above eight thousand meters! Tears rolled down my face. Except for the storm on our summit day, the trip had gone as perfectly as it possibly could have, and we had pulled off something that no one thought we could. The magnitude of the mountain and the effort it took left us speechless; there was no celebration. As well as the trip went, the death of the Taiwanese climber, Jim's near misfortune, and the reality of how difficult the past month was mentally, spiritually, and physically left us overwhelmed by the experience.

While pushing up that mountain, there was no bravado past the next step. Now, safely in my tent, the power of the highest peaks really hit me. I shook at the thought of it. The experience we gained on that trip would remain with us the rest of our lives, and it was important. We experienced success per a plan, but in the process, we stretched ourselves to our limit. My tears were of joy but not for a sense of accomplishment. Rather, I had the satisfaction of pushing myself well past what I thought I could achieve, and I understood the reality that the satisfaction was not out of achievement but rather from being in my tent able to contemplate what we didn't experience more than what we did. Shishapangma had humbled us to our core.

Our success on Shishapangma catapulted us into the media on a level that we had never experienced. When we got back home, the phone never stopped ringing, and our message boxes were jammed full. We found this ironic in that after our ski descent, we had used a neighboring expedition's sat phone to call home and tell our families and close friends. Other than that, we had not told anyone.

This was coupled with the reality that after you pull something like this off, a bit of anticlimax occurs. This is due in part to being totally exhausted, and the postexpedition letdown and depression I mentioned earlier. We were without question very satisfied and proud, but for us, it was not a lot different than any of the other expeditions. We planned the trip, went, did our best, and while I would be lying if I said this was not very special, it was not because of the accomplishment. It was just that in our progression, we had pushed it a bit further and experienced something new.

But outside of telling our families, there was no media at base camp—no platform whatsoever to push out the story—and really no experience to make us believe that anyone would really care. There were, however, a half dozen other expeditions, and as is the norm for base camp life, you get to know each other, and there are endless discussions of how other people are doing. Our success was well known in that small circle of like-minded people. But even there, we didn't hype or blow our horns to anyone, still being in awe of the reality that many of those climbers were far more experienced Europeans ticking off another eight-thousander. As I said, we were in a state of humble shock on many levels. But our success registered in general behind our backs among these folks, and word spread like wildfire.

Before we departed, we did have the odd experience of having Pat sit us down and lecture us on the need to report our success with "complete open honesty … be careful to not hype, and don't miss even small details." This struck us as a guy spewing sour grapes for not being able to join us. He pointed out that we didn't get the main summit, that we didn't make the greatest ski turns, and other details that to us seemed to focus more on what we didn't do than what we did. He pissed us off at the time in that we had never done any hyping of our careers, nor would we ever dream of it. Only in retrospect did we appreciate his message. Pat was the first Canadian to summit Everest, and from experience, he knew success in the mountains from other than well-established mountaineers was akin to throwing a slab of meat to a cage of lions.

Back home, returning calls from writers and media people became a source of initial fascination but soon morphed into an endless job of sorts, answering the same questions time and time again. It was hard work. But we all did a good job of being extremely cognizant of answering very carefully, and Pat's lecture was appreciated.

Despite a concerted effort to be forthright, the media almost always twisted the story with incorrect facts and misleading opinions. One writer claimed we had a "first ever ski descent from an eight-thousand-meter peak." Another reported that we had climbed and skied an eight-thousand-meter peak in Nepal—Shishapangma is located entirely in Tibet. The mistakes and omissions in these reports were endless.

But the controversy grew. An article I penned myself, for a prestigious alpine journal, stirred the pot when a prominent climber accused me of lying about what we did, claiming I wrote that we climbed and skied from the main summit when we actually climbed the slightly lower Central Summit. When confronted, I asked the guy if he read the article because it was clearly repeated no less than three times as the "Central Summit" and nothing more. He sheepishly admitted that he had been acting based on what "others had reported" and apologized.

The metaphor of being a piece of meat in a lion's cage was coming to fruition. While most of the climbing community were extremely supportive and excited for us, an undercurrent of naysayers was doing everything possible to discredit us. Back home, people that knew us found it hard to believe that we actually did pull it off, and word got back that the guy who bowed out of our expedition only to sit for three weeks at the base camp was secretly telling people we completely lied and didn't do as we said. We learned quickly that defending ourselves was a futile exercise, and only when the photos and footage were manufactured into stories and a film did the undercurrent of doubt subside. Photos don't lie.

The net of the situation was positive, but we learned our first lesson in letting our actions speak for themselves. Again, this was before the internet, and we would selectively allow media access to photos and began granting interviews but only if we could read the draft articles. There was little effort to self-promote or anything like that. Our careers were jump-started with a spike in our ability to generate sponsorships, but it was not the open floodgate one might expect. While over time people accepted our accomplishment as something remarkable, we were nonetheless labeled as lucky and one-hit wonders. Even in our minds, we didn't see ourselves any differently than before the expedition, and we wondered if we got lucky. It was an ironic scenario because we were even questioning if we could do it again. But it was a hook to hang our hats on, and while we didn't promote or even know how to promote ourselves, we did formulate plans for the future.

As became the norm for all our expeditions, before we left the mountain, we knew we needed to figure out how to get to the next peak. In this case it became Everest. In our minds it was a logical next step, and having pulled off two eight-thousand-meter peak expeditions and a third Himalaya seven-thousand-meter expedition, and a number of six-thousand-meter peaks, we would try to leverage our experience to make it happen.

6

The Everest Years

Up to the Shishapangma expedition, I had enjoyed still photography and found moderate success in selling photos to fund my portion of that expedition. On Shish, that passion transferred to video. When I got back and the production company started to process the video and cut their story, I found myself spending hours with the editors in the studio explaining the footage, doing interviews for the film, and learning how the process of creating a visual story came together. I became obsessed. I purchased my first video camera and in retrospect have not shot a still photo since, concentrating all my photography efforts on shooting video. The film was completed and aired on national television with a segment even playing on NBC during prime time.

Despite the one-and-done reputation within the climbing community, we were gaining better access to sponsors. We had a massive advantage in being able to tell prospective marketing people that we had a film, and it had achieved considerable success on national television. Also, I could pitch myself as a videographer that shot for the film. While I never hyped our climbing and skiing, I most definitely touted my ability to take pictures and shoot video. This forced me to practice. Almost as hell-bent as I was to climb and ski, I became obsessed with shooting video. I shot hours of Steve and Jim climbing and skiing locally. I often took other videographers to coffee or lunch and picked their brains on the technical aspects of storytelling. I watched adventure videos to the point of irritating my girlfriend. I concentrated on the angles in those videos, the light, and the kind of equipment used. I cold-called the shooters and picked their brains.

After a couple years, I found that my video of climbing and skiing was turning heads privately. I experienced the apparent failure, however, of having friends ask me to shoot other topics and soon realized that I was a one-trick pony. I could shoot the hell out of climbing and skiing, but not much else. I accepted my shortfalls and continued pointing my camera at and shooting what in my mind mattered—climbing and skiing. That passion was blended with an obsession to carry the extra weight of a large camera and batteries to get the shot.

Before we departed base camp at Shishapangma, we had already hatched a plan to climb and ski Mount Everest. Years earlier, my father had asked if we had any ambition to climb Everest, and I explained it would never happen. The cost was way out of our price range. In his typical always-positive manner, he told me, "Never say never, Mikey. You will find in life that when you set your mind to these seemingly impossible things, they have a way of figuring themselves out." I laughed, but in that Jeep looking back at Shish as we drove away, I recalled his words of wisdom. My newfound passion to shoot video would pave the path toward figuring out how to get to Everest.

I knew that getting a permit to Everest was more expensive than what we had experienced but also learned that the prohibitive cost I was basing my argument on was not valid as well. Our experiences with Broad Peak, Pik Lenin, and now Shishapangma—all major mountains in the Himalaya—had exposed us to commercial expeditions at the base camps and all the amenities that came with them. Supplemental oxygen, Sherpa to carry gear, satellite phone systems, plush base camp tents—including microwave ovens and cappuccino machines and on and on—were all perks that we did not need for our expeditions. In the planning of our expeditions, we were exposed to the costs of all these amenities, and we realized that we didn't want all the perks that came with writing large checks. We couldn't afford that stuff, but we also didn't need it, and we started to find our minimalist approach a great source of pride. As I bumped along in that Jeep away from Shish, I knew that Everest could be approached the same way and that we could afford it. Success cemented a desire for more, and there was never a doubt; we would make it happen one way or another. We vowed to leverage our success on Shish, and I laughed at the thought Dad had planted in the back of my mind: "These things have a way of figuring themselves out."

Almost immediately upon getting home, Steve took the lead on an expedition to Everest. Steve did an incredible job in handling all the planning for Shish, and he loved the endless research and correspondence with tour agencies and other mountaineers—he thrived on the organization. Everest became a part-time job that had to be completed. I was handed the responsibility of fund-raising. We had an arrow in our quiver—the first Americans to ski from eight thousand meters—and I set out with confidence. Although many saw our effort as a lucky break, the reality was that we did what we did. In the minds of many, Everest was perceived as a cocky and arrogant play for our next expedition, but facts were facts.

On paper our résumés and our newfound fifteen minutes of fame—which, by the way, graced literally every adventure and ski magazine—registered on others' minds as well. Internally, we looked at our success for what it was. While we did pull off something that admittedly we didn't fully believe we could pull off before we did, I think we understood the process and effort better than our foes. We put one foot in front of the other, hour after hour, day after day, week after week. We experienced the load hauling, the endless tent life, all the struggles involved with climbing an eight-thousand-meter peak, and while mountaineering always entails luck with weather, conditions, and health, we also realized that the process is not rocket science. It's just heading out each day and slowly getting it done despite everything.

Not for a second did we look at ourselves as like the European greats that influenced us; we were still in awe of them. The irony is that the hardship and toil of the Shishapangma expedition, if anything, humbled us more. Enormous pride was coupled with yet more questioning. In the process of approaching potential sponsors, I was not an arrogant punk looking for a handout but rather a humble guy that made no bones about being honest; I didn't have it in me to hype anything. I was inspired to do what it took to make Everest happen, but I was bluntly honest about it, almost apologizing for making my pitch. In retrospect, in today's world of social media, I see now that I missed an opportunity to catapult our careers to notoriety, but at the time, my unconscious approach somehow managed to work.

Part of our deal with the production company that produced the film on Shishapangma was that we could use the film for events and to help generate funding for the future. I entered the realm of public speaking. I was at work one afternoon, and I received a call from a boyfriend of my future wife's sister, Richard Wiess. Beyond his successful career as a prime-time news anchor and charming *GQ* good looks, he was the president of the Explorers Club in New York. He had heard the story of our success on Shish and wanted to know if I had any interest in speaking to the members of the club at their clubhouse in New York. I had never heard of the Explorers Club, but this was a chance to showcase the film, and I leaped at the opportunity. I had no ambition or knowledge of the potential that an event like this could bring me; I was just excited to tell the story. Shelly, my girlfriend, said I could stay with her mother and father, and while the club did not pay a speaker's fee, they offered to cover my airfare, as I couldn't afford it at the time.

A date was set, and I found myself in the halls of the Explorers Club, gawking at the antique wood-paneled hallways lined with artifacts from the bottom of the ocean to the top of the world— and outer space. The names and photos of the greatest explorers and astronauts depicted what I didn't know—this was the hall of greatness. This only added to my discomfort at the thought of standing in front of a crowded room to speak, but it was extremely exciting. We screened the film, and then I answered questions until Richard told the crowd we had run out of time. People continued to shake my hand as they left the show. They handed me business cards and offered support for future expeditions. The limelight was completely overwhelming. Afterward, Richard and a few of the board members took me out to dinner, and we talked about the club, some of the extraordinary achievements made by members in addition to what I had already seen on the walls, as well as high-altitude climbing. I never felt that it was a sales pitch to get me to join, but as I shook hands with one of the men, Jim Clash; he gave me his card and said, "Let's talk after you get back. I would like to sponsor you to become a member," he said.

I did as told, and the next week Jim called to say he had a packet ready for the selection committee. I was excited at the prospect but found the courage to admit that I could never accept without my brother and Jim Gile. He explained that the selection committee received thousands of applications, and we wanted to make ours as seamless as possible. He reasoned that an identical twin brother was easy to explain but that sponsoring a trio had never been done. He also realized that Jim had not carried his skis all the way on summit day for Shish, and he didn't want to push the issue of a trio. So he submitted two identical applications for Steve and me. We didn't hear from the club for the better part of a year, but in the interim, I had researched the organization and found a handful of people I knew that had not made the cut. I didn't see us as extraordinary in contrast to names like Shackleton and, literally, every Apollo astronaut, and soon forgot about the Explorers Club. When the phone call from Jim Clash came with congratulations, I was taken aback. These things are typically anticlimactic in general, but I can't say I was not totally honored. I called Steve, who at the time had more pressing issues on his plate; Steve had never heard of the Explorers Club, and I had obviously not done a good job explaining it to him. Only later would we both realize the true honor it really was.

Steve continued with the Everest planning; I did the sponsorship work, and life in general went on. When the certificate and membership card came in the mail, I was proud, but it still didn't register. Then emails came from other members, many of whom I knew or knew of, and I realized this membership was of value. One said that it will "pave the way for sponsorships, tap into it and take advantage." The light went off, and in my pitches to various companies, it worked.

Through my accounting practice, I had reached out to a small high-tech company that had started to develop a remote access system with which customers could dial into their computers and gain access to the internet. It was a crude, cumbersome system at the time, but it worked. I called the general number to Citrix in Santa Barbara and told them about the Everest expeditions and that I was making a film. A couple of weeks later I received a call from a marketing person who was duly impressed with our accomplishments but also very excited by the fact that we were members of the Explorers Club. The membership proved to be validation for yet another pitch in the thousands they received for sponsorship. Postsalutations and gabber jawing, he explained that if we could capture dialing into work from base camp at Mount Everest on video, he could use that—"Certified accountants and extreme skiers headed to Everest and doing tax returns ... that's a story I can use to sell this product!" He explained they would provide the satellite phone and technology to make it happen. One thing led to another, and soon I was signing a contract for $60,000 to be spread over a two-year period. The contract had no stipulations for supporting the film or the expedition, so I budgeted half for the expedition. This covered about half of our budget for the trip.

This was a poignant education on promotion, and I started firing off emails to every conceivable company whose products we had used on expeditions and in general. I dedicated an hour a day to cold-calling marketing departments. It was grueling, demoralizing work, with rejection after rejection, but I would pull out the Citrix contract, and it was enough to encourage me to pick up the phone and dial another number.

One company, Merck, a massive pharmaceutical company, produced an asthma drug I was using, and although I had little expectation, I pushed dial. I pitched to a message machine. Almost immediately my phone rang, and a marketing VP was jumping out of her skin, eager to explore the potential. She arranged for a phone consultation with an asthma specialist and requested my medical records and proof of my prescriptions via my insurance company. I learned very quickly that the pharmaceutical companies were held to strict compliance for how they marketed their products. In short, they didn't at that time. Rather, they used celebrities and users in internal marketing for seminars and national sales meetings. She hired a photographer to shoot headshots of me and requested footage of my face. I knew I was no model, and with a lack of self-confidence I realized this was probably a long shot.

But again, one thing led to another, and soon I found myself clad in full climbing gear with skis at the top of Buttermilk Ski Area with a full film crew, spewing answers to questions that the VP threw at me. Prior to the photo shoot, she had sent me a two-page script with directions that I didn't have to memorize it but rather know it well enough to blurt it back. "Don't worry, we will have as long as it takes to get it and can shoot all day if necessary," she told me. I interpreted that to mean the worst and memorized every line and piece of punctuation in the two weeks prior to the shoot. I wanted to sound as if I was speaking from the heart. The sound check sync slate snapped, the camera rolled, and I rattled off the script as if I were telling a story over a beer. The camera crew and VP went dead silent, and the atmosphere was broken when a grip helping with the equipment broke out laughing and proclaimed, "Well, people, I guess we don't need the lunch baskets or dinner reservations on this one." And, in laughter, all agreed, "That's a wrap!"

Much to my relief, I had nailed it on the first try. To be safe we did it a few more times, but it was never as seamless as the first try. At this point, I still did not have a contract due to Merck's reluctance to sign a deal until they knew exactly what they had, but that day sealed the deal. A month later, I received a contract for another $30,000, a DVD with the edited marketing commercial, and a disclaimer that I would never show the video to anyone or use it for personal promotion or even an example of what I was capable of for marketing.

I've held true to the agreement, but often looked at that commercial and laughed. "Hi! I'm Mike Marolt. I am a high-altitude skier, and I suffer from asthma …" and so on, babbling this, that, and the other thing about the product for three full minutes. It was an extremely well-done piece, and I often called to see if they could let me use it in pitches for other companies, but Merck has never acquiesced. I also learned another valuable lesson in the process. I only pitched with honesty—I genuinely used their product, and it was incredible—and I didn't hype what we do. Climbing and skiing the highest peaks in the world speaks for itself, and would-be sponsors do a good enough job with the hype without any help from me.

We continued with preparation for the Everest expedition, but as these things go, the initial budgets rarely pan out. Both the film project and the expedition were incurring additional costs. I often look back and realize that in my zeal I suggested to logistics people and film production companies that I had it all covered—a big mistake on my part. They smelled the blood and pushed for more. The film project was critical for my end of the sponsorship contracts, and the need for funds for that superseded the expedition itself. But word of our success and membership in the Explorers Club spread like wildfire, and I soon found another avenue for sponsorship.

Living in Aspen, we found ourselves meeting wealthy people that wanted to know more about us, more about the expeditions, and more about the films. Some of these folks lived vicariously through our stories and marveled at our ability to be normal guys who were merely following their passion to climb and ski. In Aspen, with a father and uncles who were Olympic skiers, our story became part of what people in the ski industry called a dynasty. Steve and I were not ski racers, but we had found a niche, and it broadened the general aura of being an accomplished skier in a place like Aspen. We'd meet people in the gondola on Aspen Mountain, we'd meet people at parties, and often these encounters would end with a handshake and a comment like, "If you ever need any help for your films or expeditions, give me a call. I love what you are doing and can help."

This was awkward at first, given our history with naysayers in the local climbing community. Chalking it all up to light conversation and pleasantries, we never pursued these seemingly nice gestures. It was one thing to generate corporate sponsorship but altogether something different to take personal checks. But in retrospect, what didn't register in our minds like it does today is that while we were exposed to immense wealth in our careers, we were still very young. The concept of "good times" was something we didn't fully understand—perhaps because we'd never experienced "bad times."

Bad times were something Mom and Dad talked about—her growing up on a small family farm in Wisconsin and her father having to, ironically, do accounting and deliver mail to keep food on the table. Dad had similar stories of growing up on a ranch in Aspen, where they were so poor that they couldn't afford to eat the cattle they raised for sale and instead had to fish and hunt to keep food on the table. As I said earlier, later in life my father couldn't look at a trout or wild game without gagging. Clients and companies locally and nationally were in the middle of the tech bubble, and money was flowing like water. The success I was experiencing with sponsorships at the time was perceived as normal. So, when people started asking me out to lunch or coffee to see how much it would cost to get a credit in the film project, I quickly got over my initial hesitation and took the money.

For the Everest expedition, the added funds from a handful of individuals and local companies helped me to put money back into the expedition and left Jim, Steve, and me with a nearly funded expedition. We were short only the airfare. Part of the cash budget was for the additional equipment needed for an expedition—tents, rope, climbing hardware, clothing, and food. But even there, while gear manufacturing companies were not writing checks for expeditions, we soon found success generating gear sponsorships. We started receiving shipments of just about everything we needed. It was a massive shot to our egos and added nicely to our financial bottom line. We were set and ready to go by spring 2002.

Steve, Jim, and I were planning a pure style ascent with no perks—no oxygen but, more importantly, no Sherpa. We reasoned that we needed to build a bit larger team to handle the load carrying. We opened the door to people we had previously climbed with and knew could handle themselves. John Callahan had not been on all our expeditions, but he was like a brother and as strong and levelheaded in the mountains as they come. He had proved himself with us in Alaska. We had climbed locally with Kevin Dunnette (a.k.a. Backwoods), and he jumped at the opportunity. We had climbed with Jon Gibans (a.k.a. Gibjo), an Aspen-based ER doctor who had many expeditions to both the Andes and eight-thousand-meter peaks in Asia under his belt. We valued having a doctor on the trip, and his experience along with successful local adventures and similar pace as us in our climbing careers made Gibjo a no-brainer. Our cousin Jeremy was also eager to join us, and he introduced us to another one of his Special Forces Mountain Division teammates, Tim Carlson. Although we didn't know Tim, J. O. assured us Tim could handle this, and that he was not to be compared to what we experienced with Bobby on Lenin; he simply had more similar mountain experience on par with the rest of us. (We asked Bobby to go as he was incredibly entertaining and capable when climbing, but Lenin had been the end of his expedition climbing.) We also reached out to Roger Goking from Broad Peak. Roger had attempted the north side of Everest a few years before and was eager to try it again. It was a solid team.

We were not totally comfortable with an unknown, and invited Tim to join Steve, Jim, and myself for a quick six-thousand-meter peak in Chile—21,560-foot Tupungato. He eagerly agreed to go, and we soon found he was as solid and strong as they come. The penitentes on the peak precluded any skiing, but Tim was also a Special Forces medic and had a special interest in altitude. We decided to use the trip as a test. We would acclimate to fourteen thousand feet and from there go as high as we could in a single push totally unacclimated. It was what we envisioned climbing Everest at the high altitudes would be like, with Tim monitoring us medically.

Slowly we set off up the peak. Tim took notes and interviewed us along the way. We were climbing in alpine touring (AT) boots but dropped the skis off at sixteen thousand feet. We moved slowly, preserving ourselves as much as possible so we could, hopefully, attain the summit although we had no idea if we could go that far, that high, without acclimating beforehand. This was a test. It was exciting to have an objective other than a summit at stake; we just wanted to know what we could handle. We all fell into a great climber's trance and plodded up the ridge to the summit pyramid. The ridge was bare of snow, and we walked on undulating scree the whole way. At seventeen thousand feet, all was well. We were slowing down, but we kept going. Then eighteen thousand feet; the trance made the hours seem like minutes. All was good. We had not yet stopped for a rest. At nineteen thousand feet we stopped to sip some water and eat a bit of food. Our heads were light, but all felt well. The views to our right were of the massive Aconcagua, the highest peak in the Western Hemisphere, and to the left of the peaks and plains of Chile. It was magnificent.

At twenty thousand feet, we were still moving well, although the altitude was catching up. The pace slowed to a crawl. We communicated with each other, Tim barking the adage "Remember, guys, it's not a race; there are no heroes up here.

Make sure you are okay." We kept mumbling to each other that we had to keep enough in reserve to get off. But the thrill of piercing twenty thousand feet on a peak is intoxicating. It's a magical mark. This coupled with a realization that we were really pulling off a massive day kept us plodding upward. We put our heads down and soon found ourselves at the edge of the glacier leading up to the summit. It was a short steep pitch in front of us, and we stopped to get a rope out to belay each other. We could see the slope level off just above, seeming to be not much more than a stone's throw away, but at that altitude it was a half hour or forty-five minutes distant. Our altimeters read 21,150 feet. Steve flaked the rope out, and Jim belayed him for the short pitch. Tim and I sat down to rest and have a sip of water.

Suddenly my head started to spin. My eyes dilated leaving me squinting behind my glacier glasses. It was one of the most incredible experiences I have ever had. I was not altogether comfortable, but the hypoxia created a relaxed sensation. My sight was vivid, and I rested there in awe of the day. Tim was having similar experiences. We were all mesmerized by the newfound drug. Steve yelled back at us with a question. The snow against the wall of rock we had to ascend was deep and on a steep slope. He wanted us to come up and look. This snapped us back to reality, and while we had a sense of utter satisfaction sitting there at that altitude, we voiced our concerns in unison. Steve slowly climbed back down to us, not experiencing any of what we were experiencing.

In his excitement, Steve didn't stop to rest. He never let his circulation slow and continued to feel the invigoration of the most important aspect of climbing at altitude where you can't or are not acclimated—movement. I opened the discussion and explained that I thought at that altitude, if someone were to blow a knee, or fall into a slot, or become incapacitated, there just wasn't much time before total blackout would enter the equation. Although the feeling was euphoric, the notion that this was a test and all the communication along the climb was manifesting itself in a sort of hyper repetition of "How am I doing?"

At that point, we were fully aware of where we were and what we were doing. It was obvious we had to descend and descend quickly to beat the devastating effects of severe unacclimated altitude before we lost the race. At first Steve, huffing from his effort, complained that the summit was "right there." If he could get a belay he could get through the slop, and if it slid the rope would stop his fall. But as a slight argument ensued, his circulation slowed, and he admitted it was most definitely time to turn around. Ultimately, we all agreed that Tim had the final say, and if he made a decision for safety, that decision ruled. In the end the decision was mutual, but Tim capped it off with sound reasoning medically and logistically.

Once back at camp, our faculties quickly returned to normal, but we were exhausted. We basked in the sun with a newfound confidence. We realized Tim was a solid asset to our Everest team. He had skills and a mountain sense on par with ours. He understood the game. Summits were important, but not at the cost with which they could come. We all felt an extreme sense of accomplishment in that we had never remotely pushed ourselves that far that high in a single push. The format we worked, the test of sorts, gave us an experience that we didn't anticipate for that trip. It offered something much more valuable than standing on a summit that by normal means was nowhere near as difficult or productive for what we were setting off to attempt with Everest. To that point, altitude was something we dealt with in the normal fashion. We knew we could handle it on the highest peaks in the world, including Everest. We tried to imagine what it would be like above twenty-seven thousand feet for the two-thousand-foot summit day. We reckoned that if we could go more than seven thousand feet unacclimated to over twenty-one thousand feet, that was a good estimate of our abilities. We couldn't compare that with anything we knew for certain, but it was all we had. And regardless, it was a lot. We had another expedition with a style factor that was uncommon, and we hung our hats on it, which gave us confidence and excitement for Everest.

For base camp on Tupungato, we had brought a satellite phone to communicate with our families back home. At that stage, Shelly was in the final stages of adopting our first daughter, and although we were not married, and I was not legally part of the adoption, we were together and knew eventually we would be parents. Shelly was staying at my house, a modest half duplex. It was tiny, but it was ours. While I was gone, the neighbor in the adjacent unit approached Shelly and told her he was moving. He wanted to know if we wanted to buy his half. When I did my normal call in to Shelly, she was eager.

The duplex was part of the county housing program, and while I was precluded from owning two units, Shelly—who was technically single—could buy one herself. She had enough money saved personally so that together we could afford the purchase. We reasoned we could cut a hole in the shared wall and increase the size of our small abode. With a child in the picture, the added bedrooms and another bathroom would make the units much more livable. I told Shelly to jump on it and that I'd be home in a week to get things going. She was excited, but since I had no commitment to marry her, she explained that she didn't want to end up owning and living next door to an ex. Then and there I proposed to her, on a sat phone from remote South America, something neither of us anticipated. Tears rolled down my cheeks with the realization that what we knew from the start was finally memorialized with the simple but truthful question "Will you marry me?" and "Yes." I sat in my tent realizing I was going to be a husband and a father.

After I returned home, we finalized the purchase of the unit and started the process of making our home in anticipation of a family. This was a whirlwind period in our lives, and climbing was far from my mind. Soon we received our first photo of Talulah from the orphanage in China, and it became real. By that July, we were off to China. As I flew over Los Angeles at dusk on July 4, en route to China, I watched fireworks exploding from one side of the plane to the other, I realized that my life in a few days would be altered forever with the responsibility of raising a child and caring for a wife. This was a massive change to my freewheeling approach to life, but with all the gears engaged with the adoption, the wedding, and the new house, the responsibilities thrust on me were so great I never really had time to think about them all.

My parents absolutely loved Shelly and were very excited I had committed to marrying her, but they were concerned about the adoption. Dad, in his fatherly way, never told me what to do, but he gently played the devil's advocate in the situation. Even there, I had so much going on, I didn't pay too much attention to his advice. I was on autopilot doing all I could to ensure success in all facets of my personal life. I worked long hours, ticked to-do's off a never-ending list, and carried on. Then, when we arrived home, baby in arms, and drove over to Mom and Dad's house to introduce the entire family to Talulah, something happened that made everything slow down and come into focus. As I handed Talulah, this seven-month-old beautiful baby girl off to my father and her grandfather, I had no idea how he would react. He teared up and quietly looked into the eyes of this child and to only her muttered, "Genetics are overrated." Mom and Dad were grandparents for the second time, and they basked in joy at what they held.

From that time on until he passed away, no one on this planet knew in their heart more than Mom and Dad how precious life really is, or how beautiful an infant baby really was. I was not married, nor was I the legal guardian of Talulah. All that would happen in the future. But at that moment, my bond with my mother and father was enhanced in a way I could have never anticipated, and every cell in my body was transformed. I was now a father and a husband.

Life slowly got back to a new status quo, and after time I was focused again on Mount Everest. My training was curtailed due to a parenting schedule that was tough, but my motivation was now not only for success on the expedition but to avoid the inherent dangers of climbing high peaks. You can ask any mountaineer that has become a parent, and he or she will tell you that the game changes. Justifying the risk internally is waged against a lifetime development of passion. Over the years that followed me becoming a parent, my experience proved that there really isn't a right or wrong answer.

When my brother Roger reached the stage in his life that he knew he was going to marry his wife, on Mount Logan, he unveiled his "marry me, Susan" flag, and three months later used that photo in a slideshow to propose to her. On Logan, he knew he was done. I never thought he was crazy or sacrificing something at all. He loved climbing and skiing, but his passion was always at a different level than Steve's and mine. For the buddies that have made the life change, Jim and Callahan, they had more fire to explore mountains like Steve and me.

I could give you examples that parlay into all kinds of different directions from the moment of decision. But I could also give you a list as long as my arm of climbers who simply could not handle the stress of balancing their lives as climbers with being married and raising kids. I don't know the statistics, but climbing has often broken marriages and disrupted families. In fact, enough so that when I made the commitment, I had seen it enough to know that I was looking at a slack line of life that warranted a bit of soul searching.

The biggest problem I saw was that many people believe that they can get married and have kids and not change a thing. I don't know if it was my own family dynamic or what, but that was not how I saw the situation. Again, I used words of wisdom from my father. He had retired upon marriage and having his first child, and he regretted not trying to ski in a second Olympic Games. I approached him with my situation, and he was honest. He told me that life changes without question when you get married and especially when you have kids. "Don't fight it," he said. "Go with it." But he was also very clear that change was not in itself an ultimatum to give up the passions we all find in life. He explained that after a life of climbing and skiing, I didn't have to make an ultimate decision. He explained that as I had made the decision to change my personal life, I could modify all the other aspects without giving them up. More to the point, if I tried to be a good husband while at home, and if I tried to be a good father, my actions would naturally change no matter what I was doing. "You won't have to think about it too much, Mikey," he said.

I took his advice, trying to balance out my passion, trying to not overthink it too much but pondering it, nonetheless. Having a family didn't change the way I viewed my mortality; I didn't value my life more because of it. I didn't want to die before any less than after the change in my life. So, what it boiled down to was realizing I simply had to be more attentive to the risks. My incentive to that changed. While I valued life the same, it became clear that my decisions would have greater impact on something I had chosen, namely a family. My parents meant the world to me, and I wanted to make sure that I didn't leave my child fatherless and my wife a widow. So, I had to make decisions that would accommodate this. I guess plainly put, while I still had a passion to climb and ski, my family became another even more important passion. A family obviously comes with responsibility, but I never looked at it as that, which in my mind is a burden of sorts. Rather I just loved my new life, and that impacted what I would do in the future with my mountaineering and skiing. The game changed; a level of risk was simply lowered to accommodate my new life. There was also a practical aspect to it.

That's not to say I had it all figured out. Life is a balancing act, and it's tough on a family when one member of the family leaves for an expedition. The one thing that is clear is that when we depart on an expedition, it is drastically more difficult for our wives. Not only do our spouses have the nagging fear that we might not come back, they have the added burden of being single parents when we are gone. We are out following our passions, and they have twice as much work back home. Being a parent has been referred to as the most difficult job on the planet, and I would not argue with that. Being a single parent is beyond difficult. There is no way to assure a spouse that we will be extra careful, so the task becomes being honest and talking about it. Steve, Jim, and I have a unique situation in that our spouses know we have each other's backs, but it's tough. I've never belittled that or sugarcoated it because the fact is that people get killed climbing big mountains. But what has become clear is that this thing called passion has become a vital aspect of who we are as men. There is no question that our passion makes us better husbands and fathers; climbing and skiing has, for better or worse, become part of our identities.

When I come back from an expedition, I am eager to be with my family, and again, with no concerted effort, I spend as much time with my wife and kids as possible. Not out of guilt but because I love them with every cell in my body; I want to be with them. Distance truly makes the heart grow fonder. Also, it was very important that I made concerted efforts to encourage my wife to follow her own passions. Shelly is an artist; we built her a studio. She has organized trips of her own with her friends. Same for Steve and Jim's wives. And the beauty is that when they come back, we experience the same passion for our lives together with our kids.

My father was often on the road as a traveling salesman, and my mother humorously but also seriously often told me that his travels probably saved their marriage. Couples need a break from it all, and for my family, my expeditions coupled with Shelly's ability to take off from time to time are extremely valuable. The lesson is to accept that life can change. Being rigid to the point of not accepting those changes eliminates a chance to learn something about not only yourself but about life itself. Fighting anything with rigid inability to accept change will result in one thing—a fight.

The locomotive of Everest was well along the tracks, and I set out to figure out how I was going to complete the journey. Steve had arranged all the logistics. I had successfully funded everything and obtained all the necessary gear. But the daunting prospect of climbing Everest with no Sherpa or supplemental oxygen or perks of any kind was in the backs of our minds. To that point, our lifestyle was how we trained. We raced our mountain bikes during the summer months and always used the Leadville 100 race as the end of summer test to gauge our fitness. At the time, a hundred-mile mountain bike race was mostly unheard of, but proximity to Aspen put the event on our radar, and we raced it every fall. The race was as grueling as any climb, an out-and-back trail starting in the town of Leadville, Colorado, where a fifty-yard sign painted on the wall of a massive train dock greets you with: "Leadville CO, 10,000 feet. We HEART (in red paint) Leadville and so will you!" The track never dips below ten thousand feet and tops out over high mountain Jeep roads between twelve thousand and thirteen thousand feet. Bluntly, it was a massive task just to finish the grueling course.

Having accumulated enough seasons (Steve would ride sixteen, I would ride thirteen, and Callahan twenty-five) just finishing the course, it became a true race for us, attempting to compete and do as well as possible. Callahan, with his Olympic cross-country skiing background, became our endurance coach, and we found ourselves competing well against a field of riders from all over the country. The goal was to beat the eight-hour barrier at first, and then the seven-hour barrier became the goal.

Steve had success with a handful of top five finishes, including placing second one year. Callahan was not far behind him, and I was always a minute or so behind him. Doing well at Leadville that season coupled with the success we had on Tupengato that spring was a massive boost to our confidence as we headed into the winter before Everest.

Soon after Leadville, snow flew, and the bikes were put in storage. We began to hike up the local mountains carrying our skis. On weekday mornings before work, we would hike up Snowmass Ski Area, and then on to a thirteen-thousand-foot summit well beyond the ski area. That gave us nearly five thousand feet of climbing and skiing in what had become a major part of our training. In 1999, famed mountaineer Mark Twight published *Extreme Alpinism*, a mountaineering training book that we purchased and devoured. The book emphasized a concept for success in the high peaks—power endurance—which was obtained by blending weightlifting with normal endurance but was broken into three preclimb phases: power, power endurance, and tapering with mostly endurance.

We won sponsorship with a local spa, the Aspen Club, which became a near daily ritual. On weekends, another new sponsor, the Aspen Skiing Company, provided us with complimentary ski passes to ski as much as possible. We had enough experience skiing at high altitude to understand that for skiing the high peaks, the limiting factor was direct power to ski. For lunch breaks during the workweek, we would do nonstops, top to bottom, on Aspen Mountain. We savored difficult conditions, which added to the burden.

Also, the Skiing Company had, in recent years, started to control the Highlands Bowl. The Bowl was an out-of-bounds area that started beyond Highlands Ski Area. Skiing it involved a ridge hike out and up to a series of peaks at just over twelve thousand feet. Below these peaks, there was a massive bowl that spanned about a half mile and offered sustained steep and smooth skiing for nearly two thousand feet. The hike from the top of the ski area ranged from twenty to thirty minutes. When combined with nonstop skiing, it was the ultimate training for what we were into: skiing the highest peaks in the world.

We spent weekends doing "laps" on the bowl all winter. We always used our normal alpine ski gear because it was heavier than the alpine touring (AT) ski gear we would use on Everest, but also it was a lot more fun. We took a few local adventures on fourteeners to get a bit more altitude training. We did everything possible within the bounds of being husbands and fathers and working professionals to maximize our training. We developed a mentality that we had to do everything possible to ensure we were ready for Everest. We had enough experience to know that bad luck might prevent us from success, so we had to do everything possible to ensure that if given good luck, we would be able to take advantage of it.

We knew our objective, Everest pure style with skis, was a long shot, but we were giving it our all. It sounds like a grueling process, but it wasn't. Although the training was a bit more regimented with the added guidelines of the Twight book, the reality is that we were having the time of our lives. We had a massive goal, but we also had a massive incentive to climb and ski and train as much as possible. What we didn't know at the time was that we were establishing a system for all our expeditions to come. We were formulating a way of life. Post-Everest 2003, we would find ourselves on countless peaks in our backyard, always with an incentive to take on more for the next expedition. Our passion was being absorbed into the way we lived our lives.

As winter rolled into spring, and the expedition drew near, we were ready. The snow in the local backcountry solidified, and we found ourselves climbing as high as possible as often as we could. We were scheduled to depart mid-April. For the month before our departure, we tapered our training efforts so that we'd go in rested, strong, and hungry. By this time, we had all arranged with staffing in our offices to get everything covered at work and had ensured that all the bills, mortgages, and credit cards were paid before departing. This is an extremely stressful time for most mountaineers—the pretrip scurry to make sure everything is ready.

Steve took the lead on organizing all the equipment we would be taking. Group gear—the tents, climbing hardware, ropes, cook kits, food, everything we would not be including in our personal bags—was sorted, tested, and neatly packed. The process of packing adds to the level of stress because after a few expeditions, you realize no hardware or climbing store is around once you get on that airplane; everything you need better be in a bag, or you will have to improvise. On one trip, we forgot to throw the cook kits into the bag. We found ourselves running around Arequipa, Peru, looking for camping stoves and pots and pans. Our logistics guy had an old stove that barely worked, and we cooked our food in an old coffee can. On another trip, I failed to get my Gore-Tex shells into my bag. I completed the expedition in used, inadequate, and stinky shells I bummed off another climber who was throwing them out after his expedition. Being resourceful is mandatory for expedition life, but the more of it you can eliminate by making lists and checking off gear as you pack, the better off life will be once you get there.

The day of departure came and with it the tearful goodbyes to family and loved ones. Dad drove Steve and me to the airport, and we would meet the others at various connections as we all traveled to Kathmandu, the starting point of our adventure. Dad was almost as excited as we were and gave us final words of wisdom to be safe and smart and to have fun. By this time, the leveraging our story for seating upgrades was a distant memory as the airlines had modernized, and any negotiation was over simply getting an aisle seat—not upgrading to first class. Additionally, by this point, airlines had begun charging for excess and over-sized baggage, something that had never come up before. We put the charges on our credit cards and tried to forget about it; we would deal with it after the expedition.

A day and a half later, blurry eyed, we found ourselves at the Gowrishankar Hotel in Kathmandu. Our liaison in Nepal met us and told us we had a meeting at the Nepal Mountaineering Association offices that Tuesday, so we welcomed the two free days in order to rest after the flight. The meeting came and went, and we loaded ourselves and our gear into a bus for the drive to the Nepal-China boarder. A massive bridge separated the countries, and we were forced to unload all our gear and carry it a hundred yards over the bridge to where a large military truck waited.

We ascended the steep, switchbacked roads up to the border at the village of Chengdu. Riding in the back of the truck, we sucked in our share of dust from the unpaved road as we bumped along.

We were met by a stoic gentleman in Chinese military fatigues who didn't seem inclined to let us pass. There wasn't much discussion—just seemingly endless waiting. I ventured toward the officer with nothing planned other than to eat up a bit of time. I showed him a picture of Talulah, obviously Chinese, and motioned that she was from China and that she was my daughter. The guy melted and asked his friends to look. He lit up with emotion and promptly started the process of granting us passage to our hotel, giving me a quick lesson in Asian public relations.

We arrived at our hotel, a grimy facility on the side of a steep hill within the city. There were no municipal services, and people were accustomed to throwing their garbage out behind the buildings. This resulted in many wild dogs scrummaging in the heaps, but it also resulted in a rat infestation, as a result of which we found ourselves shooing the critters from the curtains in our rooms. We were eager to get on the road the next morning when a convoy of Land Rovers arrived to take us a few hours up the road to the mountain village of Nylam. At Nylam, the accommodations were even more primitive, but the altitude, twelve thousand feet, and related cold held the stench and the critter problem at bay. We would spend a couple days here, acclimating with easy hikes in the adjacent hills. We then loaded up the vehicles, crossed over the Himalayan divide itself, and found ourselves on the Tibetan plateau.

This was our second trip to the plateau, and at the highway junction where in 2000 we turned left to go to Shishapangma, we found ourselves headed in the opposite direction, toward Everest. We crossed a seventeen-thousand-foot pass and stopped to take in the golden plateau rolling toward the majestic wall of the Himalaya, which on that clear day pierced the blue sky above. We had full views of Shishapangma, and we could see the top half of Cho Oyu. And then there was the magnificent and massive blue pyramid of the north face of Everest, plume of white floating off its summit as it interrupted the jet stream winds.

I had seen photos taken from this point in my youth, never dreaming I would one day lay eyes on the scene in person. Yet here I was, not only looking at Everest but on my way to attempt to climb and ski it. We could just see the top of the north ridge, and with the mass towering over every other peak in both directions, all pretrip excitement was reduced to quiet contemplation of the reality of what we were taking on. Our minds immediately scanned back to the effort it took to climb Broad Peak and Shish, and there was no way to reconcile the magnitude that Everest held over what we could comprehend. Our enthusiasm was suppressed. If it wasn't fear we were feeling, then it was a level of questioning that would remain with us until we finally set foot on the mountain. We loaded into the vehicles and silently proceeded to the village of Tingre at fifteen thousand feet on the plateau. We would spend three days at Tingre in the process of acclimating for the top of the world.

The Tibetan Plateau is a vast arid region that starts in the southwest autonomous region of Tibet and encompasses the entire region along the foot of the Himalaya toward the autonomous region of Xinjiang. It includes nearly a million square miles of landscape that rarely dips below thirteen thousand feet, and dozens of its passes reach seventeen thousand feet.

The Tibetan Plateau is so big it is impossible to comprehend. Nomads from various regions of the lower lands have migrated onto the plateau and made it home, creating a unique area that is extremely remote yet peppered with desolate villages. The communities of the plateau rely on the ancient but now relatively modern Himalaya highway, which connects China with the densely populated areas just over the mountains.

The road from Kathmandu to the plateau that we traveled along is one of a handful of major routes connecting the dots on the map. Tingre is one of the dots—a small, ancient town sitting next to a river. The wind blows often, and the river melts for only a couple months each year, ironically signaling the only time when the people that live in the area have a chance to take a bath. Tingre is a hub that most expeditions pass through, whether they come in from the eastern city of Lhasa or from Kathmandu and the west, as was the case for us.

The hotel we stayed in was built with state funding in a bid to promote tourism in the region. But it was rough. There were no latches on the room doors, and while we did have clean-looking beds and electricity that powered small heaters, the floors were dirt, and when the door was barricaded shut, the wind seeped through unseen cracks. It was cold. Not that we would have ventured into the bedding. We were forced to use our warm sleeping bags most of the day while just hanging out and definitely when it came time to sleep. But even in the shabby accommodations, this was Tibet, this was the plateau. And beyond the city walls, it was magnificent. We spent three days hiking to and up seemingly small rolling hills that by Colorado standards would have been major peaks. We were able to acclimate to over seventeen thousand feet, with summits that provided even better views of the carrot that pulled us onward.

As a team, we hiked in complete silence, mesmerized by the hypoxic state we found ourselves in. With no real incentive to hang around in the village, we found shelter in these hills. We discussed nothing and everything and melded into a team; we were minute dots on a vast landscape that was beyond comprehension. I will never forget the feeling of tranquility I experienced during those few days in Tingre, a standout in all the adventures to come if only because what we were doing was met at a place that seemed to make it all seem meaningless yet allowed us to focus on it regardless.

After a few days we again got into our vehicles and set off. We arrived at base camp on the north side of Everest, situated at seventeen thousand feet. Although the north face of the highest peak in the world was nearly twenty miles away, it stood there like a massive billboard that overtook our imaginations with the same fear and doubt we experienced the previous week. And yet, it was so outstanding it left us with an enormous desire to touch it.

We had more acclimating to do to attain our version of a safety net, with a situation that was identical to what we experienced on Shishapangma; base camp was very high, and even with a Jeep, retreat from altitude was a long ways down the road, and thick air was possibly days away.

Physiologically, regardless of your conditioning, it takes a minimum of eight days for your body chemistry to fully adapt to an altitude. But by the time you reach base camp you've already been traveling for more than a week. So, when you see the magnet of Everest, your inclination is to hurry up and get going. Less experienced teams get to camp and almost immediately start, literally, running toward the peak like moths to a flame. So, you must pay attention and exercise an unnatural instinct—to sit and wait. Even knowing this about high-altitude expeditions, it is difficult to sit in your tent as people start heading up to higher camps even though they arrived after you did. We held tight and talked ourselves into really enjoying the process, eating and drinking to stay as healthy as possible.

Base camp is an odd situation, one that is difficult to describe to anyone that has not experienced it. On the more popular peaks, you will find expeditions with climbers that range from the best in the world to those that have never walked in crampons. The downtime required to acclimate, to wait out storms, or just to rest between trips up and down the peak, invites enormous posturing between the teams and players, and the egotistical nature of the sport sometimes makes life tiresome and irritating.

Personally, I try to interact with other groups as little as possible, but there are so many hours in a day and after a while, it's hard to resist making new friends. It almost always leads to interesting conversations at the dinner table, often under the guise of "at the expense of others." Especially on Everest, you really come across a plethora of characters and scenarios that make for great conversation. Everest is the ultimate for the ultimate. You will see people as young as twelve and as old as seventy poised to grace her slopes. Blind people, cancer survivors, and people with a host of other diseases and conditions come to Everest, hoping to obtain the title of "first" to go with whatever ailment or condition they bring.

Often the desire for the success exceeds what to our minds is a mandatory progression to just contemplate a peak like Everest. Despite our ski gear, which we could not hide, we kept to ourselves as much as possible. We laughed but not outside our tents. Until you actually get out and set foot on the peak, you really don't know how all these people are going to perform, and as has often been the case, the small meek guy that keeps to himself ends up being the star of the season. The private conversations come with an unwritten rule to pipe down. Your personal tent becomes your private domain to escape it all despite the lack of privacy that comes with only a thin piece of nylon. It has never ceased to amaze me how I cherish the comfort and seclusion of my tent on an expedition.

Life in the mountains gelled into a routine of sorts. By the beginning of May, we had been away for nearly a month, and as we gained the comfort that comes with acclimating to a peak in all regards, our faces became chiseled under our beards, and our bodies became lean and fit. Our advance base camp offered a mirror of what we had at base camp, but it was situated at twenty-one thousand feet. Not climbing with Sherpa or oxygen, what we slowly learned was the nature of the north side of Everest—it's high, but it's also extraordinarily long.

I recalled Anatoli Boukreev on Broad Peak touting that with a pure approach, north Everest was not the most difficult technically of routes, but in his opinion one of the most difficult objectives in the world. This became painfully clear as I sat in my tent after numerous trips to establish our camp at twenty-three thousand feet at the infamous North Col of the peak. From base camp to ABC, you trek for sixteen miles up rough trail and dry glacier. It is obviously extremely high, starting at seventeen thousand feet, and despite full acclimation, amounts to a marathon. From ABC to the summit involves two additional camps at 25,500 feet and twenty-seven thousand feet and covers another five miles in distance.

The route is relatively safe from objective danger—involves no massive technical hurdles—but it is steep, long, and obviously high. The issue you have when you are climbing using a more pure style is that after spending a few days working and setting up high camps, your retreat to ABC is not enough. ABC is too high to rest. So, you must walk all the way back down the route to base camp to obtain adequate rest, only to have to make the marathon back up to ABC to continue working the mountain. Once back at base camp, we would relish in the comfort of living for a few days at the relatively low altitude, only to find ourselves massively tired once we arrived back at ABC. This was our choice, and so I don't want to complain, but suffice to say that we quickly came to agree with Anatoli on his assessment. We might have been on the same mountain as the commercial groups, but we were playing an entirely different game.

Gibjo wasn't using supplemental oxygen, but he did decide to hire a personal porter to accommodate a difference in physical strength. To say that at times I was not jealous would be a lie. Even more than using supplemental oxygen, having a porter to carry your gear is a monumental advantage. We accepted our plight and relished our style, but we were quickly learning that North Everest was a different beast. This was further confirmed through a newfound friendship with John Roskelley, who was on Everest climbing commercially with his son, Jess. John was well known to us as one of the greatest alpinists in American mountaineering, claiming more notable first ascents in the Himalaya than any other American and accumulating a résumé on par with anyone in history.

He was the first American to climb K2, among others, and he told us of his two failed attempts on the north side of Everest pure style. In his early fifties, he had decided he needed to stand on top of the world, and with Jess starting his own career as a mountaineer, John decided that he would utilize the standards of the day and try to get to the top. His stories of his pure style attempts of youth correlated well with our own but heightened our concerns in that we had the millstone of ski gear to carry.

Even our own mentor, Slowman, had tried to dissuade us from taking skis to Everest, claiming there was "no skiing on the north side," something that now that we were on the peak many people made clear to us. One Russian team scoffed at us: "Der is no skiing on dat peak! Everest is for climbing. You bring skis … you disrespect our sport!" Again, our relatively young thirty-something bodies had enough testosterone flowing to do all we could to prove them wrong. In a rare moment of reaction and a sort of flashback to a scene in the movie *Patton*, I muttered, "Yeah, just watch me, you Russian son of a bitch," as I proceeded to issue a dose of arrogant rudeness back toward our newly found Cold War adversaries. This coupled with the reality that, at least from the North Col, there was fantastic skiing, our first view of the route fired our enthusiasm to ski on Everest.

We found ourselves in the comfort of base camp after a great effort to put in our camp at the col, with the excitement that we would now be able to establish higher camps with relative ease. We would need minimal gear for the limited time we would spend at altitudes in the "Death Zone." (As a side note, modern climbers have modified Dr. Houston's phrase to encompass altitudes above eight thousand meters, or 26,289 feet. I've found no evidence of the phrase being used before Houston's studies, and he told me himself at one point that his research has shown it starts at twenty-three thousand feet.)

Regardless, you simply can't spend too much time, or if climbing pure style, carry anything more than what you will need—a bit of food, gas, a pot, stove, cup, tent, sleeping bag, and the clothes on your back. We were ready to get high, and to give the peak our best effort. By this time in an expedition, over a month, your ability to focus wanes to the memory of family and being home, and you compensate to avoid those thoughts with summit fever. When we woke up the next morning, it was not to the calm of the river running through the calm of perfect weather of base camp. Rather, it was to the yells of our base camp crew calling for help to tie the mess tent down. The weather had changed, and it had changed drastically for the worse.

In general, the weather patterns in the Himalaya are extremely predictable. You know within a few days when the major shifts in weather will occur, and the major shifts are massively pronounced. You're either in a window of very stable premonsoon or postmonsoon weather, or you're in the monsoon itself, during which moisture flows from the Indian Ocean up over the range. The jet stream plays a big role in the weather, and again, it's fairly predictable. For the normal season as it relates to climbing, you schedule your expeditions either postmonsoon in a window that equates to our fall in North America (September to mid-October) or premonsoon, which is roughly mid-April to early June.

For example, on Shishapangma, we were there in the spring, and it was advisable that we be done and out of the mountains by May 28. On May 29, the clear skies changed, and the weather turned wet and soggy gray, with a nearly constant booming of thunder. On another trip, a winter trip, we were told to be out of the mountains before February 25. We were, but on February 26, it started snowing, and it didn't stop for a month. The saying is that only fools predict the weather in the mountains and that the general rules are not etched out in some cosmic stone. Everest in 2003 was an exception. We awoke to wind shattering our base camp tent as well as personal tents, and for the next five weeks, we were in a battle not against the mountain, but against harrowing winds.

As I rushed to our base camp tent, it was blown completely over. I looked up and saw an entire military mess tent fifty feet above the ground and flying down the valley. We secured our tent with everything available, including rope, ski poles, skis, massive boulders, and blood, sweat, and tears. Our personal tents had been mangled and were now nylon tarps, which we stabilized any way we could. I was in a standard A-frame tent that had been held in place by laying boulders along its base. Inside, though, it had been reduced to a space only as wide as my sleeping bag. There was no place to hide. It was miserable to be outside, and although we were cocooned inside, we needed ear plugs in our efforts to ride out time, shifting as best we could to avoid the bruises that came with unnaturally long periods of lying around. We also did what we had to in order to ensure that the resulting bedsores were kept in check with anti-itch and bacterial creams. It was miserable.

After a week of battle at base camp, the wind subsided slightly, and we took advantage of the break to head up to ABC. We shuddered to think what the wind was doing to our high camp, where conditions were even more ferocious. We arrived at a battered camp; ABC looked like a disaster zone. Entire camps had been flattened, some by the wind, some by the campers who were flattening the tents trying to save them before the wind ripped them to shreds. Our tent was lower in the valley and more protected, but it was still a mess. We immediately started to stitch rips and secure what we had. We had to establish a makeshift cook tent, which had been destroyed. Advance base camp doesn't have the supplies that base camp has, given you must haul everything up to twenty-one thousand feet. We used personal sewing kits until we had no thread left, and then resorted to dental floss and shoelaces to patch things together.

The wind picked up after we had salvaged what we could, and we were one of the fortunate camps to still be up and running. Farther up, at the col camp, reports from stranded people who made it back to ABC in the slight lull suggested that camps were completely blown off the mountain. We watched the plume of snow off the north and summit ridges blow for miles and, based on simple arithmetic and gauging distances with a map, calculated that the winds up high were in excess of two hundred miles per hour. The weather reports set the jet stream at about twenty-five thousand feet, which was nearly ten thousand feet lower than extreme levels. Guides that had been running trips for decades qualified the storm as having the worst winds they had ever seen. Again at ABC, I watched a personal tent blowing fifty feet in the air, complete with all personal gear, probably in excess of seventy-five pounds; it floated through the air for over a mile until it smashed into a massive ice penitentes well down the glacier.

We stayed at ABC for the next twenty-one days trying to hold our camp together. We had plenty of food to wait the storm out, but it was sheer agony. You can only listen to the same cassette tapes so many times before even good music becomes irritating and stale. We started finishing a barrel of books we brought for the trip, often reading material you would never have any interest in. We read and we read … and we read. Passing the time became a mental and physical challenge that we joked was like being in prison. Of course, all of this was on top of the agony of not knowing if we even had a camp left at the North Col. We repeatedly thought of throwing in the towel and just leaving. This was not what anyone signed up for, and although weather is part of the game—and we'd had two trips before where weather shut us out completely—sitting out a storm of this magnitude, for weeks, was pushing us to our limits on all levels.

After five weeks, we had witnessed the crescendo and decrescendo of a massive Himalayan windstorm we would never forget. The clearing brought conditions that otherwise normally would have held teams down, but given the contrast of what we had just experienced, left us with some hope. We had no idea if we had a camp and set out with massive packs for a last-ditch effort to get as high as we could on Mount Everest.

But the wounds from the storm had a debilitating effect. Jim announced he was giving up the ski aspect and was going to put his ski gear, including his ski boots, away. Others followed suit, surprisingly including Steve. With good logic, the thought was that the wind would have scoured all the snow from the north ridge so that only pure ice remained.

J. O. and I were not to be dissuaded. We met in Steve's tent and discussed the situation. It boiled down to reality: we came to ski. Over the years, Shishapangma had dictated a mentality that we were skiers, and we would always carry the skis. Steve finally agreed, and with enthusiasm we utilized Steve's power of persuasion, which we'd all agreed to before the trip. What Steve said was law. The team members who were climbing would haul gear from the col to Camp 2 to allow Steve, J. O., and myself to ski from as high as possible. At this stage, we were still hell-bent on going for the summit, and we vowed that we would carry the gear as high as possible. But it was obvious, and in plain sight, that the upper face of Everest was completely devoid of snow. We reasoned that the north ridge, in turn, which topped out at over 25,500 feet, was obviously white and therefore possibly skiable. We would take the skis as far as was reasonable for skiing and drop them when the snow ran out. The other members of the team were slightly disgruntled at the plan, but we all accepted the notion of keeping the expedition a ski expedition. While skiing severely limited our personal ability to obtain the summit, carrying the gear would accomplish the skiing aspect, and it was a small price to pay for what they believed was a legitimate summit attempt. It was win-win.

We set off for the col with fairly decent weather. It was awesome to be on the route, and while it was bitterly cold with wispy winds, the sky was mostly clear. We were pleasantly greeted by tents that were only a bit shattered, and with minor repairs our camp was one of only a few left intact. Comfortably in our tents, we gathered mental momentum for the task ahead. For the first time in weeks and at twenty-three thousand feet, we found ourselves laughing. We were well acclimated, and our hard work below and before setting our camp at the col gave us a sense of immense satisfaction. We all slept the night peacefully until J. O. woke us up to the fact that while it had been a relatively calm night, it had snowed several inches. The day was gray, but we reasoned that the new snow covered the nooks and crannies in the hard snow; the ridge would be skiable.

Excitement brought us out of our tents, and we were eager to climb. We set off as the first team to hit the route. The ridge was a long, white, massively corniced ramp that lead steeply to the next camp. To the naked eye, it looked very short and quick. But with the next camp sitting twenty-five hundred feet above us, we knew it was going to be a long, hard effort. We plodded along, found the climber's trance, and slowly proceeded. At about twenty-four thousand feet, the clouds blew in, and with them, the wind picked up drastically. We decided that we would finish the next one thousand feet, make a cache, and head back down to the Col, as a continued summit bid was out of the question. Given the month we had just experienced, our hopes were dashed, and we worried that we were experiencing what we had discussed below—that this was a mere sucker hole, an eye of the storm type of situation.

We arrived at 25,500 feet and cached our personal gear for a summit bid in the rocks. Steve, J. O., and I had started out as a team an hour before the others, and we found ourselves alone at the cache. The route was made up of Coke-bottle-like ice peppered with small stones that had blown up in the windstorm. It was extremely rough. We were concerned.

The wind howled, and we had to yell to communicate. The route was fixed, and we reasoned that we would attempt the ski and clip into the rope on the steeper sections if it proved to be too hard to set an edge with the skis. Adrenaline was rushing through our veins, overloading the hypoxia we were experiencing while climbing. We took our skis off our packs, and although we were standing on relatively flat snow, it was superhard and dropped off in front of us and to the sides. The North Ridge is a feature on the north face of the peak that falls steeply to the North Col, which is shaded on the opposite side by the mass of Changtse.

From 25,500 feet, we found ourselves looking down at the summit of Changtse, which if it were anywhere other than adjacent to Everest, would be considered a giant seven-thousand-meter peak. From where we were, the wind blew the clouds in and out, giving us glimpses of the peak that caught us off guard. To be looking down at it was a testament to how high we were—superhigh. The ridge dropped off drastically to the left and down thousands of feet to the Rongbuk Glacier. One hundred or so feet to the right the ridge fell away to the East Rongbuk Glacier.

Before us the ridge fell steeply all the way back to the camp at the col. There was one way, and it was steep and riddled with rough, hard, and icy snow. We set our skis in order to click in. Immediately, the lack of weight and security of standing on a high mountain slope without crampons felt odd. We held each other's skis so as not to kick them off down the slope. This was long before AT skis had brakes—not that brakes would have made much difference on that hard snow. I stepped into my skis and returned the favor, awkwardly bending over to hold Steve's as he did the same. We helped J. O. into his skis, and we were set.

J. O. yelled the obvious: "Okay, guys. No heroes in the mountains. No falling, and ski gently. You lose a ski on this rough snow, game over." Our bindings were plastic first-generation AT rigs, and it was a concern. We realized that if we lost the ability to control ourselves with the edges of our skis, the snow was so hard that any chance of a self-arrest would be impossible. The ridge was narrow enough to leave way too little room to stop a fall, especially on the steeper portions. We discussed clipping in to the fixed rope.

Suddenly and without warning, I found myself intensely focused. Something in my brain clicked, and I knew we could ski the ridge. As I pushed, Steve yelled, "Slow, dude; be careful." Later we laughed at how I just started to ski away. My skis scraped the hard snow, and I spread my feet a bit for stability. My first turn was to the left, away from the fixed line. I turned back toward the fixed line, my potential lifeline, with the goal of staying as close to it as possible. The whiteout conditions camouflaged the drops on both sides and the rope was the only thing that contrasted the middle of the ridge, our beacon of safety.

It was not pretty, and it was not easy, but I skied to the lip of the first steep roll and leaned on my poles, breathing heavily. I somehow had the wherewithal to pull out my camera and shoot my companions as they followed me down.

We looked at each other, but there was no celebration. The slope below us was significantly steeper, and J. O. slowly step-turned into the face, testing the hardness of the snow. His edge held, and he proceeded to ramp up his technique a bit with the knowledge that this was working—we were skiing the north ridge of Mount Everest! Steve followed, and I shot video of him as he descended to J. O. My father always told us that the key to skiing ice was to relax. I concentrated on feeling my skis under me as they thrashed back and forth over the undulating, rough and hard snow and pulled up next to Steve and J. O. again. We could only manage a few turns between stops to catch our breath, but the overriding fear of the unknown was behind us. We still had to pay the utmost attention to skiing, and slowly proceeded: a dozen turns, rest, regroup, a dozen more, etc. The ridge below the steep slopes offered an accumulation of powder from the night before, which on tired legs was welcomed in that they made skiing—and more importantly stopping—manageable.

Halfway down the ridge, the weather deteriorated. We soon ran into the rest of our team, not surprised that we had decided to head back to camp. I could see in their eyes that they knew they made a mistake by not carrying the skis. No one, truth be known, believed there was skiing on that ridge. Yet here we were, skiing it. We all agreed that the weather was good enough to make the cache and that we would regroup below and assess the situation. We left the team to continue down, meeting the other teams headed up. They seemed astonished, as if they had just seen flying frogs.

We passed the Russians who had proclaimed "there's no skiing on Mount Everest" and were surprised with their greetings of accomplishment that we were actually skiing—respect. The weather continued to get worse, and back at the camp the forecast was grim. The next weather window was not soon. We waited for our mates to return a few hours later, brewing up, relishing the adventure we had just had. The adrenaline of it all was washed away in a relaxing satisfaction that can only be experienced after doing something larger than expected or anticipated.

The team found itself together at camp, and the dismal weather forecast made it an obvious decision to head down. We had not given up hope of a return, but for the moment, we were done. We picked up our packs and skied the remaining two thousand feet back to ABC. The wind was not as drastic on the lower slopes, and we were greeted with soft snow. We had to rappel a few steep slopes with skis on, but we found ourselves skiing powder back to ABC in great contrast to the perilous slopes above us on the ridge. We were in whiteout conditions, but we glided down the smooth glacier back to the moraine and our tents.

Back at camp, word quickly spread around the various teams that the Americans had skied the north ridge. Nearly four thousand feet below the summit, and turning around due to weather, we never considered it to be anything anyone would find extraordinary or even interesting.

Kari Kobler stopped by, and in his Swiss drawl shook our hands and proclaimed, "Gawt dammit, nice job, guys." John Roskelley, as only John could, stopped by with an honest slap on the back and compliment at the same time, said, "I didn't think you guys would carry the skis once you set foot on the peak, let alone ski. Nice one, guys."

The reality of what we did was so far from our minds that to have these legends stop by and congratulate us was odd. Only later would we learn that only two people had skied that ridge, and none were Americans. In our minds, we had climbed that day in gear akin to what we would use to climb around our backyard in Colorado. We cached our down suits for a summit bid, but as we skied down past people clad in down suits and sucking oxygen, even that didn't register with us until later. Skiing was just a logical way to get down if only because we carried the ski gear up. In our minds, we felt like failures turning tail on the tallest peak in the world. We were beginning to realize what we pulled off was noteworthy. But more importantly for the others on our team, they realized the essential aspect of what we were there to do—ski. All vowed that they would be taking skis on the next run up the mountain. They wanted in. We jolted them back to the reality that we were skiers, and we came to ski.

Rest at ABC was welcomed, but the weather was ferocious up high, and over the next few days, our desire to reach the summit ebbed. We were late in the season, and climbing in the pure style we had chosen combined with weeks at altitude had deteriorated our bodies drastically. We were a ragtag group with little left in our tanks to realistically make a summit bid; we were tired and beat. Physically we were emaciated. Our fit bodies were skin and bones. Mentally, we were done. But the others wanted to at least get a ski descent from seven thousand meters. Part of the team headed up the day before we would pull camp to retrieve the cache, and then the next, we met at the col. The other members had their ski gear, and we divided the loads to accommodate their intended ski. I had experienced a bit of asthma on my ski descent and was in no condition to head back up, so I stayed back at ABC. The weather cleared a bit, and I used a pair of binoculars to watch the ski descent. By midday, our team was completely off the mountain with all our gear, and we proceeded to pull our camp for the journey back to base camp.

On the trek out, there is no denying that Everest had completely kicked our asses. The contrast to our departure on Shish was drastic, and there was a somber mood as we quietly hiked back to camp. All we wanted to do was get home to see our loved ones. An anticlimactic feeling happens when you spend months training and preparing for an objective, and you come away empty-handed. In our case—at least for Steve, Jim, and myself—the seeds for Everest had been planted nearly three years before. For everyone it was a bit of a letdown; for the three of us, it was more so.

We arrived at base camp and found it difficult to look back at the giant that had beaten us. It didn't help that on the day we started the return drive, the weather was nearly perfect. That, combined with the fact that Gibjo had decided to team up with another commercial team and as we watched was making his way to the top, was hard. He had used a Sherpa throughout the expedition, something that preserved his body and mental state. He had also decided to use supplemental oxygen. We didn't begrudge him for separating, but it was bittersweet as we watched. We were happy for him, but I'd be lying if I didn't admit I was jealous.

But adhering to the notion of pure style, it cemented in our minds that our chosen style was worth more than what would amount to a meaningless summit gained by artificial means. The contrast of how even a single porter preserved Gibjo compared to how we emaciated without any porters provided us with substantiation for the disparity; there was valor in our philosophy.

But the situation made us question our decision to pull out. Did we give Everest our best effort? The answer in retrospect was a clear yes. We were in no condition to continue, but at the time, this played a big role in our further development as ski mountaineers. Many of our mates were pretty much done after the difficult experience of that expedition, but with the expedition over, Steve, Jim and I analyzed the entire experience. We were hypercritical of certain aspects of the trip that—with the luxury of hindsight—were clearly done wrong.

The team was too large. The agendas were too varied late in the expedition. People were not on the same page. The large number created logistical puzzles that took resources—mostly time and energy—to accommodate. We quickly realized that our success on Shishapangma was due in part to the three of us being almost identical in ability and having the same goals, something that would have eliminated most of the discomfort involved with a larger team.

But something else came into play. We realized that while Everest had defeated us on one level, it validated that we could carry the skis high and that we could turn around and ski down. Shishapangma was not a fluke. Jim had another ski descent from seven thousand meters, and Steve and I had skied from nearly eight thousand meters for a second time. We used the experience on Everest to not squelch our desires. Rather, it fueled our passion and confidence to want to continue. Before we climbed into the Jeep to head home, we vowed we would return—not to just another peak, but to Everest. Just the three of us, in a small cohesive unit that would give Everest another chance.

Everest faded along with that spring, and life normalized over the summer. There wasn't a whole lot of thought toward the next Everest trip. Family, mountain biking, work—all the normal life activities came into focus, and the break was greatly appreciated. I was figuring out how to be a father, and we were remodeling our home. Climbing was the furthest thing from my mind. But it was an exciting and tiring time, and I took Dad's advice that "you get out of life what you put into it." I had no clue on how to be a great parent and found myself going through the motions based on advice from my brother Roger, who was two kids into the process. When situations came up that were new, I faked it to make it. My mother and father were a great source of support, and I found my already close relationship with them even closer through the advice they offered for the new and unknown chapter I was writing in my life. By July, I was finding my groove, and life was good.

At the time, I was also proud of a trip my father was taking to go skiing in South America. I offered him advice on dos and don'ts and relished in the fact that my father, who was a massive supporter of my trips, was traveling abroad with his buddies and doing the same. Steve and I helped him put his trip together and enjoyed the ability to offer Dad advice for a change. Then life changed forever.

I had come in from mowing the grass and sat down in our living room to catch my breath. The phone rang, and Shelly picked it up. I will never forget the shock on her face and then the high-pitched shriek: "Oh, my God. *Nooooooo!*" She handed the phone to me and covered her face, crying and shaking. Steve was on the phone. "Mike, you need to get over to Mom's house," he said. "There was a terrible accident in Argentina, and Dad died."

The shock of hearing a message like that left me in a surreal frame of mind. I honestly thought that it was a bad dream and that I'd wake up. When I looked at Shelly, the horror on her face made it clear I wasn't dreaming. Next, I expected a call back with Steve saying it was all a mistake; Dad was okay. I didn't cry or get upset. I didn't know what to do or how to feel. It just couldn't be happening. I immediately drove over to Mom's house. On the way, I kept thinking "accident." Was it an avalanche? Did Dad do something stupid? My mind raced. I entered the house to find Mom surrounded by longtime family friends consoling her.

She looked at me. "Max had a heart attack and died," she said. The remainder of that day is pretty much a blur that I can't remember. The news was so shocking. Only a week before, the entire family had met the night before Dad was due to fly out and enjoyed dinner together. As we departed for the evening, I remember hugging Dad and wishing him well before he got into his car. He shook my hand, and in his palm was a hundred-dollar bill, something he had become accustomed to doing during long goodbyes when we were in college. We laughed about it. I hugged him again and told him, "I love you, Dad."

Those were the last words I ever spoke to my father, and since then I've established the habit of always telling my kids and wife the same words every night and every day when I leave for work. Over the years, our family was never a touchy-feely type family at all. Later in life, my sister, Marlis, who was also a therapist, had reinforced in the family the need to hug and say the words. By this time, even Dad had become accustomed to the concept, and we, in fact, came to not just say the words and hug each other, but to mean it.

Looking back now, years later, I find great consolation in the act that evening and knowing that my last words to Dad were really the most important words I could have said. But I also look back and know that when I said it to him—that simple phrase "I love you"—at that moment, I really, honestly meant it. I felt it. I worshiped my father, and while I had no premonition that that would be the last encounter I would have with him, something in me made me "feel" it.

After Dad died, I was on a local peak with a friend and writer from the *Denver Post*, John Meyer, and he told me that he honestly never went a day after his father passed away without thinking about him. I can relate, and one thing I will never regret is how I ended my physical relationship with dad: "I love you, Dad." And more importantly, I cherish the fact that he said it back to me. I share that with anyone and everyone now.

While life after Dad died changed forever, Steve and I both realized that his death had by far the greatest impact on our lives, and it was oddly very positive. His spirit was embodied in our desire to climb and ski.

Shortly after his death, a neighbor of Mom's came over to her fence and we started talking. He told us that while we were on Everest, Dad would give him updates from our calls home from base camp. He said Dad looked at him one day and almost in a daydream mumbled, "Damn, wouldn't you just love to be up there with them." Dad planted the seeds of a skiing life, and we could feel him in our souls, guiding and encouraging us to continue. That is not to suggest the grieving process was not difficult. It was, but there was a sense that this climbing and skiing was something we needed to play out. I lost a bit of enthusiasm to work out and train. The grieving took its toll on me mentally and physically, and we bowed out of the annual fall pilgrimage to race the Leadville 100. But shortly thereafter, as the snow began to fly, we reengaged our ski careers.

Our hopes of heading back to Everest were stronger than ever, but that trip had taken us mentally and physically to our limits. The success we did bring back was a superboost, but all the experience on that trip enhanced our ability to naturally look at Everest for what it was. And it was big. It was big mentally, it was big physically, and it was big financially. We devised a road map to get back that included four years to raise the money. In the interim we would create training camps on the much closer six-thousand-meter peaks of South America and try to get to a seven-thousand-meter peak that for years friends had suggested as "the greatest ski tour peak on the planet": Mustagh Atta.

We had read about Mustagh Atta, and it was most definitely on our radar. We knew our physical and mental fatigue after Everest would dissipate, but with the four-year plan to return to Everest, we reasoned that a few trips to lesser peaks would enhance our understanding of our ability to climb to altitude and that they would entail a lot less time and, most importantly, would be tremendous fun. Steve contacted our new friend from Everest base camp, Kari Kobler, the owner of a guiding company based in Switzerland, to inquire about a trip to Mustagh Atta. Kari had been running trips to the peak, located in northwestern China near the border of Pakistan, for years, and before we knew it, we had a permit and logistics in place to head there in the spring of 2004. With a carrot to reach for, we quickly resumed our preparation and training. Jim bowed out for this trip so close to Everest, as did Tim and Roger, but Gibjo, Callahan, and J. O. were eager to go back to Asia. We climbed and skied all winter and really enjoyed the process. Mustagh Atta was taken seriously, but the peak was more of a ski tour than a climb; it was a peak that you could skin from base to summit with no avalanche danger and only a moderate icefall to negotiate. It did have a reputation for being crevassed, but in general, it was not nearly as difficult as the Asian peaks we had climbed and skied to that point. It was very high, which was attractive given our love of thin air, and we looked forward to the trip.

What Mustagh Atta lacked in technical climbing, it more than made up with distance, altitude, and weather. We battled the peak for two and a half weeks, and in that period, we learned many valuable lessons. Primarily, we never had great weather, and the peak is a massive windsock. So, we had to break out of the normal sit-and-wait mentality we had become accustomed to on the other high peaks. We found ourselves climbing and skiing in fairly horrendous conditions. With no avalanche danger this was more feasible, but regardless, we learned that we could survive fairly comfortably at superhigh altitudes in extremely poor and cold conditions. The route up the peak was also enormously long, which pushed our physical abilities to the limit. We realized we had a lot more reserves to go out for longer and harder days, but more importantly, we found we could recover. The peak was, in fact, "the greatest ski tour on the planet," and we relished the long ski runs between camps and, ultimately, the huge ski run on the summit day.

Our summit day saw the worst conditions of the trip. We had whiteout conditions, so from the summit plateau we did not obtain the incredible views of the ranges that surrounded the mountain. But the skiing was superb, and Steve reckoned it was to ski touring what Slick Rock in Utah was to mountain biking, a mecca of sorts. Door to door, we managed the expedition in twenty-two days, and it enhanced our level of experience manyfold. It was not only a fantastic trip but also a lesson in endurance and perseverance that would enable us to better approach Everest the next time.

After Mustagh Atta, we made various training trips to South America. At home, we trained like there was no tomorrow, all the time looking ahead to anther go on Everest. We had no clue how we were going to raise the funds, but over time things started to fall into place. First, Steve, Jim, and I decided that we would not tell anyone about our plans. Gradually, the other guys who had joined us on the first trip and subsequent trips to smaller peaks began to naturally wane. Life started to get in the way, and it was also obvious that the level of passion was simply not there to sustain trip after trip.

This made planning for Everest much easier. We relished the thought of emulating our heroes, Shipton and Tilman, foremost explorers and mountaineers from generations before us. Their steadfast approach to climbing peaks in small cohesive teams eliminated hype and logistical nightmares, as well as reducing the overall cost. We idolized these men but also came to the same conclusions that they did nearly a hundred years before us: the main difficulty was the long and arduous approach just to get to the base of Everest, making climbing the peak, especially with a small team, extremely difficult but also undesirable. If we were going to go to the lengths of planning a major expedition to Everest, we reasoned that acclimating on a lesser peak would not only enable us to have a better shot at reaching the summit of Everest, it would give us a more enjoyable opportunity to experience another peak.

Cho Oyu is the sixth highest peak on earth, and its regular climbing route is only moderately difficult. It was a ready-made ski peak, and a friend, Laura Bokas, became the first woman to ski from eight thousand meters when she skied Cho Oyu six months after we skied Shishapangma. (Note that Veronique Perillat of France mono-skied Cho Oyu in 1988.) This increased the total price of the expedition but not as drastically as we feared.

If we were going to go through the hoops of raising money for another trip to Everest, we thought that doing two eight-thousand-meter peaks would resonate as a grand platform for possible sponsors. The idea had legs, especially when coupled with a statistic that we learned about a year after our success on Mustagh Atta—it was brought to our attention that Mustagh Atta was Steve's and my third ski descent from above seven thousand meters, while Jim had two (Shish and Everest). We were in the little-known realm of high-altitude skiers racking up seven thousand- and eight thousand-meter ski descents. Hans Kammerlander had managed to descend from a couple of eight-thousand-meter peaks on skis and had five (including his 8k skiing) descents from seven thousand meters, putting his résumé at the top of the list. But only a couple of people had achieved the level where we suddenly found ourselves. While we never set out to make it into the record books and almost never realized our place in the stats until long after the fact, this new recognition of what we'd done was important for our mind-sets in taking on the double bill. Added to this, no Americans had more than a single eight thousand-meter-peak ski descent.

Our experience had morphed by this time. We were trying to figure out what we really wanted to be. Even on Everest, we were searching for what we wanted to do with the sport as evidenced by the arm-twisting of getting Steve to haul his skis and Jim's initial decision to make his summit attempt sans ski gear. It was clear in our minds that we loved skiing. Those seeds were literal trees by this time, but the highest peaks in the world have a way of altering one's perception, if not in general, certainly while you are attempting to climb them. In the broad scheme of even our own careers this was clear. We didn't even bring skis to Broad

Peak, and on our initial trips to South America, we brought the skis but never used them. Much of this can be attributed to the evolution of the gear. When we started out, the gear was horrible, but gradually the technology improved.

But regardless, what we learned is that there was a cost-benefit relationship to bringing ski gear to these high peaks. On Everest, the reason Steve and Jim questioned bringing skis was because they wanted to reach the summit. Bluntly, climbing with ski gear is much more difficult than without. Once a climber steps onto a high peak, he has a fixed amount of energy and ability to climb that peak. Once you reach a certain point, as we did on Everest, you simply don't have the ability to climb anymore. AT ski boots are another issue. They are heavy, cumbersome, and don't allow for ankle angulation. They take a lot more energy to climb in than lighter, more pliable mountaineering boots. Added to that, AT ski boots are not even remotely as warm as mountaineering boots, requiring overboots, which, in turn, add more weight to your feet. And then they're still nowhere near as warm. While skiing down a high peak produces images of effortlessly swishing turns down smooth powder slopes and letting gravity do all the work while avoiding tiresome down climbing, reality and experience suggest something altogether different. On the highest peaks, when a ski mountaineer gets too tired to ski, or when the terrain becomes too harrowing, the skis end up on the pack, and crampons are strapped to one's feet.

In fact, a saying is that the higher you go, the worse the skiing becomes. With few exceptions, this is true. High faces and ridges lack protection from wind, and the snow is often blown into a hard, rough, concrete-like surface, almost impossible to ski. Ice is even worse. No matter your means of getting off a peak, it entails carrying what you hauled up. But skiing is also a fast-twitch muscle activity that normally requires anaerobic exertion. At altitude, the conditions often require not effortless ski turns but utilitarian hop-turns, as well as great effort to accommodate and balance heavy packs. Skiing is infinitely more exhausting than down climbing. Skiing is also a significantly more dangerous proposition than down climbing because crampons guard against slipping.

As Hans Kammerlander put it after attempting to ski K2, "After a few turns, the whiteout conditions forced me to step back into the safety of my crampons and to descend." In my own experience, I have pushed the limit while skiing, and on several occasions, I struggled with the decision to complete the ski or to step into crampons and shoulder my skis and walk down. The point is that skiing is a drastically different sport than mountaineering.

In our progression, however, all our experience was suggesting that the value and satisfaction of skiing outweighed the challenges of climbing. Because so few people were taking skis to the peaks we were looking at, we had very little information to assess the situation. We did what we could just to figure out how to get up and gradually let the love of the skiing define not only the sport, but our part in it. Our experience to this point gave us confidence that allowed us to look at the greater ranges with a different perspective, which allowed us to plan trips differently than before. We knew we could climb high, and we knew—despite the overwhelming negative feedback we received—that taking skis was what we wanted to do. Regardless of our ski résumés, people still let us know that the greater ranges were for climbing, and we were wasting our time trying to ski in that arena.

At home, part of this notion was driven by our inability to capitalize much on our accomplishments. We were confident about our goals, but we were received so harshly over the years by the local climbing community that we shied away from discussing what we had done and what we planned on doing. Subsequently, many people—who had no clue of the expeditions we had done—saw us as relatively inexperienced ski mountaineers who had gotten very lucky with one climb, Shishapangma. This was enhanced by a growth in ski mountaineers hitting the peaks in Colorado, as well as the proliferation of backcountry ski blogs that allowed people to tap into the new fad and to promote what they were doing.

The May-June climbing season in the Andes coincided with the ultimate spring skiing in the Rockies, and while we climbed and skied often in our backyard, most of the time we found ourselves abroad on larger objectives. At the time, it was nearly impossible to blog from the remote places where we were playing the game, and the here-and-now nature of promotion that gear companies were seeking was difficult, if not impossible. We would submit trip reports long after the fact, rendering our efforts passé. Also, we found that spending days or even weeks or months to get in a single ski run was not the most exciting or understandable thing for the average reader. Plus, skiing at altitude doesn't really offer opportunities for capturing rad photos.

The environments in which we operated weren't conducive to ski photography, and even when we took well thought-out photos, they were boring compared to the images professional photographers were creating in closer-to-home situations. It is impossible to capture altitude in a photograph, and the stock shots that impressed us were not discernable to the general population as being anything other than average. Our efforts were not to create incredible content but just to snap photos that documented what we were doing. We had little interest in the promotion game anyway, and our efforts were always pointed toward the next trip.

Steve, Jim, and I kept to ourselves and started to plan for a return to Everest, knowing we would need three or four years to raise the money and prepare. In the meantime, we found ourselves planning shorter trips to South America every six months, appreciating the region's lack of massive time-zone changes, the red tape of obtaining permits, and cost. We did trips to Ecuador, Chile, and Peru but found Bolivia to be a magnet of sorts that kept pulling us back. Our initial forays there did not include skis, but after Everest, we had enough experience to know there was good skiing. So, we climbed, and we skied down south on six-thousand-meter peaks as often as we could. Our absences were a bit of a burden on our family lives, but being able to take a ten- or fourteen-day trip to get our fix resonated much better with our wives than the typical months-long trip to Asia.

The year after our first Everest expedition, Steve, Jim, and I found ourselves back in Bolivia, licking our wounds after a difficult expedition that left us with a need for resolution after not reaching a summit. We were checking out a massive 21,500-foot peak we had viewed from every Bolivian peak we had climbed—Sajama. Sajama is a volcano that sits alone, well away from the Cordillera Real where we had concentrated our Bolivian adventures previously, and the white pyramid had always been a magnet for our eyes and a stimulant for our curiosity. We were not aware of anyone having skied the peak and didn't know if it was even possible. So, we loaded our haul bags and headed to the mountain on a quick ten-day jaunt.

We learned that we needed to head to the opposite side from the standard southwest ridge route for skiing, but we could find no beta. We were flying blind. We managed to set up a base camp a short trek from the bottom of the mountain and headed out to explore. We had no idea what to expect and subsequently took all our gear, including ice-climbing equipment and other kit we weren't sure we'd even use. We didn't want to risk not having something if we needed it; our packs were enormous.

As I shouldered my pack, the weight crushed my excitement for a magnificent peak with total discomfort. Bluntly, all the expeditions to that point had burned me out. Our enthusiasm waned, but we were there, and we reasoned we should give it a go. As we reached what seemed a feasible route from afar, we were disappointed to see that it was comprised of endless and steep water ice. This further squelched my desire to climb because I seriously doubted there would be any skiing. I didn't have it in me to take on treacherous climbing and subsequent down climbing of thousands of feet of no-fall ice considering the full loads, including ski gear, which I doubted we would be able to use. Ironically, thirteen years later I would be attempting a peak close to Sajama, and gazing at the route we climbed and skied, my fears came rushing back; looking at Sajama with the years of experience since then left Steve, Jim, and I wondering how the hell we managed to climb and ski what we did back then.

I sat on a rock depressed. Jim and Steve had geared up and started climbing. They had no need to listen to me complain and later told me that they thought if they just headed up, I would follow. I was angry and tired and yelled up: "Trip done; this is stupid; I am out of here." I started to walk back to base camp, fully expecting Steve and Jim to encourage me to join them, but they remained silent. This pissed me off even more, and I didn't know what to do.

I had a choice of two evils: sitting it out at base camp and wondering what the climbing—and subsequent skiing—might be like, or testing the waters, frozen as they were, and heading up. I also worried about them running into trouble. Given the slopes, it wasn't an unreasonable concern. I begrudgingly sat back down, strapped on my crampons, and proceeded carefully up the slippery and difficult ice using my two ice axes. As I climbed, my confidence was restored, and something came over me.

My greatest fear was that we would have to down climb all that ice. Sure, we could belay each other if we had to, but I dreaded the process given that it seemed like it would be endless. I had not climbed much ice since Broad Peak, and my skills were a question mark. We had become accustomed to skiing and ice had become an anomaly except for short sections we ran into on the high peaks. On Sajama, however, there were endless slopes of scary, pure water ice, the result of the daily freeze-thaw cycle. At one point I tried my skills and down climbed a hundred feet just to assure myself I could do it. Like riding a bike, my skills came back, and I was excited.

My mental state changed 180 degrees, and adrenaline rushed through my veins. I was going to climb this wretched peak no matter what. I had to control my excitement, and any notion of turning around faded behind a perfect day doing what I realized I was born to do. I still didn't anticipate there would be any skiing, but nothing mattered. I was a climber, and I was climbing. Later, I reached our camp situated on a small rock ledge with drop-offs on both sides but enough room to set up a tent and relax. But things got even better. Just beyond camp, we were greeted with a supersteep headwall that offered a mixture of the same dreaded ice peppered with snow patches. The prospects of skiing were looking much better. We spent the afternoon fixing ropes up the headwall. We were camped at just under nineteen thousand feet, but the views were spectacular, the weather perfect, and we all felt invigorated and strong. We decided that we would get up early the next morning and go for it.

The usual sequence of beeping watch alarms aroused us around 3:00 a.m. We boiled a pot of water, choked down some oatmeal, and hydrated with a few cups of tea and coffee. We hit the trail under a star-filled sky with the Southern Cross giving us direction. We were glad we had fixed the route, and after a half hour the route rolled off onto a broad ridge. We couldn't see much, as the sun wasn't up, but the climbing was on a moderate slope, and as we gained altitude, the ice gave way to snow-covered slopes. It was by no means smooth, and there were sastrugi lips and edges carved into the wind-blasted boilerplate snow, but it was not unskiable ice, and it was reasonable enough to validate carrying the skis. We were excited. After another hour, the sun started to brighten the sky, and we could look out over the Atacama Desert toward Chile, the view broken only by a couple of smaller snow-capped volcanoes to the side of Sajama.

The skyline took on the magenta hue we had become accustomed to seeing at altitude, and the dry air and lack of particulates combined with mild hypoxia created an experience that was nearly spiritual. The ridge rolled on, hiding the summit, so we plodded upward enjoying a climber's trance and anticipating a very long ski run. All was cool. After a few hours, we found ourselves on the summit looking across the Altiplano toward La Paz, with the Cordillera Real gracing the skyline from left to right.

The air at the summit was cold and crisp, and thin panes of ice formed in our water bottles. Drinking the water felt good. The shards melted in our throats, cooling them after hours of heavy breathing. There was not a cloud in any direction, and the air was so calm the quiet seemed loud. After a bite to eat and some more water, we readied our skis and clicked in. The summit was flat, so the normal nervousness of kicking a ski down the slopes was not an issue. We looked ahead at the rough snow and cautioned ourselves to not dig a tip into the sides of the uneven ridges on the rough surface. There were smooth patches between the rough parts, and after the normal reentry of the first few turns, the slope steepened, and we justified the normally harsh ski conditions with the excitement of skiing at nearly twenty-two thousand feet in the middle of nowhere.

It doesn't matter if it's the worst snow in the world. In the high peaks, once you click into your skis and make turns, everything is good; the effort is justified, and there are no problems. We made our way down the ridge, shouldered our skis at the fixed headwall, and rappelled the last bit down to camp. I went last and worked my way down the slope, carefully retrieving the ice screws to leave the slope as we found it. I also enjoyed testing my down climbing skills on the long, steep, and icy retreat to the bottom.

We pulled our camp and headed down, enjoying the challenge of the down climbing and basking in the sense of accomplishment. For me, the trip had been cathartic. I experienced the awful dread of burnout leading up to a big climb, the sheer enjoyment of success with a summit and ski, and everything in between. Later, we would realize that one skier had beaten us to a first descent, and although the same line had also been snowboarded by American John Griber the year before, no other American had skied the peak.

It's not that the stats are terribly important or that we perceived ourselves as extraordinary ski mountaineers, but rather the process we experienced on that peak was a great example of a progression. I am not referring to a physical progression but rather the mental progression. As I walked to that peak, I was thinking that all the expeditions to that point had brought me to a crossroads. There is no question that after Broad Peak, Shishapangma, the difficult-at-best attempt at Everest, and the other accomplishments we achieved gave us significantly more satisfaction then we ever dreamed we would experience. We had taken a zillion small steps to progress to what pop culture considered the ultimate. That's not to say we had become arrogant or complacent, but the reality was that the progression did lead us to a place where we knew we could take on the highest peaks in the world. And, contrary to what everything suggested outside of our experience of what was possible with skis, we were barraged with "it's not possible for you guys."

People were not thinking about skiing any of those high peaks. We were defined as glory hounds in a fringe sport, and our success was scoffed at. We were midcore "weekend warriors" that were willing to take on what no one else thought was fun or admirable, and many thought and even claimed they could do if they had the money and time.

In an *Outside* magazine article, one so-called expert skier who wished to remain anonymous said, "All that the Marolts have done only proves is that they have a lot of money and time to take on standard boring routes and descend them with skis on their feet." We laughed at that one. To most ski mountaineers, the guy hit it on the head. But what we slowly realized, and what was confirmed on Sajama, was that, sure, you bet, often we do our sport on the standard boring routes. But Sajama and many others were not remotely defined like that. Regardless, until you slap skis on a full pack and climb into the thin air wearing heavy AT ski boots, you really have no idea how difficult and demanding this stuff really is. But you really have no idea how satisfying it is, too, and you have no clue how hard it is to prepare to give yourself only a remote chance of success, a chance compounded by the fact that those same routes have a 50 percent failure rate for climbers, and a nearly 100 percent failure rate for ski mountaineers.

The situation is so drastic with the addition of skis that as a ski mountaineer, you must redefine what you consider success. Consequently, skiing from 25,500 feet on the north ridge of Everest, or missing the main summit of Shishapangma but skiing the Central Summit twelve feet lower than the main peak, or getting shut out on Lenin, —all antiachievements proving our mediocrity in the minds of many—became an enormous source of pride for us as we were actually out climbing and skiing the highest peaks in the world. We learned simply that sometimes the highest peaks don't always offer conditions that allow you to climb and ski them. Unless you have been there and tried, that is a difficult concept to fully appreciate.

Sajama was an exclamation point in our progression. Most of the so-called experts had never even heard of the peak. By reaching my patience limit on that peak but then persevering despite it, and then, experiencing the pure joy of the sport and the satisfaction of overcoming my frustrations, Sajama was a crossroads, and I knew we'd taken the right turn. We had summited the greatest peak of our lives, and it wasn't Sajama. Rather, it was a point where we literally became ski mountaineers. We had climbed the personal and public slopes of self-doubt and reached a maturity that allowed us for the first time to understand that none of it mattered.

This was who we were as people—ski mountaineers—and our passion became part of our identity. We stopped caring what people said or thought. We stopped caring how high or big the peaks were. All that mattered was what was next and that we had a firm desire to continue. But most importantly, on Sajama, we started to realize an important facet of our careers. It wasn't so much what the objective was but who we were doing it with—each other. We cemented the concept of "The Three Amigos" for the first time. Certainly, while Roger and Callahan and a few others often came on our trips, the nucleolus of it all was distilled down to Steve, Jim, and me. This was intensified by the contrast Steve and I found on the few trips where Jim was absent, and that absence left a noticeable hole in the process.

On Sajama, with the three of us fully engaged, our past and future became clear. We would always leave an open door for the others to join us, which they did from time to time, but it became clearly understood that they were just guests on our trips. We formulated a process to plan trips with just the three of us, and we'd accommodate others as needed. But it was us, "The Three Amigos." The power and synergy were made clear on Sajama to the point that as Steve and Jim ascended in complete silence while I pouted below; I could hear them yelling in my mind's ear, "Come on, we can do this!" We had an unspoken ability to communicate all aspects of our adventures.

The years crawled by, and each expedition gave us more confidence. After Everest 1 we had honed our climbing skills enormously, and we delved into the final planning stages for a return to Everest in April 2006. Steve was working directly with Kari Kobler and devised a plan that would utilize his infrastructure on the north side, eliminating the need to haul massive amounts of expedition gear to the peak. The idea was that we would first go to Cho Oyu, the sixth highest peak, for new terrain and another eight-thousand-meter peak, and then to head directly to Everest ABC to make our second attempt.

We had generated considerable support from Atomic and Mammut, as well as a corporate sponsorship with Under Armour, which helped defray the cost. We were still short on the total price of the expedition, but it was important enough, and we had come so far that we were all prepared to pay the difference. This was a stretch financially for each of us, but we vowed to make it happen. Then the hammer fell. I had been producing a film on our adventures to that point called *Skiing the High Himalaya*, and

I found myself in New York City preparing to premier the film at the Explorers Club.

Steve called me in a frenzy with the news that he was expecting another child in nine months; he was freaking out knowing he would be on Everest if things went as expected. I listened to the panic in his voice and pondered the situation. Jim had also had a life-altering event with his work. He was changing companies, and he was concerned that taking off a couple months was not ideal for his situation. By this time, Shelly and I had also adopted our second child; timing was simply not right, and as I paced the terrace of my in-laws' apartment, I knew we had to delay. I called Steve and said we needed another year. He eagerly agreed, and like that, the trip was delayed. He called Kari, who by this time had become not only a logistics go-to for our trips but a friend. He supported our decision with common sense. "A peak like Everest has to be with proper frame of mind," he said. "You go there with personal baggage, bad stuff happens." We breathed a sigh of relief. Then and there we decided we would spike in another quick trip to Ecuador that winter, and everyone was greatly relieved. We also reasoned it would give us another year to land additional sponsorships.

Timing is everything in life, and for us, there was no exception. I headed to the Explorers Club with the feeling that an enormous burden had been lifted. I screened the film to massive accolades and prompted such a flurry of questions after the screening that the moderator had to step in to control the excited crowd. I was overwhelmed with the interest people had in the climbing and skiing and stayed for another hour as people lined up to shake my hand and offer congratulations and salutations. While the film was well done, it was produced from shots I got as a climber and skier in difficult positions and without the greatest equipment. Bluntly, I was no professional photographer, and the footage was telling. Part of me feared that people would see the film as a bit of a home movie and not appreciate the content. The reaction from the packed house demonstrated that I had succeeded; they loved the film and were more than proud that a fellow member was part of it.

To that point, I really enjoyed the filmmaking aspect of the expeditions, and while I knew I was always going to carry a video camera, I never saw film production as anything other than just putting footage together to share with friends. The Explorers Club event changed that. I immediately saw the impact of films. My mind raced with possibilities that video brought to promoting our adventures. It added another arrow to the quiver that I could offer to potential sponsors. But, then—as people shuffled out the door—something else came up.

I was finishing my effort to meet and greet attendees, and a lady approached me from the end of the line. She introduced herself and said that she knew my wife, and that she had worked with Shelly when she lived in Aspen. I had no idea who she was, but she was into the adventure, into the Tibetan portions of the footage, and extremely excited about the film in general. The conversation moved from familiar connections when she asked me about my film aspirations. She handed me a piece of paper with her name and telephone number on it and vowed that she would help me produce the next film. I accepted her request along with others who had proclaimed they also wanted to support us, but as these things go, I took it to be more pleasantries than anything.

But this lady was different. She looked into me, and I knew she wanted to help. I didn't give it much thought in the after-show dinner with club higher-ups, but I called Shelly later that night to report the success and told her I met an old friend of hers, Jeanne Andlinger. Shelly explained that Jeanne was a fantastic friend who worked with her at the Aspen Ralph Lauren store, helping to manage their windows and set up the merchandising. Shelly loved Jeanne. She said she lost touch with her years ago when Jeanne married a "fantastic" gentleman who was hugely successful in business and had the means to help me, an aspiring filmmaker. Shelly told me if anyone could help me, Jeanne would be the person. I stayed in touch with Jeanne, who was extremely excited, and a few weeks later she told me she would be in Aspen, visiting. She wanted me to put a presentation together and said that she and her husband, Gary, would love to have coffee.

I started to reach out to people I knew in the film business to see what a presentation amounted to, and before I knew it, I was introduced to Jack Jacobs, a former defense attorney who had found a niche first in promoting major rock bands and after that had transitioned into the film industry. He was born and raised in LA and was reported to "know enough about everyone in the film business to get a foot in the door." Jack helped me understand the costs of producing a "real" film and made me realize that while my first film was received very well, it lacked basic professional aspects that were required for any kind of serious release. He made me realize that I needed an experienced team that understood the parameters of a film, but more importantly, the costs. We put together a budget that included expedition costs, a "one-pager" that detailed the trajectory of the film, and the basic gist of the story.

I met with Jeanne and Gary, presented them with what I had, and they told me they would get back to me. I patiently waited for weeks and almost forgot about them. I didn't want to be a pest and reasoned it was nice while it lasted. I also knew my budget was not small, and that it might have scared them away. Then the phone rang, and I was greeted by Jeanne. She apologized for the delay in getting back to me but said she was going to be back in Aspen and asked if we could meet. So, two months after my initial excitement, I was again excited.

We met over coffee without Gary, and she said that she would love to help. She explained that I would be working directly with her, not to bother Gary, and explained that she had the ability and desire to help me become a filmmaker. She also explained her passion for Eastern religion and philosophy and an interest in Buddhism, which influenced her a great deal. Knowing we would be approaching Everest from Lhasa, the spiritual center for Buddhism, I suggested that she should join the expedition as far as our first base camp at Cho Oyu. She said she would like that.

I wasn't sure if she was serious about joining us, but in the weeks that followed, it was clear she was going. She trained for the altitude and expected to trek as high as ABC. We stayed in touch, often discussing the details of the trip, coordinating everything to accommodate her schedule to meet us in China. We worked out a funding schedule, and all was well. Steve and Jim had not met Jeanne, and while they had concerns about bringing a rookie into the mix, the funding—which included the requisite expedition costs—persuaded them to accept the situation.

I was nervous about being responsible for Jeanne, who had zero mountaineering or altitude experience, and reached out to our mentor, Slowman, to see if he had any interest in being Jeanne's personal guide on the trip. Slowman had not been actively guiding in the Himalaya for a long time, and at age fifty thought he was pretty much done with Asia. But he also saw the request as an opportunity to go to a part of the world that he loved. He had climbed Cho Oyu, and he had the time. He accepted the invitation, and I immediately introduced him to Jeanne. He started to work with her on gear and preparation.

We were excited to be reuniting with Slowman, as we had not been on a trip with him since Broad Peak. There's a natural part of the expedition process that never goes away and that becomes more intense the closer you get to an objective: the questioning. But the questioning—the worry and the anxiety—created an opportunity for Steve, Jim, and I to value and once again learn from Slowman's experience.

We secured all the funding we would need for the trip and for the first time we were able to really concentrate on training, both mentally and physically. By that point, our résumé of high peaks attracted our first "real" ski sponsorship—Atomic—which was a great source of pride. Just as importantly, this marquee sponsorship gave us access to the latest technology in AT ski gear. We also formed a relationship with Lowa, another marquee footwear manufacturer, and many of the previous questions with regard to boots were eliminated.

The new gear we got from Atomic and Lowa was a real confidence booster—for the first time on a major trip we knew that our gear was the best available—and its arrival erased much of the doubt we'd had on other trips. We could climb and ski anything on this gear. While this sounds trivial, it was anything but. The gear was a fraction of the weight compared to the old gear we'd used on previous expeditions, and we often laughed that it was an unfair advantage. We were living in a time where AT skiing was at a grassroots level, but with interest, all our gear was evolving at a rate we never anticipated. People were starting to head out to the backcountry, and along with the desire came demand. Gear companies were anticipating a new market, and the gear reflected what was happening in the hills.

I was also concentrating on my videography skills for the film, and I carried a camera with me on every outing. I really studied the art of motion pictures and with funding, obtained two cameras. I also realized that to make the best film possible, I needed to add an extra shooter to the mix. In the process of working with the film company on Shishapangma, and with the relationship made on that trip with Cherie Silvera, I reached out to her immediately. My new film budget included an extra shooter for Everest, and Cherie jumped at the opportunity to come along. Cherie proved herself on Shish as not only a superstrong climber and skier, but also someone that fit in well with the three of us. She was a sister of sorts, and we welcomed her to the group.

Cherie was most definitely part of the local climbing community, a community that was often at odds with our small band, and she became a mediator of sorts with regard to bridging the gaps we perceived between "us and them." She took the time to get to know us and provided insight into some of the misconceptions that we perceived. At the time, we were refining our techniques and building upon our experiences in the testosterone-laden world of young guns. And while we embraced her efforts to clear up the misconceptions, there is no arguing that she inspired us to put our noses to the climbing grindstone to squelch the perceived injustices. We found her insights filled with humorous sleights and jabs but also complimentary. She explained that one of the main horn blowers admitted "we are all probably a bit jealous that those guys are out on incredible adventures, climbing and skiing, and we are drinking beer at home and slamming them." They were talking behind our backs, and we were most definitely talking behind theirs, creating what Jim described as teahouse fodder.

Critique and criticism are obviously not new to the activity of climbing, and since those days I've come to realize—partly through my own geeking out on historical climbing literature—that critique and criticism are a spice that makes the endless days in a base camp tent somewhat enjoyable. The thing about mountaineering is that it's not a sport played between two white lines or within the confines of a time limit. We experienced this on Shish when we climbed and skied the Central Summit without incident on one day, and the very next day, an arguably more experienced team of Austrian climbers was thwarted a few hundred feet below the summit because of "horrendous avalanche conditions." The difference a day makes can be astonishing. The point here, obviously, is that on any mountain, Mother Nature provides the white lines, and mountains can be painfully and drastically different from one hour to the next. This offers a climber the ultimate bag of justifications, which, when combined with hours of downtime on a typical expedition, opens the door to self-aggrandizement and the condemnation of anyone else. It's part of the game. And by this point in our careers, we were first-tier players. When the conversation stalled, it was humorous when—out of the blue—someone would blurt out, "What do you think so-and-so would do up there?" Or, better yet, "Where would you rather be, here or back home like so-and-so, shit-talking about us over a beer wishing he was here?" That always enhanced the joke because oftentimes it was obvious that being back home doing anything would be better than being where we were and doing nothing.

During the winter of 2006–7 we trained hard, making our bodies climbing machines but also spending as much time with family as possible and figuring out the payback that our wives no doubt deserved. "I swear, honey, this is the last one, the last expedition" would become a running joke for my family, but gradually Shelly came to realize this was just who and what I was. Nonetheless, I worked diligently to be a good husband and father and encouraged her to get a bike trip or something together for herself. Raising kids is a massively difficult job, and I argued that the time away was crucial for sanity, with which she agreed, and she subsequently did head out with friends on their own adventures.

My absence was also motivation to look ahead and plan family vacations, something that was important and valuable in our view. Shelly loved to travel and as a child had experienced many exotic cultures. She wanted our kids to have the same opportunities. So, she found solace in planning both her own adventures, which I faithfully encouraged, and family trips. The only downside was that this piled on the pressure at work. I was planning and saving for both family trips and climbing/skiing trips.

As CPAs, Steve and I could never leave before tax day, April 15, which put us a bit behind most Asian expeditions. The extra time, however, allowed us to get ahead of our workload and put a few extra bucks in the bank to cover the month and a half we would be gone. The balancing act of working like a rented mule and being a good father and husband at times created stress beyond belief. Yet, over the years we learned to take it in stride; it came to be expected, and for lack of better explanation, we got good at it. It was all part of the deal. Our passion came at a cost, but once on that airplane, it was all good, all worth the effort.

Soon we found ourselves in Beijing, where we met Jeanne at our hotel. The plan was to take the magnificent new bullet train from Beijing across the country to Lhasa, and soon we found ourselves in the Beijing train station. Before the trip we'd been warned that when in China expect the unexpected. Minutes before the train was due to leave the station, we were told our tickets were invalid. Why? I still have no idea.

The conductor was yelling for everyone to get aboard, and Steve was still haggling at the ticket office. He finally arrived as the train's engines roared, ready to start the journey. We began loading our gear into a carriage, more specifically into the aisle of a smoky, dirty car that reeked of a clogged toilet. As I got on the train, I realized something was wrong. Our tickets, reserved long in advance, were for private, first-class accommodations. But the carriage in which I stood was a far cry from first class. I immediately knew we were being screwed, and as the train started to roll, I began yelling, "Get the gear off the train." There was no time for discussion, and we quickly unloaded all our gear. Clearly, we were just a bunch of dumb gweilos who'd paid full price, and the train operators saw an opportunity to screw us. We argued until two in the morning, finally got a refund, and called Kari in Switzerland. Kari proceeded to berate his point man, a Chinese agent who was obviously part of the scam. Kari also told the Chinse agent to obtain air tickets, at his cost, "or you vill never see my business again!" Kari was screaming so loudly we could hear him on the Chinese agent's cell phone.

We arrived in Lhasa five days later and ran into other climbers we had met getting onto the train the same time we were exiting. They were gray and tired and told us the toilets never worked, the food was inedible, and for the five-day journey, all but half a day was spent in an old, decrepit boxcar with hard wooden seats. They laughed that we missed out on what they called "the worst experience of our lives." Life in China—expect the unexpected.

We toured Lhasa for a couple days, acclimating to its twelve-thousand-foot elevation and then made the slow drive over the Tibetan Plateau, also acclimating along the way, and finally arrived at Cho Oyu base camp. After the hectic pace of life in China's cities, we were in heaven. The views were spectacular, and Cho Oyu rose in front of us like a wondrous new toy. We studied it for hours. By this time, all things considered, Jeanne had enjoyed the adventure, but the seventeen-thousand-foot elevation was giving her anxiety and a round of mountain sickness that even after a few days would not dissipate.

Then, on the morning before the trek to ABC, Slowman entered the tent with a look of despair. He had gotten up earlier to take a pee and found his urine was completely red. We had no idea what this meant, but we knew that it was not good and that he had to get out. He was now in Jeanne's hands, and she did all she could to get him out of the mountains and back to the States. We didn't realize until we got back how serious his situation was; he was diagnosed with bladder cancer (something that he would battle for the next ten years; today, he is cancer free). The departure of Slowman and Jeanne came as a shock, as we fully planned for them to accompany us all the way to ABC, and it took a few days to adjust.

Life on the mountain with the three of us and Cherie settled into its natural rhythm after Jeanne and Slowman departed, and slowly we established ABC and started to put in our camps. The first obvious issue was snow. Looking at the upper slopes, it was clear that there wasn't a lot of it, which made a ski descent questionable. We accepted what we couldn't change and, reaffirming that Cho Oyu was an acclimation peak and that Everest was the main goal, we put our noses down and climbed.

From the outset, the task was daunting. We were planning on climbing two eight-thousand-meter peaks, one of them the highest mountain on earth. Due to constraints at home with work and family, we had budgeted only five weeks for both peaks, making the task even greater. We also had the added weight of Cherie and the film crew, which complicated matters. For the film, we hired a Sherpa to help Cherie and another to pick up the pieces with regard to bits and pieces of group gear.

Karma and Norbu became part of our team, and we started each push by dividing the gear into equal piles to distribute the weight. They were incredibly hard working and immediately joined us as if we had been climbing with them forever. Norbu wanted desperately to learn how to shoot video, and Cherie utilized an extra camera to outfit him, which added to the overall content we would obtain on the route. They had no interest in skiing, but they were proud to be part of our unusual ambition to ski from as high as possible. Their role was different from their normal commercial work in that they were really part of the team, not just there to carry loads. For Sherpa, summits offer the same glory as they do for Western climbers, with the benefit that their enhanced résumés stimulate more work and higher wages. From the get-go, it was understood that even if we could not attain the summit, if they could, they would. This resulted in a more relaxed atmosphere around base camp. For once, they were not guiding or working but getting paid to climb. Norbu, who spoke perfect English, was especially engaged. He became a brother to us, forming a relationship that continues today.

We established our first camp at about twenty thousand feet, and the next leg of the adventure was to put in a camp at seven thousand meters, or twenty-three thousand feet. Being unacclimated and hauling skis and loads to twenty-three thousand feet on Cho Oyu made for one of the most difficult days any of us had ever had. The route lacked the normal coverage of snow and involved multiple pitches of steep ice just below our camp. We were a bit early in the season to accommodate two climbs, and the reality on Cho Oyu is that most expeditions chose to climb in the fall when there is more snow, making it much easier to climb. There were bits and pieces of fixed line that we refixed, making the job easier, but it was a massive grunt to get to twenty-three thousand feet. We established the camp and headed down as a snowstorm started, happy to be headed for a couple of days of rest. The temperatures were relatively high, which also gave us hope that a bit of snow would fall, allowing for more skiing. We settled down at ABC and relaxed with anticipation as the snow slowly accumulated.

After a couple days of rest, we headed back up with newfound energy. We felt great and thoroughly enjoyed the climb. We still had fairly large loads of personal gear, but with our skis already taken up on the first forays, the task was much more reasonable. The climbing was still on bare ice, but when the sun poked out after the storm, the upper slopes were blanketed with fresh snow. It was not enough to create any serious avalanche danger, but there were patches of ice that we knew the new snow was covering. As on Everest in 2003, we knew the new snow would give us enough edge purchase so that we could ski, if not the whole route, much more than without. Summit fever set in.

The normal plan on Cho Oyu is to establish another camp at the twenty-five-thousand-foot level and then go for the summit. But since we were feeling, as Steve would later describe, "bionic," and knowing that Everest was the main goal, we decided that we would save our energy and forego the task of making another carry and camp up higher. Instead, we agreed to head down, rest for a few days and then just go for it. Karma and Norbu agreed that we were a strong team, and they also wanted to push themselves, telling us that, if we really rested, we could attain the summit. Cherie was not excited about the prospects and pushed for a high camp but acquiesced to the group decision. She was satisfied that Norbu could capture summit footage, and she would climb with us to high camp to cover the rest. We all managed to sleep at the new altitude, and the next day we headed down.

After a few restful and beautiful days at ABC, we headed back up. We stopped at camp 1 for the first night, and then headed to camp 2. We woke up around 11:00 p.m. and set off in the black of night. The air was extremely cold, and no climbers had been higher on the mountain, forcing us to break trail on the moderate slopes. The slope was too steep to utilize our skis and skins, so we shouldered them. We set off at a rapid pace, too fast for me personally, and I labored to keep up.

After a few hours we passed the normal high camp and climbed to the "gold band," a notorious band of gold-colored sandstone. We pointed our headlamps against the wall, looking for the route. In the fall, the gold band has small gullies that fill with snow to make the route not only obvious but reduce it to nothing more than a steep albeit hard snow climb. We had searched for a half hour when Jim spied the end of a rope just out of arm's reach. Karma shimmied up, grabbed the rope and tied in; we had found the route.

We had not planned on bringing any anchors or fixed rope given the information we had about the normal route, so we had to refix what anchors there were, often coming across snow pickets that had melted out of the ice. We tried as best we could but often found ourselves climbing on down-sloping slags of rock that were precarious at best and offered no protection. The climbing was much steeper than we expected, adding to our angst, and our skis dragged on the steep slopes above and to our sides. We used what ropes we could fix and relied on balance and footwork for the rest.

The new snow had accumulated deeply in some of the gullies, and we set off small avalanches that we prayed would not grow into big avalanches below us. It was tiring and exhausting work. For about a thousand feet, we picked our way up lower fifth-class terrain until we entered the more moderate ground at the top of the cliffs. We were greeted with a snow picket that was sticking out of the ice, barely held in place and offering two feet of exposed shaft. We laughed at the thought that when that picket was placed it was probably hammered into snow up to its top. But here, now, there was simply no snow.

Based on information we gathered from other climbers that had been there before us, we knew the route was normally nowhere near as difficult as it was for us. This added to the task at hand, but it also gave us a sense of accomplishment that fueled our desire to keep going. By this time the sun had started to light the sky and warm the air. The route was fixed before us, but again, we could not rely on the precarious anchors, so we ascended carefully, step by step. The terrain was steep but not as steep as it had been in the gold band, with death-defying drops all around. But more importantly, we realized that the route could be skied. We could not ski the gold band, obviously, but above and below, skiing would be doable. Difficult, but doable.

Steve was again feeling bionic, and he and Norbu and Karma proceeded ahead of Jim and me. But the day started to catch up to me. I have a history of asthma, which ironically to that point in my career seemed to disappear at altitude with the lack of particulates in the air up high. But I started out too fast, and the cold air exacerbated an attack. I felt strong but had to stop repeatedly to catch my breath. Jim was concerned, and with plenty of day and nearly perfect weather, we slowed the pace and continued. By this time, the others were far enough ahead to not have a clue what was going on. They kept going. As I proceeded, I realized that the summit for me was probably not going to happen. But I most definitely wanted to get another eight-thousand-meter ski descent.

I pulled my jacket cuff back and proceeded to climb until I reached eight thousand meters. I went an additional few hundred feet just to be safe. Then, I was done. I was not in a panic or anything, but it was clear I needed to head to thicker air as quickly as possible. Jim had climbed a hundred feet past me, and when he turned around to see me taking my skis off my pack, he decided to turn around as well. In retrospect, I question if I could have made the summit, and I know Jim could have, but the goal was "as high as we could," and not wanting to blow our reserves for Everest, we both played it safe.

Meanwhile, Steve was almost standing on top when we turned around, and he merely walked the relatively flat summit slope until he could see Everest and Lhotse on the horizon, the telltale sign you are on top of Cho Oyu. Jim and I skied to the gold band, and Steve hurried to catch us. We down climbed and rappelled the cliffs, and then skied the two thousand feet back to camp in wind-crusted powder. I labored with the skiing, stopping to rest every few turns. Jim and Steve patiently waited for me, knowing I was having a rough day. We finally slid into camp where Cherie had plenty of water heated up for coffee. I immediately dug into my personal kit for some medication and proceeded to hawk out globs of congealed crap that had been in my airway. By the next morning we had pulled our camp and with heavy packs continued down the mountain. We had to rappel down a few steep ice pitches, but besides a couple of sheer sections, enjoyed moderate skiing on near perfect slopes.

Karma, Norbu, and Steve had reached the summit; Jim and I had achieved eight-thousand-meter ski descents, and all was good. Steve was not so satisfied and cringed at the notion that he later described as "leaving my team to suffer." He vowed to never again leave the group for personal satisfaction. I didn't hold this against Steve, especially because he had no idea I was suffering as I was. None of the three summiteers did. I was very satisfied with my effort and considered their summits a team success. I do regret that there was no way for me to have encouraged Jim to continue, however.

But it brings up a pledge that to that point we had religiously adhered to: never split the group up. I would have encouraged all to continue and was not personally in any danger; I could have easily and safely descended alone, but the concept begs discussion. If the team gets spread out as we allowed, the ability to communicate is no longer within our control. Especially at extreme altitude, it is imperative that a team stay in touch, the slowest member dictating the pace. We made a critical mistake on Cho by allowing the team to spread out like we did. And it must be clear that there is a difference between making a mistake and experiencing a preventable error.

Using the event on Shishapangma where Jim entered the wrong gully and experienced a life-or-death situation, it is clear. Mistakes happen when you let personal goals guide you, and you do things that are clearly not acceptable and could expose a team. On Shish, telling Jim that we were not on the route, and to find another route, was in an effort to help. There was no ambition driving that call, and it was because that we thought there was a better way. This was a lapse in judgment, not a mistake.

A mistake happens when you break a hard and fast rule: when you plan a turnaround time and exceed it, when you break up a group, when you don't check your anchor, and on and on. There are hard and fast rules in mountaineering, and when you break those you make mistakes. Mistakes can lead to massive hardship and problems. But a lapse in judgment or making a bad decision is part of the game. Here again, if you make a mistake as we did on Cho Oyu (by breaking up the group), it subjects your ability to make good decisions to errors and bad choices. The idea is to eliminate bad decisions, and at altitude, a cohesive group allows for input that leads to making better decisions.

Unless you are climbing solo, you need to learn to make decisions as a group. But at this stage of our careers, by and large, the greatest advantage we took with us was the concept of "The Three Amigos." Steve, Jim, and I knew each other extremely well, and beyond the simple fact that we always had partners to plan trips with, we were developing an ability to communicate without even talking. Jim looked down at me on Cho Oyu and saw I was having a very difficult time. Later he told me that even had I pleaded with him to go to the summit by himself, he was not going to leave me alone to descend. Jim made the right decision, and that correct decision highlighted the bad decision that Steve and the others made.

We discussed the situation at length, and while we agreed we had collectively made a mistake, we vowed to never let it happen again. Learn the lesson, and learn it well! But in the path that we were following together, the "hollow summit," as Steve described it, served to enforce the fact that we were slowly learning; in life, what you are doing or attempting to do is not as important as who you are doing it with. Our relationships as climbers were allowing us to do great things, and we were extremely proud and satisfied, but as the experiences increased, we were becoming a band of brothers whereby the experience was not defined by what but who.

As we packed up our ABC, we experienced another situation that I consider one of the greatest mental hurdles of my climbing career—we were packing up to head down for rest to then go to Everest while other teams were packing up to go home. The postexpedition excitement of Cho Oyu left us depleted mentally and physically, and the normal process of our trips was being severely skewed. We watched the other teams giddy with the anticipation of heading home to the embraces of loved ones and to sharing their stories with friends. We, on the other hand, had another two weeks of tent life, breathing thin air and suffering the way that only mountaineers know how to suffer. Postclimb, stress levels are alleviated. And while you are mentally and physically depleted, it is easy to put forth the effort to get out and get home.

Instead, we were looking at four or five days of discomfort on the high Tibetan Plateau, living in a dirt-floored hotel as we tried to rest, then heading back to another massive peak, the most massive on the planet, to do it all over again. We were cranky, slightly depressed, and tired. We had to justify the situation to ourselves, ignore the giddiness around us, and force ourselves to stay focused. At a minimum we tried to get excited about sleeping on a real bed for a few nights at a relatively lower altitude. It was a trying time to say the least.

Rest was very much the goal as we fumbled casually around the town of Tingre, and in contrast to the postmonsoon season, during which many climbing teams could be found lingering around the streets, we found the small town deadly quiet. In an odd way, this was comforting. There was none of the common posturing or preclimb jitters, and we were fully acclimated, which did bring restful and welcomed sleep. There was also a sense of pride in that we were not heading home. Rather, we were playing the game at the ultimate level, which allowed us to enjoy our brief stay without the usual nervousness and preclimb grab ass. Our attitudes slowly changed, and the general feeling rose back up to excitement. After four days, we put our noses to the grindstone, loaded into our Land Cruisers and headed back toward the towering Himalaya with Everest filling the view out the windshield as we drew closer.

Unlike the normal Everest north side base camp—a buzz of teams and camps, noise and activity—we found most people had by this time departed. We were welcomed to our camp with little pomp and circumstance. The next day, we loaded up, and being acclimated, we started the long trek to ABC. As we marched the grueling sixteen miles to ABC, we found that we could remember specific rocks that we'd seen on our first Everest expedition. We were happy we would only be making this massive marathon once on this trip, satisfied that the plan to acclimate on Cho Oyu was paying off. We enjoyed the trek, and we were welcomed at the end of the day with Kari's staff providing us with hot coffee and cake inside a heated and insulated tent. The experience stood in stark contrast to the windy cold camp we spent weeks in on our previous expedition, and all was good—very good.

We spent the next day on a go-for-broke attempt at the peak. We were now very late in the season, and although the weather was magnificent, the weather reports told us that the monsoon was to hit in five days. This allowed us plenty of time to take what we needed and to head up immediately the next day. Kari had run a commercial expedition that fall—now long over—and he had tents and camps already established. We welcomed the fact that all we needed to carry was our personal gear and ski equipment. At first glance, this was something we deemed as cheating, but Kari made it clear that what we were taking on had never been attempted: to climb and ski one eight-thousand-meter peak and then Everest, without oxygen, and with the monsoon on our backs. He suggested that if we wanted to climb, it would be by his rules. We acquiesced and accepted his belittling for the logical and conservative thinking that came with it. At that stage, we just wanted to get going. Our egos were checked, and we would take the mountain how it had been set and see what we could do, knowing our chances for success were extremely limited, regardless.

The climbing began, and the weather was perfect. Contrary to the weather on Everest in 2003, which left a sheet of windblown snow and ice, the 2007 postmonsoon season had seen little wind, and small scuds of storms had deposited a blanket of soft snow on the north ridge and slopes back down to ABC. We knew we would have tremendous skiing. The upper slopes, however, above 25,500 feet, were completely void of snow. We spent the first night at the North Col at twenty-three thousand feet, and the next day headed up to Camp 2. Again, the weather was perfect. In contrast to our first trips up the ridge in 2003, during which we had little or no visibility, the vistas in 2007 were extraordinary. Halfway up the ridge, we found ourselves above most of the peaks surrounding us. There was no wind, and we could gaze over the range and into Nepal on the left, and we had an unobstructed view of the entire Tibetan Plateau to the right. We gazed along the range at Shishapangma, in awe of a view we had dreamed about but had never experienced. This fueled our desires further, and any sense of dread we felt from not being done was reduced by the anticipation of moving higher.

We settled into Camp 2 satisfied and giddy. We were totally acclimated, and we felt great. I had been concerned about my asthma on Cho Oyu, but even that had completely vanished. The next steps, however, were discussed at length. We were late in the season, and the upper slopes were completely void of snow. It made no sense to carry the skis any higher. We did discuss hauling them to the summit to ski a little bit of snow higher up, on the final three hundred feet leading to the summit, but eventually decided that climbing in AT ski boots was a limiting factor given that while the weather was perfect, it was an extraordinarily cold season. We figured we needed every bit of energy to just attempt the peak and decided to leave the skis behind. We wanted to get the peak at this stage, and while the letdown of leaving the skis was great, with no snow, we deferred to common sense.

We broke camp early the next day. Our goal was our high camp at just over twenty-seven thousand feet. We hoped to get there and get settled in early in the day so we could make a go for the summit a bit earlier than teams normally would. Kari had suggested that climbing without oxygen would slow us down drastically, and that we needed a couple more hours to establish our position on the northeast ridge. We agreed this made sense and wanted to have several hours of rest before we departed.

Our arrival at high camp was on schedule, and once we settled in, we experienced a first and dismal aspect of climbing Everest without oxygen. Most climbers start using oxygen at about twenty-three thousand feet, which obviously aids in actual climbing, but more importantly, it eliminates several thousand feet of thin atmosphere while sleeping and resting. As we sat in our tents and hydrated as much as possible, we had to force ourselves to eat. We sat in utter discomfort, our hearts racing, leaving us in a pant, which at times felt like it was for our lives. We had to concentrate on relaxing and staying calm. There was little conversation beyond the deadpan reminders of making sure we all were packed and ready with food, water, extra mittens, etc. Despite our depleted states, we had to make sure no one was forgetting anything that would be necessary.

There was a natural, nervous anticipation of heading to an altitude we had never experienced. Above this camp, we would be pushing ourselves into a complete unknown. We had no idea how it would be. We had no clue if we could pull it off, and outright fear engulfed our thoughts. We had to remind each other that it was one step at a time. We had to stay together, to communicate, to watch each other's backs. Sleep was hard to find, and we quietly laid back in our sleeping bags. I prayed. I justified my existence in this odd place, but I also laid down the mental boundaries that I would adhere to. I was not going to lose any fingers or toes, and I told myself that I had already attained success just being there. I did not personally know any climber that had reached the altitude we were at without supplemental oxygen, and while I was still driven by ambition to reach the summit, I vowed I would concentrate on being reasonable and realistic. I convinced myself that the only thing I had to fear was making a dumb decision to move past realistic limits—limits I well knew based on my experience to that point. The thought process occupied much of my time and slowly built a level of confidence that allowed me to look at the next day with enormous anticipation and exhilaration, which left me at peace. I was in a slumber of sorts when all our watch alarms started beeping within a few seconds of each other.

We slept in our climbing gear, so all we had to do was get up and get moving. We did manage to gulp down a few sips of coffee, but we were all eager to start climbing. Moving at altitude increases circulation, and with adrenaline starting to flow through our systems, we were ready. Our organization paid off, and we were soon outside, stepping into our harnesses, pulling on our overboots, and clicking into our crampons. Steve was in a huff. He had a hard time getting his overboot on, but I had too much on my mind to worry. Only later would I notice that he was climbing without his overboots, something that I found odd but would later understand.

We climbed as a team, and using only the rays of our headlamps, we climbed steadily, at a pace that was comfortable. We worked our way through the Yellow Band at just less than twenty-eight thousand feet, and contrary to our original expectation, found ourselves passing a few other groups that were on the route ahead of us. We were most definitely moving slower than our norm, but we were still climbing significantly faster than many groups with oxygen. This gave us a dose of satisfaction. We were not climbing too fast. Indeed, we were in a sort of conservative trance that included sporadic encouragements to keep going but watch the pace. Passing other teams became a source of confidence that allowed us to really enjoy the climbing. The route wound its way up through more cliffs and ledges as we negotiated the Band. We could do this! Fear and anticipation were diluted by the reality that here we were higher than we had ever been, without oxygen, and it was not a whole lot different than any other climb we had been on. We were pumped.

The trance drew us up with each step, and suddenly the route leveled off. I pointed my head lamp ahead of me, but there was nothing to see. Just a black hole with no reflection. Norbu welcomed me to the northeast ridge. I looked at my watch, and we were two hours ahead of the sunrise. This was not good at all.

The route ahead required negotiating precarious, down-sloping slags of rock ledges, including the infamous steps leading to the summit. We needed to have the light of day to tackle these. Added to this, it was extremely cold, and our feet started to go numb. We were hours from even the physiological warmth of the sun. Steve, climbing without overboots, decided that he had to go down, and with little hesitation he started back down to the tent.

We were at just over twenty-eight thousand feet and Jim and I, along with Norbu, proceeded to walk the ridge. My feet were starting to go numb, to no feeling whatsoever. We looked ahead at the second step, and there was a logjam of climbers who were at a standstill. The steps on the ridge are the only avenue of passage, and often there are fixed ropes and ladders to climb. With numb feet, I looked at Norbu and proclaimed I was not going to lose any toes. "I have to get out of here now," I told him. He was surprised at this and simply said, "[If] your feet are numb, you will lose them. We can make the summit, but your toes will be lost. It's not worth it." I immediately turned around. Jim was a few hundred feet ahead of me but soon followed a few minutes later; he could not get his fingers warm.

At the time, there was no shame or disappointment. At altitude, you really lose all sense of emotion. It was just an obvious point of fact, and I chalk up all the experience before as contributing to my obvious then-and-now decision. The only thing that I do know for certain is that I was not even remotely disappointed—I felt a great sense of satisfaction. Being that high without oxygen and feeling as normal as I did was something I really appreciated. I descended back to camp. I was quite cognizant of the fact that while I did not conquer Everest, I had conquered fears about being at superhigh altitudes that had built up during my career. In fact, the fears simply never materialized. Looking back, I find those moments oddly surreal.

When we all got back at our high camp, Jim continued to Camp 2. It was still dark, so Steve and I waited for the sun before heading down. The toll of the summit bid followed by a cold night at twenty-seven thousand feet caught up to me personally. I found my asthma creeping back into the situation from the exertion of breathing the frigid air so hard; the expedition really stretched me personally. Steve immediately descended the next morning, but I was hammered. I struggled to the point of finding myself at a rock with another guide smacking me in the shoulders; I had stopped and fallen asleep. I woke up scared thinking, "This is how people die up here. They fall asleep and never wake up." Coupled with the emotional drain, I was near the end of my wit. I'd be lying if I said we were not slightly disappointed, but we still had a ton of work to do, and at a minimum, with soft snow down below, we knew we were in for a massively attractive ski. Truth be known, as much as we wanted to climb Everest, by this time, the absence of our skis was disappointing. We had put so much energy into the goal of skiing from the summit of Everest that when we packed up and started climbing without them, our hearts were never really in it. Ironically, once I got back to Camp 2, even skiing wasn't enough to perk me up. I had to stay there another night to recover from utter exhaustion. I slept until the next morning. When I woke up, I was feeling extremely tired, but I was infinitely better than the day before, and my ambition returned. All I wanted to do was go skiing. We didn't even brew up; we wanted to get back to the North Col, and we wanted to ski.

I had coined the phrase on Cho Oyu that "climbing without skiing is pain and suffering with lousy food at the end of the day," and from that perspective, we have never thought of ourselves as climbers. Skiing was all that mattered to us. This is difficult to explain, but during the pretrip buildup and preparation, the activity that we were preparing for was pure and simple skiing. By this time in our career, we had enough experience to know we could climb the highest peaks in the world, and although the additional height of Everest was unknown from a climbing perspective, the real concerns revolved around skiing.

Simple things like the transitions from crampons to skis and from skis to crampons—activities that at altitude are extremely dangerous and physically demanding—were a typical challenge for which we trained. We also knew how difficult just skiing was at high altitude. So, while we wanted the summit of Everest, doing it without the skis created a sort of psychological detachment that left a gaping hole in our minds. While we waited in the tent for the light of day, we chalked it up to the caprice of the mountain and dressed the mental bruises with the thought of the skiing we knew we were about to experience.

As the sun rose, we packed up our camp and headed down. The idea of a second ski descent of the north ridge was intoxicating, and we pulled apart the cache containing our skis. The north ridge was blanketed with soft snow, a stark contrast compared to our previous descent of the terrain. The day was supercold but crystal clear. This allowed us to see the slope as it rolled out of sight ahead of us, and the narrowness of the ridge was overwhelming. Both sides boasted sheer drops to the glaciers below, and it was clear that regardless of snow conditions, there was absolutely no room for error. Our hearts raced with anticipation and fear. The cache was fortunately on a small flat ledge, which allowed us to easily stand and take off our crampons and then to click into our skis.

Standing there, however, during the transition when neither the spikes of crampons nor edge of ski was securing our position was an odd, uncomfortable feeling. With the click of our bindings, we were on familiar ground. Our edges were razor sharp, and all the days standing on skis brought a welcomed feeling that, for a ski mountaineer, is blissful security. The snow was soft, but it had an annoying crust. Here we were, again, ready to ski, but as was always the case up high, the moment before commitment brought out feelings of inadequacy. Until you make that first turn, you literally feel like you forgot how to ski.

Steve jumped in first, and Jim and I watched him go through a couple of awkward first turns then relax into a more normal style, something that a life of skiing had instilled in his legs. This excited us and tempered the initial question marks we thought and felt. Jim followed suit as I filmed the show—skiing on the north ridge of Mount Everest. I put the camera back in its bag, which hung around my neck and was secured around my waist, and I pushed off. The first turn felt horrible, and I traversed farther across the face than I anticipated as my altitude-numbed mind caught up with my body. The next turn was not much better, and as I made a herky-jerky hop, I remembered one word of wisdom my father had instilled in me: "relax."

I recalled in total clarity that I was thinking the exact same thoughts on that ridge four years before, but my brain translated the message to my body, and I soon found myself making ski turns again on the north ridge of Mount Everest—at over twenty-five thousand feet! I skied a few turns, reached Steve and Jim, and let out a burst of "yahoos" that had built up inside me. All the feelings that had been building during the years of anticipation of skiing Mount Everest—compounded by the hardship of getting all that gear up that mountain, the disappointment of dropping the skis, and not standing on top—boiled over and required something, anything, to be released. It is not uncommon to see the best climbers in the world with tears rolling down their faces as they stand on the tops of their objectives. We were no different. And while we didn't achieve a summit, skiing that ridge that day validated all the effort, all the planning, all the everything that we put into that expedition. Tears rolled down my cheeks, and I knew more definitively who and what I was. There was no fear, no anticipation of what it would be like, just three best friends out skiing where only a few others besides us ever had, enjoying the fruits of all our labor. Nothing else mattered.

We continued our descent, and back at ABC we were satisfied. All question marks of what it would be like up high were answered. We had progressed in the sport to a level we had not expected, and the knowledge of ourselves and our capabilities opened an entirely different perspective for our climbing and skiing. That day, skiing that ridge, validated everything we had ever done to that point, and it changed the way we viewed ourselves and the way we would approach our passion from that day on.

When we arrived home, it was not without condolences from just about everyone for not standing on top. Everest generates a broad spectrum of emotions from people who have climbed it. But because it's the highest peak on earth, it's not just a mountain. Everest is a natural benchmark of what is possible for human beings. In general, people don't understand even remotely the disparity involved in the thousands of ascents of the peak. To most, the concept of a pure style ascent is superseded by summit photos and stories relayed by the people that have been there, regardless of the style by which the peak was climbed. Nothing else matters in the spectrum of Everest in pop culture. If you don't stand on top, the story is over. It doesn't matter if you attempted it without supplemental oxygen or without porters.

Skiing on Everest is almost always thought of in terms of Yuichiro Miura, who in 1970 tucked it down the Lhotse face in the Academy Award–winning documentary film *The Man Who Skied Down Everest*. His descent included a harrowing fall— with a parachute that slowed his drop—and involved only a few actual ski turns. His was a bumpy, two-thousand-foot slide. For us, making controlled utilitarian hop turns down the north ridge was appreciated by only a small number of climbers and ski mountaineers. All this fueled the local climbing community's disdain for us, and many people appeared almost relieved we had, by the normal definition of Everest, failed.

It's not easy to explain why we found such satisfaction in what we had achieved on Cho Oyu and Everest. The reality was that except for our ski descents of the north ridge of Everest, only two other people had skied that ridge, and a ski descent from above twenty-five thousand feet on any other peak than Everest was a rarely accomplished feat. Only a handful of people had ever dragged skis up and skied down from that altitude at that point in time. In that total, starting with Shish, we had logged many of the high ski descents ever recorded. Everest was our fifth ski descent from above seven thousand meters, placing us in a tie for the most ever. And with Cho Oyu, we had become only the fifth people in history to obtain multiple ski descents from above eight thousand meters. We had climbed to over twenty-eight thousand feet, experiencing an altitude that only Everest held over every other point on earth.

We knew all this, but it was difficult to explain to people who had not had the experiences we'd had, and our efforts to explain it left them with nothing to compare it to. Indeed, most people who heard our story gravitated to the only thing they could really understand—we didn't summit Everest. Nothing else mattered. Our excitement was sometimes perceived as sour grapes for not making a summit, so we gave up trying. But regardless, it was a theme that we had developed in our careers, and we were extremely proud of the accomplishment. But more to the point, by this time, after all the trips, it was another check mark in the "I don't care" box.

We were getting older and wiser, and the sheer joy and satisfaction we derived from what we were doing superseded any need to blow our horns. Plus, we knew most people didn't care. From time to time reporters would call to interview us, and we would try to relay the facts and circumstances, but even then, they almost never understood the story, and almost always got it wrong.

At times, this served the naysayers who berated us, especially when clueless writers hyped their stories with headlines like, "Skied Mount Everest." It was clear we had skied on Everest, but taking the advice from Pat Morrow on Shishapangma, we never relayed our story with delusions or deceit of anything but the truth. It was what it was, and any effort to relay all the other facts was missed and contorted. Effectively, we stopped doing any interviews and kept to ourselves. Even when writers got some of it right, it was almost always watered down with qualifying opinions. In a feature article in *Outside* magazine, the writer understood the magnitude, and we were referred to as "the most accomplished ski mountaineers alive" in one sentence while being referred to as "weekend warriors"—with an emphasis on the fact that we were accountants—in another.

Granted, we understood the irony of CPAs who were also climbing and skiing the highest peaks in the world, but to anyone who saw us working out at the gym, or understood the tally of peaks we had accumulated, or understood when we were out hiking and climbing the Highlands Bowl that it was not just about a day skiing but hard-core training. We weren't household names in the various ski rags, but we were as committed to the sport at a level few if any athletes in any sport have ever been. Our ski mountaineering careers had spanned nearly twenty years; we were approaching age forty, and we were still pushing the boundaries of the sport. The article would help generate acclaim and sponsorships to keep it all going, but despite the plug, it bruised our egos. But as they say, any press is good press, and soon another platform came that would change the way we looked at our part in the sport.

A call came through that the late Warren Miller was doing a segment on Aspen, and they wanted to film "the Marolt Brothers" skiing down Aspen Mountain. For a skier, Warren Miller films are pretty much the ultimate venue for validation. We spent a couple days and then appeared in the film, which more than healed the bruises to our egos. But more importantly, it generated my own ambition to carry on with film. Jeanne was eager to push me into production. I had funds, and I set out with enthusiasm to make something out of the opportunity. Seeing how Warren Miller produced not just our segment but all his company's films in general became a course of study. I saw the chance to create a film that "got it right" because I was the producer and not some writer looking for content. We were satisfied with what we had accomplished, and we learned to accept it internally, but it came with a level of the game that, bluntly put, cost a lot of money. We had a desire for additional expeditions, and I was not hell-bent on notoriety, but I realized a bit of it could be leveraged to obtain funding for more trips.

I reached out to Cherie, who had been the field producer for our Shishapangma film as well as for our Cho Oyu/Everest expeditions, and we set out to tell our story. While we had been pitched by various production companies and even networks to do both films and segments for other films, we kept our cache of footage to ourselves, not wanting to expose the content before we had a shot at making our own film. And, while we gave the shooting our best efforts—in terms of footage that meant the high-altitude material—I was not a professional videographer, and the objective of climbing and skiing superseded any notion that I was there for anything beyond the obvious. While I took great pride in getting the shot, my footage, bluntly, lacked continuity and creativity and was generally what you would expect from a guy who at times questioned carrying the extra weight of the camera equipment. We didn't have hours and hours of footage but rather minutes.

We had to piece together the good shots I was able to obtain under wraps. We didn't want to share that until we were ready. We reached out to an aspiring editor who lived in town, Danny Brown, a guy who had a natural talent for telling a story and was equally talented in the difficult nature of editing the relatively new technology of video. He knew the complicated programs involved in putting a video together and was also a ski mountaineer. We loaded the footage onto his system, discussed the arc of the film, and set him to work. A month later, he produced a thirty-minute film that I still regard as a work of art. But Danny did not have the money to purchase the expensive programs for sound sweetening and color correcting that were being used at that time, so we had to find a studio that could. Our ideas carried a six-figure price tag, and the only options available were with the studios in Los Angeles.

As Danny pieced the footage into a film, my excitement grew wildly; the sense of seeing my footage put into a story was intoxicating. I loved the process. I reached out to people in Aspen with connections in LA and in time was connected with Jack Jacobson, who "knew enough about everyone in Hollywood to get a foot in the door." Jack loved the concept of the film and connected me with Kenny Fields, the owner of a large production house, West Post Digital (WPD). The cost Kenny quoted was extremely high, but he was also a passionate skier, and we worked out a deal to cover the processing at cost.

I soon found myself in LA with a haul bag of computer drives that contained all the footage as well as the film we'd made with Danny. I couldn't help but marvel at his beautiful facility, complete with a half dozen fully operational editing bays and editors wearing headsets entranced on various video projects for a client list that included all major networks, including a massive MTV feature project. The bays were in use 24/7, and the studio included a full kitchen complete with pantries and food closets, enough to run a restaurant. People worked around the clock at WPD, and WPD ensured they never had to leave, even to eat.

Soon I was sitting in the dark of a pristine video bay jamming away with Kenny. I was blown away at what the system was capable of, and my otherwise mediocre footage was transformed into a professional, polished piece of work with color and sound that radiated as if in an IMAX theater. We worked for a week on the film, and then the project took a turn that would change the way I viewed the process entirely. As we watched the finished piece playing on a massive screen in a viewing theater, I noticed a gentleman who seemed entranced by the film. Before I knew it, he was sitting in with us, mesmerized by the images on the screen. As the film concluded, he simply said, "Oh, my God. That is skiing on Everest. I need to make this film."

The gentleman was Les Guthman, and he was working on a film of his own. As I reached to shake his hand, I immediately recognized his name as the producer of a film I had just watched on mountaineer Reinhold Messner. Later I would learn that in *Men's Journal* magazine's list of the top adventure films of all time, Les had produced three. Les was the director and founder of Outside Magazine TV and was regarded in the adventure genre as one of if not the top producers of all time, often referred to as the "Spielberg of adventure documentaries."

At first, my heart sank. Les was not at all interested in what we had painstakingly produced. As only Les could do, he managed to compliment me on the film, but tactfully he explained that it was too short and lacked continuity that would allow for the film to be included in major film festivals and ultimately for mainstream distribution platforms. He explained that what we had was totally unique footage regardless of the quality and that the story was on par with "anything I have ever produced." Les didn't ask; he demanded that he take this project on and produce a "real" film. My initial reaction reflected my longstanding goal to never let mainstream media take this on simply because "they" never seemed to get it right. I hesitated. But Les made it clear that I would be a producer and director along with him and that he could not do what he envisioned without me, and he put my mind at ease.

Before I left LA, Les had formulated a budget. The fact that he never asked how I was paying for the film enhanced my ability to understand that he was not looking for a paycheck and that he really wanted to tell the world our story. But his budget was huge. I didn't have a commitment from Jeanne for the kinds of numbers he was talking about, and I had spent almost everything she had given me. I tactfully told Les I needed to pencil it all out and get back to him.

I headed home, not with the anticipated completed project, but empty bagged as all the content remained at WPD until I could figure things out. I rehearsed my stilted pitch to Jeanne over and over, trying to perfect how I would explain being empty handed with regard to a finished film that we'd all anticipated and resolved that the truth would set me free. I'd explain exactly what happened. Certainly, I did have a finished film, but I'd clearly stumbled on a new opportunity in the process.

I researched Les Guthman and built a version of his résumé from scratch. My findings were almost too good to believe, and I let the facts speak for themselves. I met with Jeanne over coffee. She explained that while she and Gary had attempted to produce other films, films were generally a financial black hole—they rarely made money. But she explained a bit about Gary's story and how after a successful career he had a propensity to want to help others with their careers. It was as if she understood what I experienced in LA better than I did. She vowed that she and Gary would help me, and they not only wanted to create the film; she encouraged me to consider filmmaking as a potential career.

By this time, I had produced a few different films, and while I never saw myself as a career filmmaker, I absolutely loved the process. In contrast to my square-pegged career as an accountant, telling the stories, writing scripts, putting footage together, finding music, and doing just about everything, making films was becoming a passion. Also, beyond the movie *The Man Who Skied Everest*, which captured high-altitude skiing via a massive telephoto lens at the bottom of the mountain, I realized I had the first actual skiing footage from above twenty-three thousand feet. Shooting this kind of material was becoming a massive draw for me, and I developed an enthusiasm to do whatever it took to get the shot. Jeanne realized all this and was eager to help. I left her barely able to contain my excitement and immediately called Les to start cutting.

I spent the next several months making many trips to Santa Monica and working with Les in the studio. We had limited ability to use technology, but we were able to piece the film together with the use of the internet. Les realized that I would need to learn the editing program and arranged for me to take a crash course on editing with one of the professors at UCLA's film school. Although I would never consider myself an editor, I learned enough to communicate with Les while using footage to tell the story. I loved the process and was learning from a master storyteller and producer.

We finalized the film, and almost immediately it toured in a limited release with Landmark Theaters, as well as a prominent West Coast chain. The tour had limited success, but it put the film on major theater marquees in 2009, exposing the film to a national audience. We screened it in many domestic film festivals as well as major international festivals like the Dingle International Film Festival in Ireland. That led to a distribution deal with Cinetics Media, which was the largest digital distributor in the world. They brokered a deal with ESPN Classic, and the film ran on their network "until people stop watching," which amounted to a two-year run. The film aired on PBS, and segments landed on NBC and a variety of other networks. It was available on every major digital pay-per-view platform and is still available today.

The film wasn't even remotely a financial success, but for my first film, the exposure generated was a massive hit. I was flooded with emails and messages from people all over the world saying they watched the film as well as requests for private screenings. Sponsors flew me around the country to do private screenings, and various nonprofits requested screenings for fund-raising events. I was a board member of the Jimmie Heuga Center for MS, and we used the film to raise money for the fight against that disease. I generated a bit of a name for myself in the film business, and my efforts for the Jimmie Heuga MS organization led to Jimmie Heuga himself requesting that I do a legacy film on him.

Jimmie was the first American to medal in alpine skiing in an Olympics, and he subsequently succumbed to multiple sclerosis. He spent the second half of his life proving that physical therapy was a means to obtaining a more normal life despite the disease.

I was able to raise nearly a hundred grand to produce the film. We made the film with West Post Digital for about $25,000, leaving the rest as a donation for the cause. We toured and sold the film via Cinetics Media, generating a ton of money in addition to that as well. Whether I realized it or not, Jeanne's efforts to create another career for me were panning out. But in my mind, I wanted to make another film on my real passion, climbing and skiing. I had enough experience with two "real" films at this stage and several other lesser films to obtain funding from sponsors and various sources to set out on more expeditions.

After *Everest 2*, life was crazy for me. My accounting business was growing, I was making films, I was traveling around the world doing screenings, and I was trying to raise my two children. This forced me to hire people to help at the office. I took advice from my brother Roger, who at this time was raising three kids. "Don't fight it," he told me. "Go with it; but kids have to be the priority." I tried to never miss school events and to help Shelly with the kid wrangling, and while I often felt I was in well over my head, things were good.

Steve and Jim were experiencing the same thing minus the film stuff, but life was a balancing act, keeping deadlines met and priorities in line. We still had great ambition to do more expeditions, and while the long Asian trips were difficult to sell, our families realized the importance of our passion and encouraged us to head to the lower-hanging fruit in South America. We found we could plan and execute short ten- to twelve-day adventures to six-thousand-meter peaks and found ourselves in Bolivia, Ecuador, Peru, and so forth climbing and skiing, despite criticism from the local climbing community that "there's no skiing on those peaks; they are for climbing."

Our gear sponsorships flourished, and the new gear and technology allowed us to push our passion well beyond what we ever imagined. We found ourselves out on our local peaks as often as possible, really enjoying our progression within the sport. But we also learned that too much of a good thing can, if nothing else, burn you out.

7

Beyond Skiing Everest

After Cho Oyu and Everest, we still had a great desire to give Everest another shot, and we understood the changes we had to make with regard to preparation as well as for the logistics of climbing the peak pure style with skis. The dream was still alive. But a sea of change came around the time we were on Cho Oyu and Everest, and it would impact not only our lives but the lives of adventurers in general.

The economic tech bubble and the mortgage banking industry imploded, and along with it, the world economy. This had a drastic impact in the Aspen community, where many of the wealthy people who are big players on Wall Street have second homes. Their property taxes pay a lot of bills for the full-time residents. Steve and my businesses flatlined, and although you must have accounting for black numbers, you also must count the red numbers. The situation was depressing at times. In Aspen, real estate drives the economy as much or more than skiing, and it was painful to witness real estate agents who had become accustomed to seven-figure salaries relegated to literally being street people. In multiple instances, I knew people with beautiful homes and families who became alcoholics and lost everything. On the other hand, it was ironic to see clients and friends who were worth hundreds of millions crying because their fortunes were cut in half. Poor is a relative concept. Bernie Madoff had scammed many locals out of their fortunes, real-estate prices dropped through the floor, and many people who were able to obtain loans well exceeding any sense of reasonableness found themselves with little or no income stream. Many lost their homes. Steve and I continued to work and were counted among the more fortunate, cementing the idea that we had chosen great career paths, but it was tough.

The situation, however, had a drastic impact on our passion to climb and ski the highest peaks in the world. Along with the economic decline, the adventure industry in general and the skiing industry specifically suffered greatly. For the next several years, funding for expeditions and films was nonexistent. To that point, I was successful in generating relationships with companies like Merck & Co. (the big pharmaceutical company), Citrix Systems, a technology company, and Under Armour. I could literally send them an invoice for $30,000 and with no communication whatsoever would receive a check in a couple weeks. People stopped offering to fund film projects, and those who had, pulled back in hesitation. Gear companies completely got out of the funding game, but they did continue to offer what they could: gear. This was the only bright spot in the sponsorship game, and the technology was advancing so quickly that we had to keep up with it. We welcomed the gear sponsorships, and the value was enormous.

At the same time of the decline in the economy, however, there was an odd spike in adventure-seeking in general. The commercial climbing industry flourished on major peaks around the world. Wealthy segments of society suffered like everyone else, but the decline in the economy seemed to leave many doing a bit of soul searching. Combined with ample free time, they seemed to formulate bucket lists of exotic adventures—going places they'd never dreamed of nor had time for and doing things they'd never imagined. In the flurry to "live life," the more popular peaks began to see a spike in commercial expeditions.

Everest has always been a magnet for adventure seekers, and guide companies took advantage of the situation. We sat back and watched. Technology was well developed by this time, allowing all these people to set up websites and report to the world what they were doing on an hour-by-hour basis, from their tents to the summits and all points in between. The numbers at base camps exploded from hundreds to thousands. Pictures of fixed lines with people climbing ass to nose by the hundreds appeared online regularly. On Everest, both the northern and southern routes played host to horrendous stories of people waiting for hours at the bottlenecks. Along with the masses, the death counts rolled in, and they were horrific. Death had historically been part of the equation on Everest and the other popular high peaks, but over the seasons, the counts were by the dozens. All the other issues that come with masses of people became exacerbated: trash, physical altercations at camps, Sherpa strikes, and on and on. The local Chinese and Nepalese governments and climbing associations tried to control the situation by raising peak fees, Sherpa fees, garbage deposit fees, rescue deposit fees, and basically taxing everything. Armed guards were even deployed on the mountains to control the situation, but nothing worked. People with means continued to write checks, and the guide companies continued to cash them.

For us, this was a terrible situation. On our last Everest trip, the bottleneck ahead was really the ultimate factor in our decision to turn around. With cold feet, we could not afford to move higher, especially with the prospect of having to stop for twenty minutes at one of the steps, which was the norm at the time. Looking at the mess on Everest even a couple years after that made it clear Everest was not going to be possible given our pure style. But the price of climbing drastically increased in the effort to control the situation, and coupled with the economic reality that sponsorships and funding disappeared, Everest became a pipe dream. The deaths and garbage along with thousands of people made the dream a nightmare.

We took a step backward to let the mental dust settle from Cho/Everest and started to research other peaks and places. When you don't experience total satisfaction on any trip, there is a need to fill the void that it leaves, and our desire to find a fix was strong. Our personal success generated a need to keep climbing and to look for other projects.

We didn't have the funds or really the desire to head back to Asia, primarily because it entailed too much time away from family. So, we sought the easier and cheaper solutions that South

America offered. We wanted something totally different to our previous southern experiences, so one evening with nothing to do, I sat down at my computer and opened Google Earth. My initial reaction was to head directly to the normal hot spots—the Cordillera Blanca in Peru, the Cordillera Real in Bolivia—but it was too familiar after dozens of previous trips.

Then, on the corner of my computer screen, I noticed a white dot on the edge of the vast and bare Atacama Desert. I took my virtual spaceship in that direction and lowered in for a closer look. When no text appeared, even when close enough to see the peak was glaciated, my interest piqued. The mountain was located about a hundred miles northwest from a large city called Arequipa and as far inland from the coast. The peak was massive, with glaciers cascading from numerous summits. I then googled "mountains near Arequipa" to find its name—Coropuna—as well as those of several smaller white dots in the area. I further googled the peak to find it was a volcano that rose to 21,500 feet, and immediately knew this was a peak we wanted. I bounced the idea off Steve, who was immediately intrigued and without hesitation ordered me to plan the trip.

Beta on the peak was sparse at best, but I learned that there were a handful of tour operators that had taken trips to the north side of the peak. Being skiers, however, we were looking at the longer glacier lines of the southern slopes. I could find nothing on that. Operators had no clue and no time to offer suggestions. Almost giving up hope, I managed to talk one guy into helping us with the promise that if he could get us to the southern side it would come with a bonus of $100, enough to set him into action. He called back a week later and explained that he had it figured out but that he could find no one who had ever climbed the mountain from the south. He offered no guarantees past a drop-off point several miles from the peak. We hesitated slightly at the thought of another wasted effort, but the excitement of having to figure it all out fit our definition of "no people," and we accepted his offer to get us there. Two weeks later, we found ourselves in Arequipa.

Jim had issues with the short notice and could not join us for the quick twelve-day itinerary, but Callahan and Gibjo were excited to join us. We toured the ancient city of Arequipa, which sits on the flat edge of the desert with massive volcanos in every direction.

The main streets were the same streets used hundreds of years before by the Inca; their handiwork was on display everywhere. But we were on a tight time budget and didn't have time to see the sights. We immediately headed to Coropuna.

The paved road soon ended, and the Jeep road paralleled the steep side of the world's deepest canyon, the Colca, a journey that even without climbing and skiing would have made the trip a success. The canyon left us in awe. Eventually, we stopped at the end of the road at the village of Barraco, a totally self-sustained community of farmers and ranchers that live on the beautiful foothills of Coropuna. We learned that they had first seen white-skinned people only two weeks before, when a team from Poland had set off from their village to climb the massive peak. No one had any knowledge of people climbing the peak from the south before that. They touched our faces in amazement and welcomed us warmly with a delicious lunch. We could sense their excitement, knowing we would be attempting the peak as well. The reality that people had climbed the peak was at first a disappointment, but it also allowed us to realize if they could climb it, so could we, and without question no one had ever skied the peak. Our fears of getting shut out from a great adventure evaporated. Our tour operator negotiated with a local rancher to help haul our gear from Barraco up to a base camp, and we were off.

We followed game and cattle trails up to a beautiful green plateau, noticing vegetation none of us had ever seen. The position offered unobstructed views of the vast landscape, with the stark, grand Colca canyon winding its way to lower climes. Our first camp was about 13,500 feet, meaning we didn't gain much altitude after leaving Barraco. Still, we respected the altitude with a rest day before setting off to a higher camp. The first issue we came across was that the stream that irrigated the green grass of our camp ended only a short distance from the barren and dusty volcanic slope that was the start of the peak.

Upon further investigation, we found that the next sign of water was at the toe of the glacier, somewhere between seventeen thousand and eighteen thousand feet. This was further complicated by the fact that much beyond a flat ledge only five hundred feet or so above our base camp, there were no suitable camp spots. We discussed the situation and decided we would camp at the next appropriate spot, a flat, grassy field where there was a small stream. When we pulled our gear out, we were astonished to find that we'd forgotten to get the camping stove out of the back of the Jeep. It was classic complacency, neglecting a hard and fast rule to always manage the gear before the vehicles leave. Now, we would be learning another lesson the hard way. There would be no possible way to put in a high camp, and we would be relying on the base camp stove, which was too heavy to carry by ourselves.

Every foot mattered now, and five hundred feet became a huge obstacle; we had to get to the next flat ground. We managed to get the rancher to bring his strongest animal up the steep and rugged slopes to the next camp, five hundred feet above. While that was successful, the poor beast subsequently fell down a steep bank, much to the horror of his owner. Thankfully, no bones were broken, but we would have to carry the heavy stove half the distance. We took the task on gladly, partly as a diversion from the embarrassment of our carelessness in planning and partly as a diversion from the embarrassment of making the poor animal lug the two-hundred-pound load.

Our shame was only overshadowed by the fact that he was not injured and happily and confidently descended to unlimited grass and water. Another lesson learned; don't disrespect the enormous effort that animals often play in expeditions. They are living, breathing beasts and without them, we wouldn't get too far. Since that day, we have paid greater attention to the animals on our trips, and more than a few times we've chastised their owners for overloading or otherwise abusing them. They, like us, have limits. Whenever we can, we use human porters for approaches. They appreciate the work and need the money.

As we settled in to our second camp, we realized that we would have a monster of a day on our summit bid. We were situated at about fourteen thousand feet, and at twenty-one thousand feet, the summit would require a significantly longer push than we had ever taken on. We spent a day hauling all our ski gear to the toe of the glacier, which was located about half the distance to the top. That was a massive day, not only because we had to move loads up for the final push, but because we were still acclimating as well.

Thus, we reasoned we would rest a day longer than normal to allow ourselves a better chance to reach the summit. We were thinking, "Sure we will get some climbing and skiing in, but reaching the summit has a snowball's chance in hell." Steve and I had climbed nearly the same distance to just under twenty-one thousand feet on Tupungato, but we had no loads, and the effort left us dizzy sick and at our limits with hypoxia. We had little confidence we could manage a longer effort with the weight of skis. John and Gibjo had never experienced a push this high and long, and even with Gibjo's background as both a climber and an emergency room MD with significant altitude experience, they thought the idea to be ridiculous. We justified the attempt with a "we are here; we don't have a choice on camping higher" and "Let's just go as high as we can safely and reasonably." We spent the next day and a half resting and talking ourselves into climbing the peak.

Our schedule had us on the trail at midnight, and with stable dry weather, we were not terribly concerned with weather issues. We set off slowly. We reached the cache at about eighteen thousand feet as sunlight hit the peak and chuckled at the thought of having to climb unacclimated for another three thousand feet. But we felt strong, and the light lifted our spirits. We traversed a glacier basin on our skis to the steeper slopes leading to the summit. There, the snow crust thinned out, and the lower layers were avalanche prone. Our day was long and going to be even longer considering our idea to continue around the right to see if the sunbaked slopes were more consolidated. We crossed a barren dirt slope where a vapor hole melted the glacier to the dirt, climbed down and across this, and to our delight, the snow crust was thick and hard.

We ascended without a rope until I fell in a slot up to my waist, and we broke out the safety line. The climb was steep, and we were gaining altitude as we went. In a trance, Steve finally crested the skyline, and he said he could see the summit. At this point, our hypoxic brains stopped worrying about much of anything but climbing. We all felt relatively strong, strong enough to go a bit farther. Then a bit farther, and so on. The rope in front of me continued to inch along, and suddenly I crested the slope and found myself on relatively flat ground with a small rise ahead. The rise looked close—too close to bother pulling the skis out of our packs to skin across the terrain we found ourselves struggling through, postholing in the deep snow. The slight rise of the final summit went on forever. Forty-five minutes into the complete suffer fest that it was, Steve put his arms above his head in a victory salute. The wind on top was strong, and we struggled to speak to each other—but we did it! Ten hours and nearly seven thousand feet of climbing to twenty-one thousand feet.

We clicked into our skis and skied the steep summit cone. As we descended onto the lower slopes, the hard ice and snow became corn, offering a massively long ski on near perfect smooth soft snow to the end of the glacier. We shouldered our skis and walked back to camp. Our base camp cook and guardian had pulled our camp and hauled it down to a lower elevation where the horses could then take it down to the flat green meadow. We carried our personal gear and tents back down, and fifteen hours after we started, we were done. The next day we headed back down the valley to Barraco, and two days later we were home.

Coropuna became a catalyst for taking our climbing and skiing in another direction. We realized that our decision to head to remote peaks where few if any people had climbed let alone skied was paying off. That no one really knew about this massive peak and that we were the first people to ski it and that only one other team had climbed this route, left us in amazement. That skiers had not discovered the mountain left us bewildered, but it also left us in wonder for the endless places we could take our passion.

So many climbers and skiers gravitated toward the obvious and explored peaks of the world, but the vista on that trip left our imaginations spinning out of control. The contrast of big crowds on mountains like Everest and other popular peaks compared to peaks like Coropuna was drastic, defining a completely different activity. But it also opened our eyes to the vast possibilities in the world's greatest ranges. The ease of entry and craze of people entering the sport had not in fact saturated climbing to a point of no return. Rather, the boom in climbing and skiing had created a community that had barely scratched the surface of what was possible. Many, it seemed, were content to repeat trade routes and descents. If you took a bit of time to research and took chances on going to places with little or no beta, those places were countless. But it also reformulated our interpretation of our passion itself.

To that point, our past experiences were based on what was known by others. We picked peaks based on a popularity contest of what we could research and what other climbers had experienced. This served a purpose and was part of a progression based on a ratio of experience to information. It's quite natural and somewhat unavoidable to pick an objective with a known pretrip experience, even if it is not yours.

Climbing the highest peaks in the world is drastically different than, say, climbing peaks in our backyard, where after decades of playing around, there was little if any thought needed to take on just about any summit. We'd just decide on a peak and without much thought, the gear, the food, the fuel, and everything else that was needed simply made it into the pack, and we knew what we needed to do. When you decide to head to a massive peak in Asia or the Andes, it takes a lot of preparation. There are so many unknowns that you naturally gravitate toward any objective that is known. Consequently, you end up picking peaks that have been climbed, often where things can be researched on the internet or about which other climbers are available to talk; information is critical.

Our experience on Coropuna told us a different story. We could not find any information on skiing the peak, and for the southern slopes, there was no beta on either climbing or skiing it. Standing in Baroco's town square, we learned that there was no beta because no one had climbed there before the Polish team climbed it, the week before we did. Yet, there we were. Our progression had by no means allowed us to be as comfortable as we would be heading out to a peak in the Elk Range near home, but we had accumulated enough experience to risk heading into the unknown and sorting things out as they happened. The name of the peak or who had previously climbed it was unimportant, and while climbing and skiing were the goal, the trip became an adventure in and of itself. The rush of heading out with haul bags and no map or guidebook to extremely remote parts of exotic ranges became a massive incentive for us to explore.

We fancied ourselves somewhat as explorers and obtained some insight into the experiences we had read about from history's greatest explorers like Shipton, Tillman, Shackleton, and others. Shipton, specifically, is regarded as one of the foremost mountaineers of his time. But when I read his words, there was a general theme that while his passion was climbing, he found enormous satisfaction in exploring totally unknown regions. The title of one of his books, *Blank on the Map*, sums it up nicely.

Up to 2009, for us, the idea of trekking and merely walking in the mountains came as an unnecessary evil to obtain the real fun: climbing and skiing. Thus, we could never figure out if Shipton was being honest with his readers. On Coropuna, though, as I walked through the grazing lands and saw plants I had never seen or heard about, and got lost numerous times along the way, I started to understand what Shipton was talking about. That's not to say I would ever compare my own experiences with those of Shipton or any of his contemporaries, but regardless, I felt I could understand them.

While no area on earth today is a blank on the map, we were still in far-off areas beyond much research when compared to the popular peaks. We took enormous pride in the fact that the skiing aspect of our adventures was most definitely a blank on the map. While few if any climbers had heard of some of the places we found ourselves, far fewer skiers had thought of skiing where we had left tracks. This left us with greater respect for our historical heroes and framing our point in the context of how those great men approached the activity. We were realistic that we could never replicate their achievements, but we aspired to be as much like them as our experience and skill would allow. Our new objectives were sought not out of disdain for the ills of the modern sport as much as for the satisfaction we derived from throwing a dart at the unknown and heading to the point of contact on the map, regardless of what information we could obtain. Subsequently, we developed a great deal of satisfaction inversely related to what we knew before we got to the base of an objective.

There were also other factors that came into play with our approach to climbing and skiing. Our families were growing. Steve, by this time, was a father to three kids. Jim's two kids were getting into high school, and he was trying to balance everything with the millstone of funding their college careers. Our jobs provided the needed financial support for everything on the home front, and with experience, paydays were larger. But as for most people, life was about making ends meet.

Our desire to continue climbing and skiing was deeper than ever, and we continued to plan and execute expeditions to various six-thousand-meter peaks in South America. These trips were affordable and relatively quick, which helped us stay involved with our families back home, and we often found ourselves back in familiar haunts and with familiar friends in places like Bolivia, Peru, Ecuador, and Chile.

These were great trips, but they also gave us an opportunity to get better. We learned to climb much more efficiently, and with the improvements in gear, which in the 2000s were considerable, we found that our aging bodies could not only still climb and ski well but improve in all aspects of high-altitude living. But it left us with a void of sorts. We pondered what we could do next.

After Cho Oyu and Everest, we realized that we had done not only two descents from above eight thousand meters, but along the way, Steve and I had racked up five ski descents from above seven thousand meters. According to what we could find on the internet, seven-thousand-meter peak ski descents were not exactly common. But with a bit of effort, we pieced together that only a handful of other ski mountaineers, all Europeans, had as many. Skiing from above seven thousand meters in the face of eight thousand meters was not something that many people claimed along the way, but having skied from that height as many times as we had, it became something we started to consider seriously and took a great deal of pride in. The reality was that with two eight-thousand-meter peak ski descents under our belts, we knew enough to understand how difficult that objective was, both physically and mentally, but also financially; eight thousand meters was our goal, but reality (i.e., our back account situation) was a different story.

So, we focused on seven thousand meters if only because it was an enormous objective while still being tremendous fun. And it was financially a fraction of what eight-thousand-meter peaks cost. With a bit of money in the coffer from the film business, and a pitch to do a sequel called *Beyond Skiing Everest*, we hit up a handful of previous sponsors to obtain ski footage from another remote seven-thousand-meter peak that was both relatively unknown and, by comparison, extremely affordable. We called Kari Kobler, the owner of a guiding company based in Switzerland, whom we'd met and befriended on Everest. We let him know we wanted to go to a seven-thousand-meter ski peak where there would be no people.

"I've got just the peak for you," he said. "Norjin Kansang, 7,206 meters [23,642 feet]." The peak was difficult to find information on. It was well off the beaten path for the Everest hordes, and the cost was minimal. Perfect!

By early 2009, we had formed a team. Jim couldn't get away from work, but we persuaded Callahan and Mike Maple, another childhood buddy, to join us. John had not been on a trip with us since Coropuna, but he was eager to get back to the mountains. He was still strong and levelheaded. Maple had little experience with altitude, but he was incredibly strong both physically and mentally and had a huge capacity for endurance. He had joined us as often as anyone on the peaks in our backyard since Everest 2, and we welcomed him. He had also been an extraordinarily talented ski racer in his youth and was as passionate about a good adventure as anyone. Being relatively new to the international mountaineering game, Mike often succumbed to altitude and stomach issues, but even at his worst moments, he was always positive for the climb. He has a unique ability to rebound and is always positive—a great guy to have on a trip.

We also wrangled a new but close friend, Ham Mehlman, who had reached out to us in his quest to write a book on high-altitude skiing. He was a former editor of the *Harvard Crimson*, a diehard skier, and always up for an adventure. He wanted to join the trip and get a firsthand taste of the subject matter. Ham was also a successful hedge-fund manager and helped defray part of the expedition cost. At the last minute, Gibjo also joined the team. Like Callahan, he hadn't been on a trip since Coropuna, and he was eager to get back with us. And as always, we also welcomed his medical expertise.

We all met in Lhasa, toured the city—including the Potala Palace—and were off. We drove west and came to a familiar intersection in the road. One sign pointed right, to "Everest." Another sign, with some Chinese writing, pointed left. When the bus turned the opposite direction of Everest, we knew we were on an adventure!

We arrived at base camp with a tight schedule. The plan was to head immediately to advance base camp, a day's walk from base camp, but when we got out of the Jeep, our heads were spinning. Our altimeters told us we were at 15,500 feet, and we needed to acclimate. We set up base camp at the end of the road below a beautiful monastery that was occupied by several Tibetan nuns. Other than them, and a few yak herders, no one had been at this camp for years. Our driver spoke to the yak herders to arrange for us to move in a couple of days. It was still too early in the season for yaks, which were far down the valley grazing, but he said he had ponies that could do the job. We settled in with the anticipation of a rest day.

A day later, we felt better, but we needed an additional day to acclimate. We decided to do a quick, easy hike. We stopped off at the monastery, where the nuns were excited to see us, but with the language barrier, no one had much to say. We headed up above the monastery for a bit more altitude. We weren't prepared for what came next. As we crested a small buttress, the entire south face of Norjin Kansang rose up before us, dropping sharply into a vast lake that was still half frozen. A serac cliff at the foot of the peak shed immense chunks of ice that calved off into the lake, leaving us gawking in awe. There was little beta on this peak, and we had no idea that this lake even existed. The sky was clear, and the sun was warm, and we sat gazing at this unexpected jewel that few—if any—had ever seen. And jewel was an understatement. We sipped a bit of water, ate a quick snack, and descended back to base camp in utter amazement. To us, the trip was already a success.

The next day, we headed up the valley, which gained very little altitude as we walked around the base of the peak to where we would set up our advance base camp. As we entered the enormous, glacier-carved cirque, another lake greeted us. It was a magnificent place, and we would happily call it home for the next two weeks. The north face of the peak was sheer and steep, with a massive glacier flowing from its base to just above our camp. We had no idea where the route was; we didn't even know if we were on the right side of the mountain. We spent another day acclimating and scoping the various and unlimited routes through our camera lenses as well as going on another hike up the slopes behind camp. The only feasible route—a long slog up scree slopes to a small glacier that ended at a small buttress on the left side of the peak—eventually became clear. There would be a long traverse on what appeared to be a steep rock ridge to the main glaciers on the peak. From there, we figured we could climb steep but doable slopes to the steep summit pyramid. It was a long route, but any direct route was barred by massive ice cliffs near the summit, which calved off with horrendous roars farther up the glacier. We decided on the route and settled into life at camp.

Ham, however, was not doing well. Although at sixteen thousand feet advance base camp was only slightly higher than base camp, coming from Boston, he was not acclimated as well as the Colorado contingent. He labored for two nights with a headache and sour stomach, and on the next day showed signs of pulmonary edema—most notably, he was coughing up pink sputum. We immediately brought out the oxygen, which had leaked on the carry in, and suddenly we were desperate. We called our logistics guide on the satellite phone, and then Steve and Callahan loaded Ham's gear into their packs and escorted the hobbling man down the valley to a waiting Jeep. The retreat was, thankfully, a success. The event was a wakeup call, too. We were high, and despite the added rest day at base camp, we were higher than was practical. We spent the next two days at advance base resting.

We managed to get in light acclimating hikes up the hills behind camp, which ate into our time, but we knew without properly acclimating we were subjecting ourselves to potential disaster. With very little relief on the route back to the road and potentially a day's wait for a Jeep, the need for everyone to be fully acclimated to advance base camp was critical. Descent is the only way to combat deadly high-altitude edema, and where we were there wasn't a lot of descent to be had. We felt lucky getting Ham out safely, and we didn't want to push our luck.

We finally felt good enough for the long climb to Camp 1 and set out with huge loads. The climb started on steep, unstable talus. We circumnavigated a small glacier on the first trip because we had no idea how to get onto it, or if it was even possible. The talus ended at an area of flat shale on top of a broad buttress, which made for easy walking. Our loads were extraordinarily heavy, and our legs felt wooden. We moved slowly, letting our legs swing under our bodies, and by the time we reached camp, at nineteen thousand feet, just at the top of the glacier, we were wiped out. All our loads were of group gear: tents, stove kits, food, fuel, and our skiing equipment. With no Sherpa support, and this being a very big mountain, the stroll along the ridge brought the reality of the situation into focus. What we were attempting was substantial. But each step brought us a bit higher and closer to the end, and with that, confidence and satisfaction fueled our tired bodies. We arrived at Camp 1, set everything up and secured it and immediately headed down to thicker air, three thousand feet below. We rested for a day after the effort and then the next day headed up to sleep.

After a fitful night at Camp 1, the next objective was to set up Camp 2 at about twenty-one thousand feet on top of a steep glacier. This entailed down climbing a rock ridge for several hundred feet and then gaining the glacier. It didn't look far, but we knew that it was deceiving. We took the climbing hardware—pickets, screws, and ropes—not knowing if the slope was ice but knowing it had crevasses. The snow slopes were steeper than we thought, but they were a perfect consistency for climbing. We didn't need protection.

The objective was thus coming into focus, but as soon as we started, progress was slow. We labored on, noticing the grand north face of the mountain to our right and the dots of our tents at ABC far below. As we rounded a knoll at the top of the slope, we came across some old tents, abandoned and shredded, left by uncaring climbers too lazy to haul them off. I wondered how the slopes ahead had thwarted them. Were they truly lazy or simply too fagged to take the equipment back down the slopes and then back up to the next camp? Looking ahead, we also became aware of the next major hurdle: climax slots—deep dirt-to-air cracks in the glacier—that dotted the face from one side of the peak to the other. Crevasses are part of the game, but these were unusual in length. We used our camera lenses to search for snow bridges but immediately realized our summit push was going to be a lot longer than any direct line with the commensurate back-and-forth effort to stitch a route together through the gaps. We had failed to bring nearly enough wands to mark our trail but were happy when the nuns at the monastery presented us with about fifty bamboo wands with red tape on their ends. The wands were so old that the tape was pink, and it disintegrated to the touch. We wondered how old they were and who had left them but we were nonetheless happy to get them. We would be able to leave our "bread crumb" trail to help us descend, which we'd do unroped. They'd be critical, too, if a whiteout blew in. Hopefully, we'd be able to stick to our line and get off. Twenty thousand feet was an altitude personal best for Maple, who was fatigued but, as always, positive and excited. We headed back to camp but during the descent realized that Camp 2 was a long distance and a Herculean effort away.

By the day of our summit push, we were running low on time, and we opted to forgo the second camp, reasoning it was more effort than just going for the summit with only ski gear. We also wanted to learn more of what we were capable of. On Broad Peak, Shishapangma, Mustagh Ata, and Cho Oyu, we had eliminated high camps in favor of long summit pushes, so we had a track record to support our reasoning. But on Norjin, our timeframe was stunted, and the six thousand foot total descent, including the dip above Camp 1, seemed a monumental proposition—we wanted to know if we could do it. Physically it was a big day, but mentally, with no other climbers and no established route, it was a huge undertaking.

We were guardedly excited and had a healthy level of nervousness. We didn't know if we could reach the summit, but we didn't care. Our ambitions shifted at this point. We knew we could climb and ski the highest peaks. We had been on enough expeditions doing things in the accepted fashion, and we'd gained an appreciation for pushing ourselves a bit harder each time. Norjin presented us with a time crunch, thereby forcing us to look at pushing ourselves a bit further than in the past. We were also exceptionally aware that we might be able pull off another seven-thousand-meter peak ski descent. So, we were fueled by ambition, but there was a hell of a lot of excitement, too. We were fit as we had ever been, and we had a superstrong, well-congealed team. We rested for three days and set off.

The climb up the glacier to Camp 1 went as planned. We felt great, and the clear skies allowed us to enjoy views that were as magnificent as we had ever seen. We managed to sleep well that night—too well in fact—and we dozed a half hour past our watch alarms, which were set for midnight. The panic that ensued when we woke up and realized that we were running late sent adrenaline through our bodies. But Steve quickly calmed us all down, noting, "No big deal; we have a bit more fuel in the tank, and we'll make up for it." We gained the snow, which was hard after the previous night's freeze. The climbing was perfect. Just as we gained the missing Camp 2, the sky lit up, and with it, for the first time in a week, clouds and wind buried the upper slopes. The weather was changing. The temperature was nauseatingly cold.

For the sake of moving fast and light, we took minimal shells and light parkas so we didn't—we couldn't—stop long. We continued up steepening slopes and began to weave our way back and forth, looking for snow bridges. The back and forth was frustratingly slow. We had to climb roped, the slopes were steep, and the direction changes were cumbersome. Without the slots, our line would have been simple, short, and straightforward. Because of them, our time was tripled. But we managed slowly to gain the summit pyramid at about twenty-two thousand feet. We had about fourteen hundred feet to go.

Spindrift blew violently off the summit, but we were on the opposite side of the mountain, somewhat protected from the storm. We continued to climb, but the snow kept accumulating and formed a thick but hollow slab, which we were soon climbing on. At just over seven thousand meters, Callahan suddenly piped up, "Boys, I am not comfortable on this slab."

My stomach lurched inside as I halted. I wasn't sensing the danger, but red flags went up inside my head: "What am I missing here?!" The slope was easily forty degrees—steep enough to break away—but the crust was fairly consistent. Steve looked at the snow and then at me with denial and disdain.

Later he would recall, "We were spitting distance from the summit and I wasn't concerned about the snow conditions. And I wanted it badly. I was pissed! But Callahan is a brother to me. We've been on many climbs. I had to listen."

During all the previous expeditions, we had an unwritten rule: defer to the most conservative ideals. In this case, Callahan was adamant. The risk that we were taking at that moment kept us in check. If, God forbid, someone had gotten hurt or killed, we would all have had to live with that for the rest of our lives. Turning around was a no-brainer. At over twenty-three thousand feet, after ten hours of climbing, it wasn't an easy decision. However, Gibjo spoke up and pointed out that the weather was coming in. Plus, it was already late in the day. The decision was discussed no further.

We carefully—slowly, methodically—stepped into our skis. A fall or losing a ski would have netted a near free fall down the entire north face of the peak, ending nearly at ABC. Once we were secured on the edges of our skis, getting going on the chalky crust was all that mattered.

Callahan and Gibjo achieved their second seven-thousand-meter ski descent, Maple his first, and Steve and I got our sixth. At the moment, however, we didn't have time to celebrate; we had to get off that slope. After we were off the slabby face, the knowledge that we had avoided a catastrophe came as a great relief. We still had to negotiate the numerous slots, but the failed summit, barely missed as it was, was forgotten. We were still a long way from camp. We carefully proceeded one at a time skiing between the crevasses, watching for possible hidden slots that we may have missed. At the wands, we straight-lined unroped over the snow bridges until everyone was safely on the downhill side.

We made sure that the last skier always carried the rope. I also always carry a fifty-foot piece of 7-millimeter cord in my pack in case of a fall so we always have a rope on both sides of the abyss. The snow was a bit rough below, but it still offered great skiing, and the slopes were steep and exciting. We found ourselves back at our would-be Camp 2 and stopped for a drink. The lower slopes were hard and icy and fell away to the north, exposing a fall and a death slide on the forty-five- to fifty-degree slopes. It required extremely delicate skiing back to the rocky ridge. Safely back at the ridge, we shouldered our skis and headed back across the ridge and up to camp.

We were beyond tired, totally running on fumes, now fifteen hours into the bid. We pulled camp and then hauled everything back down to ABC. Callahan mumbled how he wasn't looking forward to "hauling all that gear back down to base camp." The lower glacier presented extremely difficult skiing compared to our descent a week earlier as the snow had deteriorated to rough snow fins, and with our eighty-pound loads, skiing the last five hundred feet was impossible. We down climbed back to camp, and twenty hours after we set out from Camp 1, we were safely off the peak.

We barely missed the summit, but we knew if the conditions were better, we could have tagged it. Regardless, we had the satisfaction of one of the harder days in our careers. As Maple put it at the turnaround point high on the face, it was his "hardest day by a factor of ten." For Steve and me, attaining our sixth ski descent was a mark that we never thought would happen until that expedition, and while we still looked up to the greats of the sport, we knew that in the small circle of high-altitude skiers, we had etched a mark in the conversation. But more satisfying was the knowledge that we could go a bit harder, a bit farther, and a bit higher in large pushes. But perhaps most importantly, we had assembled an incredible team of players we could tap for more trips. We missed Jim severely on the trip, but later our success fueled his passion for more as well. We were high-altitude skiers by the only definition we had ever heard—ours.

The peak fees made the Himalaya extremely difficult, although we did manage another eight-thousand-meter peak expedition to Manaslu in 2010. Even there, the commercial guides had started to operate aggressively, and the crowds were extremely annoying. Manaslu also proved to provide a great lesson for us. The following is my trip report that was used eventually as the basis for an article that published in *Outside* magazine that offers a glimpse of the situation on the popular peaks at the time:

I woke up yesterday morning and did my usual scan of Facebook and was alerted to what I and others have long expected—a major disaster. This one had killed eleven people and left dozens of others severely injured after a massive avalanche on the slopes of Manaslu, the eighth highest peak in the world. The magnitude of the disaster is beyond comprehension, and thoughts and prayers and condolences go out to the families and friends whose lives this major event will touch. It is terrible and so very sad.

I found myself on this amazing peak a couple years ago, and as I mentioned, this major disaster was absolutely expected in my mind as well as in the minds of others who have ventured to Manaslu. I am not suggesting this was not an act of God, but after being on the peak for a month, and reflecting on it for a couple of years since, it was no doubt an act of God that was manufactured by man to be a major disaster. In a post on my Facebook page on July 25 of this year, after posting pictures, I responded to one viewer that in twenty-five years of climbing and skiing on some forty of the world's major six-thousand-, seven-thousand-, and eight thousand-meter peaks, this was the only peak that I could not recommend for anyone. It is avalanche central.

One also must understand Manaslu in general to properly understand the peak and how this disaster could have possibly taken place at the level it did. This is possibly the largest single disaster in mountaineering history, so it warrants discussion.

The history of Manaslu up to about five years ago was comprised mainly of serious, relatively small private expeditions. Being one of the world's fourteen eight-thousand-meter peaks, it was a sought-after goal for hard-core and elite climbers looking for off-the-beaten-path eight-thousand-meter peaks. The peak in and of itself is short, by Himalayan standards, sitting off one of the more popular trekking routes. It is in an incredibly beautiful part of the range and is a magnificent-looking tower above the valley floor. When you see it, you want to climb it.

However, as history would dictate, short is not congruent with easy, and the peak has a history of death almost by the year. Under ideal conditions, the peak can be easily climbed and has seen approximately three hundred summits over its history, making it the fifth most climbed eight-thousander; however, it has a death rate of just over 35 percent relative to summits. It is regarded as the easiest eight-thousander to climb, yet it is one of the most dangerous. Human nature being what it is has therefore placed it as an easy peak to climb, but unless you experience the peak, or research it closely, you have no idea what Manaslu will throw at you. When you look at the peak historically, this is clear: it is an avalanche chute.

Manaslu's history is peppered with avalanches and fatalities with few years untouched. When you review this list, virtually no section of the peak from base camp to high camp is safe from the objective hazard of avalanches. Manaslu in my experience is unique in that there really is no safe zone. Unlike other seven-thousand- and eight-thousand-meter peaks, virtually no safe place exists to retreat on the mountain.

We researched the peak, decided to make our attempt, deferring to the easy quick nature, and prayed for good weather, something rare for Manaslu. We arrived on the peak in early September at the end of the monsoon, and what struck me, even compared to all the other Himalayan peaks I had been on, were two major factors; it is an incredibly warm peak with temperatures even around the higher parts of the mountain rarely dipping below zero, and generally around freezing or warmer on the lower slopes, and second, the incredible accumulations of warm heavy snow. The amounts of snow were likened to that of Alaska in the Wrangell-St. Elias Mountains where snow is accumulated by the yard; however, temperatures are as cold as it gets, a major difference compared to Manaslu. At Manaslu, we experienced multiple days of snow and rain accumulating by the yard, which is very typical for the peak. At base camp, I described the sound as if we were pitched in the middle of Denver International Airport; it sounded like continuous jets taking off. At one point, I used my video camera to capture six four-thousand-foot massive gullies sliding at the same time with avalanches that were by all definitions Himalayan in size. It was absolutely mind boggling and beyond anything I had expected based on my previous expeditions, but per other guides, typical for Manaslu.

As we ascended the mountain, the next hurdle of Manaslu became apparent. From base camp to Camp 1 includes travel up a glacier that is as crevassed as anything I have ever experienced, often at the base of large avalanche-prone slopes. The commercial guides had attempted to alleviate this potential problem by placing fixed lines across the slots, but even those were typically not used as being on relatively flat glacier, and ironically a nuisance for just about everyone on route. Having lost a friend to these same slots a few years before, we broke out a rope and noticed the church-sized holes we were walking over. How anyone could pass this section of glacier not roped is simply beyond reason, but almost everyone, including many guides and Sherpa, passed this section free as you would to walk to the store for a quart of milk. A solo fall would have resulted in never finding a climber; there were simply too many crevasses that fell into seemingly bottomless black holes to find someone. This combined with massive avalanche debris flowing well into the line of ascent made for a nerve-wracking trek to Camp 1.

Camp 1 was safely perched on top of a small peak and was the only safe spot on the route. Beyond this camp, the route included a traverse of a massive ice fall that also had continuous debris falls, and in fact when we reached it, we found a fixed line completely covered by a truck sized block of ice that had fallen across it the night before. Heeding to the herd mentality, we climbed over it, in retrospect something that makes me question my own intelligence as a mountaineer. Mountaineers take risks, I get that, but this was a seriously active ice fall with crashes almost by the day. But it gets worse.

After an hour of negotiating the ice fall, we climbed steep serac faces to find ourselves at the base of a fifteen-hundred-to-two-thousand-foot headwall in the middle of the ice fall referred to as the hour glass. It is a steep forty-degree smooth patch of snow, perfectly angled to capture enormous amounts of heavy wet snow, primed for the first avalanche section of the route. Over time, it has slid to the demise of more than a few climbers, resulting in a catastrophic pile of debris at its base. As I climbed to the upper section of the slope, a down climbing Sherpa needed to rappel past me. I courteously stepped off the beaten path to find myself in armpit deep bottomless mush! The beaten path was ice and hard as rock, but inches to either side revealed something different. How it failed to slide is beyond me. Granted, we were climbing it on a fixed line, but a slope that large would have more than likely wiped out any attempts to fix it in the event of a slide.

We reached the top of this steep slope and were surrounded by massive crevasses that entailed climbing on flat ground back and forth to navigate, and the only section, albeit a short one, where the risk of avalanche was fairly minimal. We arrived at the first level of Camp 3 at just under seven thousand meters. Many guide companies choose this bench as a place to camp in lieu of a higher camp that sits at a col about an hour higher on the peak as it was a safer spot. My initial reaction to the spot was to wonder what the ice cliff above the camp some three thousand feet above looked like from there; we were in a complete whiteout, and while I knew the cliff was above us, deferred again to the herd mentality that this was a safe spot due to the other tents there, but my extra sense told me this was not a good spot. We grabbed a quick bite and drink and started onward toward the next camp. We were immediately greeted by a Japanese IMGA patched guide who was as gray as the sky. He told us how the entire face (same face as the avalanche that blew out both these camps for this recent disaster) had slid as he climbed down. The look on his face told us everything; he was done with Manaslu. We walked another one hundred yards to find the debris pile, which covered in the words of the guide, "three hundred meters in width and included the entire face." We retreated to the rest stop and hashed it out. My brother Steve, Jim Gile, and I had had enough of the herd mentality, and after ten minutes, finally made what was in our view the only logical decision. Trip over. Ironically, the clouds cleared a bit, and it was painfully obvious that there really were no "bomber" camp spots below the ice cliff separated from us by the three-thousand-foot thirty-five-degree slope above. This is the main dilemma of climbing Manaslu; from base camp to the summit, except for Camp 1, there are no safe places to camp on the route. None!

We left Manaslu with our tails between our legs; we had climbed and skied some of the greatest peaks in the world, and here, this "easy" peak Manaslu had proved to be well beyond our level of comfort. Guides and clients continued up, some even smirking and laughing, some shaking their heads. "Why would they haul their entire camp up and pull off altogether in the same push?"

I have mentioned the herd mentality in all of this, and this is also a relevant aspect that needs to be understood. No one is immune. When you enter any typical base camp, the camp members including the guides generally discuss everything from weather, to conditions, to logistics. If in this mass discussion, one group decides to move up the mountain, any success generally dictates a mass movement of all other teams. As it relates to commercial guide companies, this aspect is magnified. It is extremely difficult to stay put as other climbers ascend, and it pressures guides to often be aggressive, in my view, in that it makes clients want to go too; happy clients are good for business. It impacts even noncommercial climbers as I have painfully depicted in my own experience here, and it creates a herd mentality. It is rare for guide companies to make their own decisions. I have seen master guides (companies)—Russel Brice and Kari Kobler and a few others—make painful decisions to not go on Manaslu and other major peaks, and I've witnessed the impact on their clients when they do. It is not good for their businesses at the time. But these guides understand the reality. There is a great difference between mad clients and dead clients. But not all guides have this level of experience, and what we see are the mass ascents of these peaks when reality would dictate other. Add to this that the money aspect has reached the discussion; we are talking huge fees for these trips, and what we see are guide companies offering guided trips to peaks like Manaslu, and recently even Nanga Parbat, and K2, ironically all the statistically most dangerous peaks.

Bluntly, the herd mentality is dangerous, and I believe there are some peaks that simply exceed what should be commercially guided en masse. When you do the research and look at the peak and its history, you will find that Manaslu is not a great alternative to the normal guided peaks, and in fact as many well-seasoned climbers have noted to me, Manaslu and some of the other eight-thousand-meter peaks are simply not peaks that should be recommended or advertised as commercially guided trips. Take Cho Oyu and Shishapangma and even north Everest. The typical scenario is to set the routes with fixed lines and send the climbers out to reach the camp with experienced Sherpa. Climbers can come and go by and large as they want with little danger to even think about other than altitude, which is mitigated with supplemental oxygen, and lots of it. Routes are fixed a to z, and there is little or no chance of clients venturing into trouble. There is significantly less objective danger, and the model works incredibly well as statistics of summits and relative fatalities and problems would attest to. Cho and Shish have death rates to summits below 2 percent. Manaslu, on the other hand, is so riddled with objective dangers, this model simply doesn't work. Its death rate to summits is as I mentioned over 35 percent!

Climbers in commercial groups and even simple guided climbs rely on their guides to make practically every decision from the time they arrive until the time they depart even if they have the experience to climb the peak without a guide. The guide rules no matter. If he says go, you do; if he walks through the crevasse field not roped you do too (even if he set fixed lines) and on and on. This is crucial to understand because it takes the thought process out of a climber; they are not controlling their destiny even if to a limited degree. When you add the major objective dangers and conditions of a peak like Manaslu, if you are not there controlling every aspect of your climb, you have no choice but to fall into the herd mentality. Others are going up; therefore it must be okay. Again, this places enormous pressure on guides to let clients climb, and the problem compounds itself by mass movement. It is impossible to tell one client no when you just let another client go, and experience matters very little; they are all there for the same reason, paying the same fee to do so, and it becomes a situation where everyone goes or no one goes no matter the conditions. If a guide has even a slight lapse in judgment and lets anyone go, not only does he have very little control over his group, but generally every other group follows suit.

On Manaslu, I saw one experienced guide handle this extremely well, climbing as a team with Sherpa to assist those who could not go on to get back to the last camp, but this particular guide and one or two other guided groups were the anomaly on Manaslu. We saw other teams in various groups at various stages of the climb, some even climbing solo. If shit hits the fan, and it did with one climber falling into a crevasse, there is lag in the time it takes to organize and manage a team for a rescue when everyone is all over the mountain. Keep in mind, even on a commercially guided trip, a team has a responsibility to take care of itself. This is nearly impossible under the model of most commercial guide companies on some of these peaks. On the standard guided peaks, the problem is eliminated by the numbers when other team Sherpas and guides take on the burden of rescues very successfully. But along these lines, when you are in a commercial group that has decided even under ideal group dynamics to go up, and you are not comfortable saying no, it becomes extremely difficult to buck the system. It is far easier to defer to a certified guide combined with all others heading up than it is to make your own decisions starting with the fact that you are paying for a guide to make the decisions even before you get to the mountain. On Manaslu, we didn't have a guide, but we were part of a guided base camp, and the guide put a great deal of pressure on us, and when we backed off the peak even ridiculed us. Our decision made his team question him. It made us question our decision. Had he not been there, we would have accepted it for what it was—the right decision. We stuck to our guns and went home. The guide eventually followed suit but not before trying where conditions proved us right. No one was hurt, but his decision exposed his team to more of the exact same dangerous conditions that forced us all to pull the plug on an attempt in the end.

Today we have guide companies offering alternatives to the normal, safe, and totally guidable peaks like Cho Oyu, Shishapangma, and even north Everest, all very guidable peaks and significantly more difficult objectives to prove a climber's mettle, yet they are significantly much safer. When these peaks become too crowded, or as the case was this fall at Cho Oyu when the Chinese closed the peak for any climbing, guide companies attempted to preserve their season income with offers to ascend Manaslu as an alternative. Case in point as it relates to this recent Manaslu disaster. I have a buddy who was slated to attempt Cho Oyu, a peak that based on his experience and conditioning was a great choice for entry into the game. Cho Oyu has been successfully guided for twenty years or more, and while it is a long, high, difficult climb, the guide companies have it down. They know exactly how to do it and how to do it safely. The peak has incredibly safe camps where even if a storm blows in, climbers can retreat and wait things out safely. Or, if a climber reaches his peak before the summit, he can safely call it a trip with an enormous spectrum of altitude and success notwithstanding the summit. When it was closed off, the guide company talked him into Manaslu as a "great alternative" and an easy peak. With the guides twisting his arm, there was no talking him out of it. He was not alone. As the reports come in from Manaslu, it is apparent that many people who were slated for Cho changed plans to Manaslu.

The normal fifty to one hundred people at base camp ballooned to three hundred. Combined with the lack of safe camps as per the discussion, this is a recipe for exactly what we have. One could argue that it is by the grace of God that the number of fatalities in the Manaslu tragedy was not significantly greater than what it is. At the time, there were only about thirty people at that camp, but there was enough space for just about everyone at base camp. But another issue that occurs in these changes of venues is critical in my view.

While the guides become well acquainted with many of these peaks trip after trip, the same cannot be said for most of their clients. What the guides fail to realize is the mental change. It is not reasonable for most climbers, let alone commercial clients, to comprehend what they spent months even years planning for, to suddenly change gears for a different peak and find success. In the seven-thousand- and eight thousand-meter peak game or for any peak for that matter, any change—a change in team, a change in logistics—is monumental and as depicted in Johnathan Waterman's book *Surviving Denali* can have a potentially fatal impact. When you look at the statistics in his study of Denali as a mountain ranger for years on the peak, almost all fatal accidents involved changes of sorts that impacted the mental aspect to the expedition. His premise is that when an expedition experiences monumental shake-ups, trip over, and he recommends this in no uncertain terms. Statistics prove him right. He didn't even begin to touch the subject from the point of view of changing objectives. In my own experience on one trip, we arrived at the base of a seven-thousand-meter peak to find the Chinese military doing live-ammunition exercises at the base of the peak. They offered an alternative peak in lieu of the mix-up, but as a team we came to climb a specific peak. Similarly, with our logistics guide company twisting our arm to do an alternative peak in the area to preserve his income, we realized the impact. We had no research or mental preparation for a different peak, and we went home. It was, plain and simple, not a good idea. I know a handful of ski mountaineers that were faced with the same situation here, that went to Manaslu, and fact is, they had a few weeks at best to try and recapture a year of research, planning, and mental preparation for a major objective, an eight-thousand-meter peak no less. It is not reasonable to believe this is acceptable or even possible without, as Waterman's book suggests, serious risk. As it relates to Manaslu, the change in venue came so rapidly that there is little chance many of those climbers had properly researched what they were getting into. I had a year and didn't do my homework and completely missed the mark!

The only alternative is to refund or have expeditions return when the situation permits it. With few exceptions, modern guide companies and the combination of economics in an industry that is difficult at best are providing the base for disaster, which has been painfully proven during this season on Manaslu. What we have are extraordinarily large groups of climbers in places where any climber is exposed to high levels of objective danger—some not qualified to make decisions and some where their ability to make decisions is effectively mitigated—where they shouldn't be, or at least should not be encouraged to be. Climbers need to take control of the game, and guides need to better understand that the way they have been operating in recent years is nothing more than a short-term economic fix that is effectively destroying the industry on which they are relying. Routes are being destroyed, and people are getting killed. After a season that depicted three hundred people on a single fixed line on the south face of Everest and almost a dozen deaths, the recent tragedy on K2, and now this tragedy, it should be apparent that large commercial international groups are being sold on expeditions by guide companies that are pushing the limits of the game they play to levels that are neither realistic nor safe let alone enjoyable.

As the saying goes, mountains don't care who you are, what experience you have, or anything at all. If that doesn't demand a bit of reverence and respect, then we shouldn't attempt to climb them. The slope that killed all those people on Manaslu slides virtually every snowstorm and has gone that big many times in the past for hundreds if not thousands of years. Seracs fall, and if the slopes they fall on are loaded with enormous amounts of warm heavy snow, they will avalanche. It's a fact. Rolling the dice is part of what climbers do, but without respect for what we are rolling the dice over, we are doomed. Manaslu is simply a mountain that warrants a bit more respect than I and all that have attempted it recently have given it. Look at Manaslu's history and statistics and consider that eleven people were just killed and dozens seriously injured by a naturally released avalanche that took their lives while sleeping in a camp that offered no alternative safe spots to camp.

For Steve, Jim, and myself, Manaslu was one of the only peaks in our career that, even today, I just couldn't recommend to anyone. But Manaslu also played an important role in our development. We let our anxiety and excitement get in the way of our normal planning. We failed to properly research the peak, and like many climbers, we jumped in the deep end with little thought for where we were going or what we were doing. The fear and discomfort resulting from not taking more time and care to plan it right was a wakeup call to not get ahead of ourselves and to be more patient with regard to picking the right peaks. But the experience also provided us with confirmation that our gut feelings about the popular peaks were spot on. We needed to continue our progression; we still had the power of passion leading us toward something new, but we knew we needed to do it on our own terms. We also wanted to do it all without the crowds that were heading to the peaks and all the related issues they brought with them. Our mission was simple. We needed to move beyond skiing Everest, and the criteria were simple: places and peaks we had never been to that offered us a chance to achieve first or near-first ski descents and had few if any people.

Life had evolved. We were no longer free from most responsibilities, and we had to make family life and our professions the main priority. In my own situation, I didn't have any personal funds to allocate toward trips. The financial environment for sponsorships was still dry at best, yet we had to rely on it for the adventures. Not helping matters was our newfound desire to head to very obscure peaks. With that, a lack of sponsorship interest followed. The only good news was that while the cost to climb the popular peaks continued to skyrocket, we found that the places we were seeking were extremely inexpensive. The issue of how to fund even the cheaper price, however, was still something that had to be figured out.

By this time, my only option was to continue to use my filmmaking as a means to an end. *Skiing Everest* and *Can Do* continued to successfully sell via Cinetics Media, relatively speaking; it was not a massive financial windfall, but in the difficult world of independent filmmaking I found distribution. I knew that I had to capitalize on that success as much as I could; we simply were not ready to throw in the towel on our ambitions to climb and ski high peaks. Although I never referred to myself as a filmmaker per se, I leveraged the label, and I wanted to produce another film. I envisioned it to be a *Beyond Skiing Everest* sequel of sorts.

I pitched the concept to sponsors, and I brought it up at cocktail parties with wealthy individuals that liked the mountain life culture, and I found success. While the days of the major corporate sponsorships were long gone, I was able to pick up small cash sponsorships from our gear manufacturers, and the occasional larger hit from individuals who enjoyed seeing their names in the credits of our films. I was also amazed that there were individuals who really appreciated our careers and what we had accomplished.

The fact that we weren't household names in the climbing world ended up working to our advantage. People realized that we weren't glory hounds in a niche sport. Bit by bit, the films and various articles portrayed us as what we were—guys who just loved to climb and ski and got out often, more than most. Magazines referred to us with catch phrases like "the most accomplished ski mountaineers … that you've never heard of" and asked, "How is it that they have flown under the radar?"—both actual quotes in magazines.

In mountaineering, there are most definitely those that are so far beyond the rest of the pack that they are bestowed the title "professional" and are indisputably respected. However, in the digital age, in which people take advantage of social media to hype everything they do, nauseating self-promotion becomes the norm, and the title "professional" often gets applied to anyone with a computer and some climbing or skiing photos. Our experiences at the dawn of the social media age scared us out of the self-promotion game, and by the time we realized how valuable social media was, we had long missed the boat.

As our list of climbs and skis was hyped by writers over the years, what developed was a narrative of sorts on three guys who loved to climb and ski and didn't care too much about hype; it was painfully obvious as the stats became public. Films I made about our exploits fanned the fire, but over time, the facts remained the facts—we'd achieved a hell of a lot. Point being, everything was coming together—the story, the filmmaking, and respect for a solid track record that had been misjudged from the start.

The table was set, and somehow, we always managed to obtain the funding we needed to continue with our adventures. During the earlier days where our egos were crushed by it all, my father often told me, "Forget about what people say and think. Just have fun, go hard, and be kind to people, even your enemies. Trust me—cream always raises to the top." We have never considered ourselves to be the cream, nor have we ever believed we were at the top, but it is ironic how wise that man truly was, and looking back today, I do see what he was talking about. It's not about rising to the top as much as how you approach what you do. The process is ultimately what matters.

The trips continued, and we enjoyed the newfound pleasure of climbing and skiing peaks off the beaten path. To suggest that Everest was not still a goal would be a lie. It was just not practical, and the commercial guiding environment made it cumbersome and unappealing. Our new direction, which avoided all the fuss, was incredible, and as we ticked the trips off, our experience increased even further. The natural progression we were experiencing created a desire to do something that would take us to an even greater level than climbing and skiing Everest in a pure style. But what?

One winter day in 2010, I found myself out climbing Mount Baldy with Steve. It was a rare moment in our lives; we had no plans for an expedition. It was extremely cold, and a storm was blowing wildly. We reached the summit at just over thirteen thousand feet, and I voiced a question that came to me while skinning up: "How much colder do you think the Himalaya is right now?" Steve shrugged it off with an "I don't know," and "I am cold enough here now." But later, when we were driving home, the discussion came up again. Steve mentioned, "Well, it's probably ten times colder than it was up there today, but one thing guaranteed is there aren't many climbers out there climbing, that's for certain." Then and there, the seed was planted. We didn't outright decide that was the "next big thing" for our planning, but it was enough discussion to pique my interest to look into it. I got home and googled "winter expeditions Himalaya."

I quickly learned that in the three decades since the well-known Polish expeditions of the early 1980s, there had been only about fifty total winter expeditions. Successes were sparse, with the information I found indicating that the only successful expeditions to summit were also the only expeditions to attain eight thousand meters, and the vast majority of other expeditions, roughly 80 percent, failed to climb above seven thousand meters. The prospects of climbing in the winter Himalaya were dismal. This, however, was not a source of dissuasion. The lack of crowds, and reliable windows of hard clear days—despite the extreme cold— were a source of great enthusiasm. Added to this, I could find no discussion whatsoever of skiing in the Himalaya in the winter. It appeared to me that while the extreme cold and wind were the main obstacles, winter climbing and skiing in the Himalaya might offer the ultimate pioneering objective that even exceeded a regular-season ascent of Everest. I planted the seed with Steve and Jim, and to my surprise, with very little hesitation, they both agreed it was something to consider.

In my mind, the Himalaya in winter was a bit of a stretch. I threw it out almost in jest and was certainly not expecting much reaction from Steve and Jim. I had heard of people climbing in the winter, and the names of the few who had tried left an impression and piqued my interest when the subject came up. But it was one of those topics that was so outlandish that I hadn't really taken the time to investigate the subject aside from the rare blips I came across. In fact, I had been approached by one friend several years before to go to Pakistan for a winter attempt at Broad Peak, with the notion that "No one has climbed Broad in winter; it will be a major first." I didn't give it a second thought then and brushed it off as a bit far-fetched. Now, however, my interest—stimulated by experience and a new desire to go to places where no one else wanted to go—was building. With Steve and Jim's interest, I started to look into the matter. I took a break at work to further my research. Again, I typed "Himalaya Winter Ascents" into Google, and started surfing the internet.

Initially, "outlandish" was an understatement. Certainly, major winter ascents in the Himalaya were underway by the early 1980s, but it was the characters involved that caught my attention. The men tackling these objectives were not just your average Polish mountaineers. They were the best their country had ever produced. Only three decades before, it was thought that climbing in the Himalaya in winter was impossible. That myth was expunged when Leszek Cichy and Krzysztof Wielicki climbed Everest in February 1980. That opened the floodgates, and over the next several years, the Poles made six more first winter ascents on eight-thousand-meter peaks. Throughout the next few decades, the Poles continued the charge. A few others entered the winter climbing arena, but not many. Since the first winter ascent, I could find only seventy-five or so climbers going on winter expeditions in more than thirty years.

But more remarkable was the fact that the success on those initial forays was extremely limited. Summits were almost nonexistent. A rough estimate showed that nearly 100 percent of all expeditions failed to reach summits, and roughly 80 percent failed to climb above seven thousand meters. During my research I learned that a more modern leader of winter ascents was a chap I met on Pik Lenin earlier—Simone Moro. Simone is an Italian who's as hard as they come. At that time, he was attempting to obtain the coveted Snow Leopard award, whereby all five seven-thousand-meter peaks in the former Soviet Union are attained, including the peak we were after, Lenin. He attained that in that single season, something that had never been done. Not to my surprise, my winter study concluded that after the half dozen ascents in the '80s by Poles, no eight-thousand-meter summits were attained until 2005 when Simone reached the summit of Shishapangma.

Winter climbing became Simone's game, and he became the winter guru, knocking off four winter eight-thousand-meter peak first ascents. The trajectory of his career left me with my jaw hanging. My firsthand experience meeting Simone combined with his unprecedented climbing résumé was topped off with a short film on one of his eight-thousand-meter peak first winter ascents. It included a visual of him and his partners on top of

Gasherbrum in Pakistan when they had attained that peak's first winter ascent. Before Simone and his partners succeeded there were sixteen attempts spread out over twenty-six years—he was and is the real deal. The photos depicted men with ice mustaches and beards, drawn eyes and worn faces—obviously at the limit of what is possible in minus-sixty-degree temperatures. Initially, my reaction went from awe to horror. I could not imagine. Then I started to reflect on the only experience I had to compare. On one of our Alaskan adventures, we found ourselves approaching Mount Logan on the Yukon border in March. It was not winter, but it was close enough. Being in a region that is contained by the largest mass of glaciers in the world including the North Pole, it's always cold. We climbed and skied for a month on that trip, never stripping much below our down clothing and doing battle with the most severe wind and snowstorms of our lives. We did not attain the altitudes we later sought in the Himalaya, but we were moderately high—up to nineteen thousand feet. Experience and common sense dictate that there is a significant difference between nineteen thousand feet in Alaska and the seven-thousand- and eight-thousand-meter altitudes of Asia. Combining extreme cold with the highest altitudes in the world made us wonder how we might do.

For me, the breaking point in terms of altitude generally happens at about seventeen thousand feet. I can be in any range, and without an altimeter, I can tell you when I arrive there. But as it relates to winter climbing, the subject warrants a bit of discussion.

Not many mountaineers let alone people understand much more than the general concept that the higher you go, the thinner the air becomes. Most people think that the ratio of air quantity to height can be represented by a sloping line. In general, that is true. However, there are many factors that dictate the quantity, and while the ratio of air to altitude follows an upward slope, it is not a straight line.

The atmosphere (from the Greek *atmos*, meaning vapor, and *sphaira*, meaning sphere) contains the air we breathe. It is several miles thick and envelopes the earth on all sides. Despite our terrestrial perceptions, the seemingly weightless air has substance that equates to weight. At sea level, the weight of the entire atmosphere of air above your head weighs the equivalent of about thirty-two feet of water. It doesn't crush you because it is easily displaced around you, but it's still a lot of weight.

As you go up, that air pressure is eliminated merely because there is less of it; there is less air, so there is less air compression. As the air gets thinner, there is also less gas per unit of volume, which means, ultimately, less oxygen. Point being, as you ascend a peak, there is less pressure from the weight of less air, and that decreases the amount of oxygen that you can obtain in a single breath—less pressure, less air, less oxygen. It all adds up to a drastic change on the human body, which has evolved since time immemorial to allow humans to master the available oxygen in the "window of life"—between sea level and five thousand feet. When you climb, your body is thus forced to deal with the changes in a process that we refer to as acclimation. But along the bumpy path to altitude, the upward sloping line depicting the ratio of altitude to oxygen is also bumpy. We do not live in a vacuum, and other factors have drastic impacts on the air pressure and the levels of oxygen necessary for life.

The location of the peak you are ascending has an impact on air pressure. Not many people realize it, but the world is not a perfect sphere. It's slightly squashed on the top and bottom—at the poles. Therefore, there is no uniform sea level. The lowest portion of the atmosphere is farther from the center of the earth at the equator than at the poles. So, the farther north or south you go from the equator, the lower the air pressure will be at a given altitude.

Many climbers believe that the variation by location is due to the gravitational shifts, but this accounts for a very minor difference in the air pressure. For example, many climbers suggest that Denali climbs two thousand to three thousand feet higher than other peaks due to the gravitational pull and shape of the earth "squeezing" the atmosphere and making it thinner. Denali does climb higher than peaks farther from the North Pole, but it is almost exclusively due to temperatures, which drop drastically as one gets closer to either of the poles. Hence the greatest glaciers and icefields are located nearer to the poles.

Cold air is denser than warm air, so at low temperatures the entire atmosphere is compressed downward. Specified air pressure will lie at a lower altitude in cold compared to warm. The cold air does, in fact, present more effective altitude for Denali's 20,320 feet, and it feels like it climbs much higher—scientific calculations suggest about fifteen hundred feet.

Everest offers a different kind of example because it lies relatively close to the equator. During the climbing seasons, which are significantly warmer than the winter months, its altitude ranges from barely eight thousand meters in, say, May, to three thousand feet higher in January. By comparison, K2 in July, its climbing season, falls off the eight-thousand-meter list in summer, and then in January, it attains the same physical altitude as Everest (8,800 meters), creating a difference in effective altitude of over three thousand feet! The impact on K2 is more drastic compared to Everest because it is located farther north and is thus colder.

The obvious conclusion is that because the Himalaya is located closer to the equator, the effective altitude due to pressure is more drastic due to temperature. While peaks like Denali effectively climb higher than their physical altitudes and while the Himalaya's effective altitude is lower, the reality is that for Himalayan climbers seeking seven-thousand- to eight thousand-meter peaks, regardless, the altitude is just high.

So, for winter Himalayan mountaineers, climbing in this odd season, the winter, is not even remotely the same game as climbing in the premonsoon and postmonsoon, or regular, seasons. Pop mountain culture would suggest that the "Death Zone," the altitude where without retreat the human body will eventually die, starts at eight thousand meters. Scientifically speaking the Death Zone starts lower, at about seven thousand meters or twenty-three thousand feet, and with plenty of normal-season experience to that point, we knew well Himalayan climbing was extraordinarily difficult due to altitude. Climbing there in the winter was literally like adding a three-thousand-foot mountain on top of those mountains simply because of the cold.

The extreme nature of climbing in the Himalaya in winter scared us, but the notion of going to major peaks and not seeing another soul was exceedingly attractive. By this time, the dream of Everest had not disappeared completely, but the reality was that it was far-fetched. While we had found great satisfaction with various trips after 2007, they also provided us with a great deal of experience. It's not to say that we had become as comfortable as we were on our local peaks, but naturally, more trips gave us more knowledge, of not only the higher peaks, but more importantly what we were capable of personally, and it was substantial.

So, although we were really enjoying ourselves, we had an almost unconscious desire to seek something on par with how we approached Everest on those two previous expeditions. Again, Everest not being practical forced us to look at our mountaineering with a different perspective. Any seasoned mountaineer will tell you that while Everest is the tallest peak, it's not the ultimate test. I could put up an argument against that, which only made our effort to find the next big project more difficult, but we continued to think it out.

Winter Himalayan climbing was beginning to fill a void. We really didn't have a clue as to how difficult it was, but on the small list of characters that had been there, it was almost exclusively made up of the greats. At least, winter climbing was not something just anyone took on to get away from the crowds. Cautiously we looked in this direction. The idea was tantalizing. We wanted to see what it was like.

From the get-go, we didn't look at winter climbing with summit fever. Not even remotely. The overall implications from the bit of information available on winter climbing eliminated any serious thoughts of glorious summit photos. The few images we'd seen—like the photos of Simone Moro and partner on top of Gasherbrum—showed men who were cold, miserable, and physically and emotionally worn. But behind the obvious suffering, the photos showed faces that were full of satisfaction. There is something about the victory of toil seen in a photograph of men that have pushed themselves to the limit of human endurance and perseverance. We wanted a small taste of that. The more we read, the more fuel we put on our fire to find that next big thing. With little to go on, we made the decision to put a trip together.

The bad news is that climbing in the winter is obviously a very risky and dangerous endeavor. The good news is that a properly outfitted expedition can take on the risk, which by nature is not objective—things like falling debris or avalanches. While there is nothing to be done about the main hurdle, the cold, by properly approaching the mountain with safe havens, the cold can be approached as a subjective danger—one can get in out of the cold. This notion has obvious limits that are compounded by the reality of being at high altitude and exposed to severe negative temperatures. The basic premise is that the human body at altitude is severely limited—it's just trying to stay alive. Extreme cold enhances the ramifications of every aspect of altitude. As I have mentioned, the cold places a climber in an effective altitude that is significantly higher. Bluntly, bodies in motion have no choice but to stay in motion; in the winter at altitude, you stop, you die.

We would find out soon enough what all climbers reported: that even clad in the most modern clothing and technology, especially at altitude, one cannot stay warm enough for survival once stopped much longer than twenty minutes when the temperature dips below minus thirty. To address this, only one solution exists: get out of the cold. This is obvious. What is not so obvious, however, is the simple task of setting up a camp.

Depending on the campsite, setting up a camp rarely takes less than twenty minutes. All the tasks—hacking out a tent platform, setting up tents, building snow walls for protection, storing snow and ice for melting into water, and on and on, is often a job that can take two or three hours. From firsthand experience that I'll describe later, this is always hard work. But in minus forty temps, the process of deploying camp requires forethought, and it is one of the most miserable and dangerous tasks imaginable. We did all we could, even reaching out to Simone for advice, but the reality was clear. We were basically starting out in a completely different sport.

The first objective was figuring out the first objective; this was not just another mountain for us. All things considered, we at least realized we needed a very safe and familiar peak. Earlier in our careers, we had enjoyed a ski tour of Mustagh Atta, which was not what some would describe as a climber's peak; its regular route is a broad and very long ramp that crests at just under twenty-five thousand feet. There was no risk of falling off it or even any avalanche danger, and with the evolution of AT ski gear, most parties that headed to Mustagh did so with skis. The ramp was heavily glaciated and crevassed. On ski gear, however, a party can rope up and climb to its summit with only a minor section of the route passing through a moderate icefall.

But Mustagh Atta is high, and its location subjects it to extreme wind and weather. It is located on the Tibetan Plateau at the hub of the five great ranges of Asia: the Kunlun, the Tien Shan, the Pamir, the Karakorum, and the Himalaya proper. Mustagh Atta is a solitary mountain. It rises attached to no other peaks, and the relief from start to summit is more than twelve thousand feet; it is massive!

What it lacks in terms of actual climbing challenges is more than made up for in weather challenges. Several parties have been caught in windstorms and literally blown off the peak, never to be found. It is a ski tour, to be sure, but its height (seventy-five hundred meters) and the length of the route make it a great test of perseverance and endurance. Our climb and ski of the peak during the normal climbing season (June) in 2004, proved extremely taxing. But Mustagh Atta also provided us with what Steve later described as "the ultimate ski tour." Mustagh Atta is to ski touring what the Slickrock trail near Moab is to mountain biking." Serious without a doubt, but about as much fun to attempt as any peak we had ever been to. The skiing was not extreme, but it offered seemingly endless wintry snow.

Our experience on Mustagh Atta came rushing back to us during a discussion of a winter ski attempt. We were concerned about weather, obviously, but we had little to go on. Considering that Simone had successfully climbed Gasherbrum II, a peak that we looked at from Mustagh Atta, the previous winter season (2011), we reasoned by proximity that our goal was at least possible. "How could Mustagh Atta be more difficult than Gasherbrum?" we asked ourselves.

Also, we had no way of knowing if there would be ten feet of snow or no snow at all. At least the Karakorum Highway skirted the base of Mustagh Atta, and we knew it was a major year-round transport line. Access was thus not an issue. But the main consideration was that the peak was a ski tour. We needed to establish safe havens—camps. Then, if we got out on the route and the cold became too much, we merely had to take our skins off our skis, lock our bindings, and glide back to safety; exposure was limited as skis were tools for efficient travel going up and, especially, going down.

This concept had clearly been a factor in our Alaskan adventures, where we experienced firsthand the benefit of retreating on skis to a camp during periods of miserably cold and stormy weather. We reasoned the gentle slopes of Mustagh Atta in the winter would be like our experiences in Alaska. We were not delusional, though. The altitude would still present a major challenge, but the setup of these safe havens was our "out," and we would figure that part of the equation out in due course.

We had little to go on, but the excitement of the unknown and our desire to find out more propelled us onward with guarded optimism. We immediately reached out to Kari Kobler to get his logistics contacts for the region. He was excited about our prospects, but in a fatherly way he took on the role of devil's advocate and pointed out the obvious. But Kari was a climber, and Kari was an adventure seeker. In a sense his enthusiasm was a kind of blessing, and he helped us to find the contact. He also helped us through the process of making sure we had the proper setup to accommodate the expedition. It was obvious we would need a substantial base camp, including standard propane heaters, proper stoves, and clothing. Steve was in charge of group gear and logistics, and he worked diligently to ensure we had everything in order.

A substantial base camp was key, and that involved finding an equipment sponsor that could provide a dome tent big enough so that we could eat and sleep in it. In the regular season, a standard military tent is the norm, and expedition members set up separate sleeping tents, leaving the group tent for eating and hanging out. But we reasoned that with the cold, we would need room to also sleep with the propane heaters. Steve reached out to Ed Viesturs, who had become a marquee athlete at Eddie Bauer First Ascent, and arranged a beautiful and sturdy dome tent, a $10,000 mobile home. The company representative was proud to provide a simple piece of equipment that could arguably be the difference between life and death.

We also felt that having a medical doctor along would be a very important aspect to the expedition, and we reached out to Gibjo. He was tied up in the winter at an on-hill clinic at the

Snowmass ski area, and besides not having much interest in "freezing my ass off for a month," could not find the time. We had formed a friendship with my family vet, whose brother was a climber and MD. He had experience on expeditions to Alaska, and I reached out to him. Doug Dolginow was a world-renowned cancer researcher who had nearly won the Nobel Prize for his ground-changing research on prostate cancer detection. He had found enormous professional and financial success with his field of work—but along with it a heavy schedule loaded with stress.

When I called him, he was ready for a personal break. With little hesitation, he said, "Count me in." His background as a general practitioner and experience with mountain medicine was an added benefit to the expedition, and it left us with a great sense of confidence that we—with little medical experience and extremely dated mountain medicine cards—were in good hands. Doug had a home in the Aspen area, and we knew upon the first clink of the beer glass that he would fit in well with our group. Although his mountaineering was slightly in his past, and his career had severely dampened his fitness, he vowed to train before the trip, and just wanted to get on the peak and "not be in the way." He had a great ability to laugh and pitch us shit; he fit in nicely.

The larger issue in accomplishing our mission was the foot gear. Alpine touring (AT) ski boots had proved on Everest to be marginal at best for high altitude and cold. The problems came at over twenty-eight thousand feet, when we experienced that elevation's unusually cold temperatures.

Mustagh Atta might prove a double-edged sword in that regard; we knew it would be colder in the winter, but we also knew we'd be four thousand feet lower. With a bit of preexpedition engineering, we deemed the challenge doable. We were able to secure a sponsorship with a company called 40 Below, which gave us confidence; they made neoprene overboots, which were, we felt, mandatory gear, but we needed more. We had experimented with chemical packs on previous expeditions, including Everest, with only marginal success. There simply wasn't enough oxygen at high altitudes to mix with the chemicals to create any lasting heat. We needed to find something else. We had heard reports that the latest packs had been engineered to work better but not by much. In the interim, we had to come up with another plan.

My father had sold a product called Hotronics, which was a battery-operated system for alpine skiing. The battery pack was wired to the boot's insole. It required an installation whereby the ski boot was drilled and cut to accommodate the system. The wire ran up the back of the boot between the hard-plastic shell and liner to the battery, which was mounted to the outside of the shell. It was a very static system. The upside was that the system in the static environment of an alpine ski boot had a proven track record. The downside—based on our own testing of the product in AT boots—was that the back-and-forth movement from walking proved too much for the wiring; the thin wires soon broke under the stress. The system was also heavy and bulky and limited to the pair of boots it was installed in.

Also, the battery it used was a standard battery, not lithium. In severe cold, standard batteries lose energy quickly. Lithium batteries are much more stable. The manufacturer was keen on us using the system and connected us with a boot fitter in Boulder, Colorado. He claimed he had worked with other mountaineers and had it all "dialed." He knew how to protect the wires, using extensions that ran from the boot up a climber's leg. The batteries could then be stored in a jacket pocket, out of the cold, for normal use. It all sounded great, and before we knew it, we found ourselves in Boulder, Colorado, at Neptune Mountaineering's workshop making orthotics and customizing the system to our specific boots. We were excited!

Back home, with our new overboots, the system—clunky as it was—worked fine. We weren't able to test it at great altitudes, nor did the Colorado winter ever get remotely as cold as we anticipated we'd be in Asia, but at minus-fifteen degrees at thirteen thousand feet, the warmth was appreciable.

The next issue was the tent and sleeping bag system we would need. We had obtained a sponsorship a few years before from Nemo Equipment, and their single-wall tents on previous expeditions proved their tents to be among the best we had ever used—another check mark on our list. By this time, Nemo had started to produce sleeping bags. They sent us prototypes of a superlight minus-forty-degree bag the likes of which we had never seen. Upon opening the box, the bag was so light and thin that we immediately doubted its authenticity. I tested the bag at home, on concrete with no pad, during a night when a short cold spell dropped the temperature to minus-twenty degrees. The results were astonishing. This bag was (and is to this day) one of the most amazing technological advances in expedition sleep systems ever. This alone added to our overall confidence like nothing else; camp was the retreat, and the sleeping bag was obviously the most critical element of any camp. We were excited!

We also negotiated a sponsorship with First Ascent for down suits via Ed Viesturs. Ed included a note that said, "These suits are overkill for a normal expedition," which bolstered our confidence, and along with a few other cold modifications, we were ready to go. Steve had nailed down the logistics, I had raised the money from sponsors, and all was good. We spent the fall season training for the expedition, and by the end of December were wrapping up last-minute work details—no small task, but we were soon ready to go.

Steve and I had massive workloads before we left, and while the holidays were spent working, the fact that most clients were not at work created a perfect scenario—I accomplished what normally would take two months in three weeks. It was difficult with the stress of it all to remain well rested, but we delegated to staff as much as we could, and we tapped into something we knew well by this stage: treat your employees well, and they will always return the favor. Our staffers also knew that climbing and skiing was our passion, and they rose to the occasion to get us out of their hair for a few weeks. They understood from past expeditions that when we returned, we were always more relaxed and able to accommodate their passions as well.

One member of my staff is a passionate transoceanic sailor. I came to realize she needed similar blocks of time. Another staffer was a passionate bike racer; I didn't push him when he needed time for races or training. Others just liked to travel. My own goals created a work environment that not only encouraged the staff to chase big goals outside work but supported it. Along with my personal goal to climb and ski, I developed a desire to create an accommodating and fun place to work. It's paid off over the years. I'm not bragging that I am a great businessman or boss or anything. Rather, I'm trying to emphasize that positive environments support positive lives with positive outcomes.

We never played the "professional" card to accommodate our expeditions. This wasn't planned. Rather, it was just how things unfolded. There were "professional" mountaineers who could generate the funds required for expeditions, as were we. But the notion of earning a living at it was difficult at best, and as it were, those that did often found their income streams—from speaking and writing books—to be very meager indeed. They spent most of their lives in the mountains and were by and large the foundation of the term "dirtbag climbers." By contrast and necessity, Steve, Jim, and I had found careers to supplement making ends meet, and at the same time we really established passion for the international expeditions, and when we were not out climbing and skiing, we were working. It's what our parents did, and it was all we knew. However, there were times when we did explore other options. Before I headed into the exciting world of accounting, I vividly remember a discussion with Dad in which I pushed the notion of working in the ski industry as he had. Ski rep, patrol, working for a ski company—I wanted to do that. His answer resonated to me to this day: "Mikey, when you make your passion your job, it becomes work."

That was enough to push me to become an accountant. At the time, I didn't have two nickels to rub together, no trust fund to look forward to, and I had to do something. I wasn't at all thrilled with my position at the big firm, but what I did enjoy was the freedom a paycheck gave me to do whatever I wanted. That pointed toward climbing and skiing, and as I proceeded into my career, another progression developed. As I gained experience and know-how, my checks got bigger, and my freedom increased. After a few years, as mentioned, the freedom allowed me to live in Aspen, and, further, to create my own life by creating my own practice.

It was a means to an end, and it worked. I began to appreciate my job and, with experience, enjoy it. I can't tell you how many climbers and skiers cringe at the thought of a desk job, and even more so at the thought of crunching numbers all day. But here I am today, after twenty-five years, looking to take my other career, climbing and skiing, to the winter Himalaya. Somehow, Dad's words of wisdom prevailed.

But the impact is not just on me. One of the most satisfying aspects of my life is to know that what I have created is doing the same for my employees. I don't expect my office to be listed in *Outside* magazine's list of the greatest outdoor employers. But if longevity is any indication, then I think I've done pretty well. I can't even remember how long my individual staff members have been showing up, making it all happen. Again, this was not some magnificent plan, and I am not suggesting I am some brilliant accountant or businessperson at all. Instead, I got lucky with how it all unfolded. Work drove my passion, and my passion drove me to work. Somehow, it all helped me to balance my life out.

By mid-January, we all were ready to go. Few things feel better than stepping into an airplane headed for a remote land. The grind of planning and preparing is done. There is no sense in worrying about what you may have forgotten because you can't do much about it. You use lists to eliminate problems, and by and large at that stage, we had it all down and were able to totally relax.

The flight to China takes the better part of a day and a half with all the connections, and we rested the entire way until we reached the final stop before our destination—Kashgar. As we landed on the deserted landing strip and taxied to the terminal in Urumqi, China, the monitor in the seat back in front of us listed the particulars of the flight, including the temperature. Men bundled up in warm clothes and running around while working the flight from the outside suggested how cold it was, but the monitor told us the truth. It was minus forty Celsius! Our initial reaction was to translate that into Fahrenheit, to which Jim quickly noted that the two scales—Fahrenheit and Celsius—meet at minus forty.

This scared the hell out of us. If it was that cold at twenty-five hundred feet in Urumqi, we didn't have much enthusiasm for what we were taking on. We looked at the map in the in-flight magazine, relieved slightly that Urumqi was slightly farther north than Kashgar. The reality of it all was sinking in. This was cold country! Later, after the plane took off and headed to Kashgar, we were slightly relieved to see the "air temp at destination" a balmy minus-twenty-five degrees Celsius.

Upon arrival at Kashgar, we found all our gear had made the destination, and we loaded into a bus and headed into the murky, polluted city. It was bitterly cold, and the pollution limited our vision to a couple hundred feet. Kashgar is the last ancient city on the Silk Highway, the terminus of the Karakorum Highway, and it is the capital city of Xinjiang province, an autonomous region in China. Its population is by and large Uyghur Muslim, and has been part of the Turk, Tibetan, and Kyrgyz culture for thousands of years. As with Tibet, the Chinese government lets the region govern itself as the drastically unique cultures that converge in the province have been self-sustaining for centuries.

The pollution is worth noting because in either the heat of summer or the cold of winter it is terrible. There is no denying that the very limited regulation on air quality plays a role. But the real problem is the city's proximity to the Taklamakan Desert, from which dust and sand blow constantly. But despite the smoggy atmosphere, Kashgar is an incredible city with a unique culture and friendly atmosphere. To an outsider, the history of strife and infighting among regional tribes that has taken place in not less than a dozen "wars" on the streets is not evident. Rather, one can walk the streets, where he will find an old city center as well as a modern metropolis.

Contrary to the belief that pasta is Italian, it originated in the region, and a standout of the Kashgar experience is the plethora of restaurants that serve only fresh pasta with a variety of meat stews and sauces. But bring a flask. Kashgar is Muslim, and while the locals drink, it's tough to find alcohol in restaurants. It's a cultural experience that was extraordinarily unique in all our travels. Regardless of culture, however, cold is cold, and no matter how incredible the culture may be, the cold trumps much of the enjoyment. The irony was that while we feared the minus forty cold in Urmqui, Kashgar's more reasonable minus-twenty-five gave us mental relief of sorts. Our first line of business was to get to the local market to stock up on our mountain food. Bundled in summit parkas and cold weather boots, we accomplished the task and were set.

A dark, murky dawn greeted us as we hauled all our gear bags to a waiting bus that would take us to base camp. Inside the bus was not much warmer than it was outside, and we broke out our down suits for the ride. The small heater in the back of the bus was blowing, barely, a small stream of warm air that was immediately swallowed by the cold surrounding it—it was totally useless. Our logistics crew included a young liaison who was pleasant enough but young enough to never really warm up to "wealthy Americans" poaching his stomping grounds, and unless the discussion revolved around money, he barely spoke English.

He was accompanied by a driver who never said a word and a Chinese authority liaison officer whose responsibility was to guide us through the half dozen military checkpoints along the route. It was just after five in the morning, dark and smoggy, extremely cold, and the atmosphere surrounding him, clad in a lightweight jacket, slacks, and loafers, extinguished any chance of pleasantries. To the contrary, his presence reinforced the notion that he had zero desire to be where he was, and his badge was going to be used to make sure we had just as miserable a ride as he would. We soft-shoed around him but realized he didn't know a lick of English beyond "passaports," and the expense of our conversation was his. Our main contact, Wayne, sent us on our way with a business card and message that we would have cell coverage along the way. If any problems came up, he suggested, "Call me."

The road to Mustagh Atta is as amazing as the city we started out in, and while it's paved, it's often diverted because of rockslides, washouts, whatever. The route to the mountain rises slowly out of the Kashgar basin and enters the beastly peaks, running between two seven-thousand-meter peaks at one point, something that in our experience as well as imagination was beyond unique. You can stop for photos, and in the distance of less than a mile gaze up at the summit of Kongur at 7,649 meters on one side of the road and a neighboring peak just under seven thousand meters on the other side of the road—the name of which I could not decipher.

As the road continued, the altitude increased, and the temperature decreased. The smog of the plateau was left behind. After crossing a high pass, we entered another high plateau that offered magnificent views of Karakul Lake with the massif of Mustagh Ata rising over twelve thousand feet behind it. To our delight, the temperature was no colder than it was in Kashgar—we expected much worse—and on our arrival in the basin, the sky was crystal clear. Our attitudes soared in anticipation of what we were about to take on. By this time, we had shivered in the bus—which really never warmed up—for several gloomy hours. But now all that was behind us, forgotten in the moment.

Behind all the hype of planning an expedition to a major peak, there exists lingering self-doubt, in this case enhanced by the severity of what we were taking on. The closer you get to the trip, the greater these feelings become. Am I ready? Did I prepare properly? Do I have all I need? Am I really experienced enough to take this on? So when you see the objective for the first time, it is always more significant than even the mind's ability to exaggerate it, but as you get closer, there is also a reality that it is what it is: it's just a mountain. Somehow before this point, the reality that you have no choice but to take it a step at a time is diluted by the extreme nature of what you are taking on.

The approach in a Jeep or, as it was in this case, a bus, also brings perspective. Despite seeing a mountain that has influenced so much of the past weeks and months, in my mind, anyway, it's clear that I don't have to climb the thing if I don't want to. While I have never actually acted on this notion, it does allow for a bit of a release as you get closer. Your frame of mind comes to grips with the whole idea of things. You learn quickly that while you must constantly look ahead when playing this game, trite as it sounds, being in the moment is where the action is but, more importantly, also where the next action is deciphered. So, from this perspective, taking the peak on really does manifest itself one step at a time. It all sounds like a cop-out, but this notion, and I believe I speak for Steve and Jim as well, was not something that always was, or that we forced along the way, but rather just how after twenty-five years things evolved. I also believe it's a realization that has contributed to the body of work we have accumulated over the years with all the expeditions we've been on. It is well put by a single comment in *Outside* magazine: "They don't even care about summits."

Looking back, this wasn't always the case. Take Denali, for example. That was our first major peak. For twenty-one days until we set foot on the summit, the summit was really all we thought about. Getting to the top of Denali was not even close to a given. Instead, it came with a high percentage chance of failure. If you are not living in the moment, you are living with the pressure of wanting something that very well may never happen.

It's like buying a lottery ticket and focusing on it until the draw a month later. And don't kid yourself: base camps are riddled with climbers who literally worry themselves sick over the prospects of taking all that time, spending all that money, and winding up with no summit. Having been there, it's a horrible way to exist. The older I get, the more I realize this is not just how some climbers approach an expedition; I see many clients living their lives the same way.

In our evolution, I think the misery of focusing on a summit slowly dictated our ability to focus on the process instead. Nothing can eliminate the negatives in life. But by living in the moment, the negatives are sidelined, and the sheer beauty of life becomes the focus. Philosophically, we gained an understanding that we had a gift for this stuff, but more importantly, we somehow managed to know we should. Practically, it allowed us to savor the moments, because we realized what we were doing was the same gift. As each objective drew closer, we saw it for what it really was, and the pictures in our minds of a summit party evaporated with the satisfaction of just being where we were. As Steve has often said, "Once boots hit dirt, all anxiety goes away." It's so true. You don't have to do anything but decide on the next step. The more you do that, the more experience allows you to make the next step count no matter what direction it leads you. In that bus, at that moment, everything was cool.

The next step in this case, however, was soon to be another lesson in the fact that life throws you curveballs. And sometimes, the steps are tough. We finally reached our disembarkation point, a dirt platform on the side of the highway on the edge of a herders' village—Subache. We knew the place well from our previous trip to the peak, and excitement soared as we stepped off the bus.

What happened next took place so quickly that I don't even know how it went down. Nearly as soon as our boots hit the dirt, Chinese military Jeeps came and surrounded us. Grumpy Pants, our liaison officer, nervously herded us back onto the bus. His demeanor changed from cocky arrogance to submissive cheerfulness as he offered cigarettes to the fully armed soldiers. Another Jeep pulled up; the soldiers stood at saluted attention, and another man, obviously the commander, stepped out into the cold, not happy to be where he was but appearing somewhat pleased because he had something, if not different, interesting with which to deal.

He was just as cocky as Grumpy Pants, but age had softened his ability to take his obvious power too seriously; it was granted without posturing. We watched as pleasantries were exchanged. Our permit to climb the peak was produced, and we could easily tell the officer was bewildered. Our logistics guy was standing to the side and came in to offer a translation: "The Chinese Mountaineering Association failed to notify the Chinese military that there was a permit issued to climb the peak at this time. They are involved with live ammunition winter survival training. You cannot climb the peak." He headed back into the conversation, and the officer started laughing. Steve stepped out and asked, "What is so damn funny about this?" The translation came back: "Who is dumb enough to be here to climb this peak this time of year besides the Chinese military?" Even we laughed.

The officer came onto the bus and, with hands together, bowed with mumbled Chinese in what was his offer of an apology. Grumpy Pants and our logistics guy conversed, and with little or no communication with us, the driver cranked up the bus, and we continued onward. "We have been given an alternative for your expedition." We accepted this and thought maybe we were headed to an alternative drop-off that was closer to the peak. But the bus continued. The peak in the rear window got smaller. And we soon knew something was up.

We were told, "Only forty-five minutes longer; we have another peak for expedition." Ha, you can't imagine how large this curveball was. One would think you would immediately put a stop to the madness if only to get a more definitive explanation. But at this point, after months of planning and raising a massive amount of money, the only solution was to go climbing and skiing. Maybe there was an alternative. Our only question was whether it would be a seven-thousand-meter peak, which we were told it would be. But no name was given, and only a slight bit of relief could be seen on our host's face as we drove on.

The bus rolled to a stop, and we were told to get out. We gazed around not knowing what the plan was. We were shown an icy and rocky peak in the distance and told this was the alternative. Only later did we come to realize that the peak was just shy of seven thousand meters, had only been climbed one previous time (in season no less), and there was not a speck of snow to be skied. The only relief was utter laughter. Our hosts were not amused.

This pushed Steve to the brink, and he said we needed to call Wayne. The beauty of the day was totally overshadowed by the biting cold wind that blew and the pathetic miscommunication that had occurred. The meeting with the military was now obviously a farce, a part of the game that had been structured long after we had written the large check and flown halfway around the world to China. Steve composed himself enough to lay into Wayne on the other end, in a manner that left him crying on the other side. Wayne had obviously long since spent our money, and a refund was impossible. He literally begged us to climb the peak before us. Steve made our argument painfully clear: We don't have the gear to climb a massive high-altitude wall, and, more importantly, "There is no fucking skiing on this peak, Wayne!"

We formulated the idea of attempting Mustagh Atta from another side, for which we didn't have a permit, but which Wayne happily said he would fix. We drove back the way we came and, as the military approached us a second time, a herd of yaks suddenly came out of nowhere to assist us in getting to a skiable ridge on the peak.

For the moment, all was good. We sank back into our default state—"What the heck, we are here, let's make the best of this." As we got into our cold-weather gear and even loaded the yaks with our haul bags, excitement grew. If nothing else, we laughed, it would be one hell of a story. But trouble came as we were about to take our first steps. Our base camp team of locals were clad in jeans, driving gloves, and fake leather jackets, and as the bitter cold penetrated my own clothes, I had a vision of hauling out three dead and frozen Kyrgyz men.

My next thought was for the sponsors who helped foot the bill for this expedition-turned-circus. The excitement of our logistics team was a bit abnormal as well; the smiles on their faces as they nearly pulled off the scam was clear. "Guys, look at these people! We take one step toward that mountain, it's game over. There will be no recourse for anything in my mind. No refund, no accommodating, just an ill-prepared team heading into the most inhospitable environment on earth. These fools will die before the light of day."

It was one of those moments in life where reality comes crashing through and the massively ridiculous nature of a situation becomes clear. Again, moment by moment. The game was over, but we pulled together to make a difficult-but-obvious decision. Steve called Wayne again, and still there was no refund available. We called Kari in Switzerland. He told us he was going to call Wayne, and he told us to tell Wayne that we were entitled to a 100 percent refund in some way. We knew this expedition was over, but we bargained with Wayne so that he would be responsible for our deposit for an attempt the next January. This would obviously come at a great cost to Wayne, but with the threat from Kari, who provided him with massive business, he finally accepted the situation. Through tears, he admitted he knew about the military situation but had no solution and finally apologized for straight up lying to us. "Please be my guests next year without fail," he said.

One cannot imagine the mental anguish we experienced standing out there in the cold. All the time, all the money, all the hype. It was devastating. Added to this, it was getting too late in the day to return to Kashgar, and we knew we would be spending the night in the bitter cold all for naught. Our despair was great, and one of the yak herders noticed our sadness. He felt so bad for us that he offered to let us stay in his house down the road—a mud-thatched cottage with dirt floors that every generation of his family had lived in.

The gesture was great, but how great we had no clue. An hour later, we walked into his primitive hut to find a yak dung stove burning and were greeted by his wife and kids and led to a back room with benches covered in beautiful handwoven rugs complete with sleeping pads. Beers appeared, and shortly thereafter, our host provided us with a meat stew served on homemade noodles. I am not exaggerating when I say it was one of those moments you will never forget. That evening—spent living on the high plateau on the Pakistan/China border, breaking bread with complete strangers in the coziness of their home—ranks as one of the most extraordinary experiences of our careers. In some weird way, the day, the scam, the entire failed mission came into focus as an adventure that illustrated just how wonderful human beings can be. We relaxed, and anger and frustration turned into calm enjoyment. We spent the night laughing and planning our return.

We returned with excitement that we had another attempt in place exactly one year in the future, but ironically, with all the fund-raising and planning totally in place, we were at a complete loss in terms of what to do next. The planning for these trips takes an enormous amount of time and energy. But because we had never experienced a situation where the planning didn't lead directly to the first steps of the expedition, there was a massive physical and mental gap to deal with. With everything in place but new airline tickets, coupled with the nagging need for a climbing release of sorts, our mental state was oddly blank. It was fantastic to have another carrot to push our training until the expedition, but to that point, with few exceptions, we had not gone two years without a major peak and altitude. We had blown our travel chit with our families for the feted attempt but reasoned that we had only been gone for a week and that maybe we could sell everyone on a really quick trip to South America to at least get to twenty thousand feet to stay if only mentally acclimated. We had previously made a couple of attempts on 20,561-foot Chimborazo, where a variety of issues prevented a successful climb and immediately concluded that we should head there for a quick week trip to get back a bit of sanity. We realized that we would also need to modify our style by eliminating camps in the winter. It was clear that standing around was simply not possible, and the thought of setting up all the camps was nauseating given the cold temperatures we anticipated. But also, by this time, we found ourselves in position to really want to push ourselves in general.

The whole winter concept—despite not having stepped foot on the peak—pushed us mentally, nonetheless. The thought of blitzing, or climbing Chimborazo in a single push, would not equate to the difficulties of climbing anything in the Himalaya in winter, but it would take an otherwise fairly standard peak and make it something we could hang our hat on. It wasn't about finding glory but finding personal growth; we had no clue if we could climb that high, that far—nearly seven thousand feet of elevation gain—with skis, and then turn around and ski back down. Tupungato and Coropuna provided a stepping-stone that showed us we had the experience to try, but just adding the skiing aspect was totally unknown. At that point, we didn't even know if anyone had done it on Chimborazo, but our inclination that it was special was confirmed later upon the realization that only one other person had skied the peak, and he didn't blitz it. It was a massive objective. So, we decided to give it a go and put a trip together.

We had befriended another Aspen local for the attempt, a medical student studying in Buenos Aires—Jesse Durrance. Jesse was from another Aspen ski-racing family, the Durrances, and had similarly hung up racing skis in lieu of adventure skiing. He was several years younger than us but had reached out when he heard that we had been on many forays to South America. Jesse had likewise ventured into the Andes to start his own ski mountaineering career. He spoke perfect Spanish and had enough years in medical school to practically be a full-fledged doctor, making him an attractive recruit to our team. He was also a superstrong climber and fantastic skier. We met Jesse in the capital city of Ecuador—Quito —and quickly made our way to Chimborazo.

Chimborazo is located near the Equator in the Cordillera Occidental range, which is a string of active volcanos that are part of the southern arch of the Pacific Ring of Fire. Interestingly, the peak is not the highest in the world, obviously, but at the equatorial bulge, its summit is the farthest point on the surface from the earth's center. When we first attempted the peak several years earlier, the only information on the peak we could find was in old guidebooks. We found pictures of perfect snow slopes from the Whymper Hut, which works as base camp at the foot of the two main routes, all the way to its glaciated summit.

The peak used to be popular, and guides took hordes of mountaineers up it each year. The Carrel refuge at the base of the peak alone suggests better times, its massive, three-story structure lined with bunks to accommodate the masses. The guidebook pictures we saw from the 1980s were impressive and tantalizing from a skier's perspective. Looking at the peak from our first attempts and then at this time, it was clear that the massive crowds, as well as the beautiful slopes, were long gone. The refuge sat totally empty, and the slopes to the upper glacier were, as Steve would later say, "one ugly peak." Over the years, global warming as well as volcanic dust from nearby erupting volcanoes had reduced the lower slopes to steep water-iced steps encrusted with pumice gravel falling from upper slopes, rendering the route nearly impossible to climb. The pumice ate at our crampon points and destroyed the points of ice screws, leaving a climber to scratch his way up and over the vertical steps. This thwarted our earlier attempts, but on this attempt, we came with titanium screws, ice stakes, and hammers.

We arrived at the Carrel refuge, nearly seven thousand feet below the summit, and immediately hauled the skis as far up the peak as we could, to around seventeen thousand feet above the smaller Whymper refuge that served as the normal advance base camp. We then retreated to the Carrel refuge below and waited a day to further acclimate. The weather deteriorated into a fog and sleet that got so damp and cold we lit a fire in the refuge's fireplace. The Whymper refuge is named after Edward Whymper, the first climber to scale the Matterhorn in 1865. He subsequently attained the summit of Chimborazo in 1880. He did not ski Chimborazo (grin), and in fact barely made it "off the peak with the skin on my back," the altitude being the greatest he'd ever experienced. At the time, Chimborazo was thought to be the highest peak possible to climb, although early surveyors incorrectly estimated the height to be close to eight thousand meters.

The third day dawned, and we were skeptical that we'd do much. We were barely acclimated to the refuge (base camp), and even less so to where we dropped the skis, and worried about the great effort we were about to undertake. Regardless, we set off in the dark. The stars occasionally poked through the mist, and we followed the beams of our headlamps. We arrived at the normal starting point for climbing the peak, the upper Whymper refuge, and over a hundred years later, we found ourselves at the same point of Whymper's third camp. We halted for a rest and to fuel up for the difficult and dreaded climb to a saddle, another two thousand feet above, where the rock and ice turned to snow. At this point, there was no trail, and in the foggy dark we had to reckon our position as best we could using the hut and a GPS point taken two days before to point us in the general direction.

The scree slope steepened until we reached the first ice step. Our effort to bring better equipment was soon found to be in vain, and we could not protect the twenty- to thirty-foot steep cliffs. We did our best to work around to the lesser exposed slopes and kicked and scratched as best we could. Steve and I had two hammers with points that we used to claw our way up, at times passing them back and forth to help each other. The exposure was harrowing—a fall certain death—but with small flat ledges between cliffs, we managed to rest and take on each obstacle, finally stepping onto a steep, gravel alluvial shelf leading to the col where a rope length ahead we could see smooth white snow. The snow slope was steep and icy, and there was a sheer drop thousands of feet just to our right, but the ice was not riddled with pumice, and we easily set the ice screws and ran belays for the next five hundred feet to a point where the ice turned into wonderful, flaky snow, eliminating the need to protect. This was a massive relief.

We could now relax a bit as we climbed, and it also was clear that the skiing was going to be amazing. We had never seen snow like this; Chimborazo's famous penitentes—which we had feared may thwart any skiing—were not to be found. Penitentes are thin blades of hardened snow, often several feet tall that are found at high altitude on many South American peaks.

At this point, the penitentes were just a few inches tall—not the four- to five-foot fangs of unskiable and barely climbable ice teeth we thought we might encounter. The altitude seared our now unacclimated bodies, but our spirits soared at the thought of skiing this peak. Ahead, the slope was steep to a false summit a thousand feet above us, and as we looked in the direction we had climbed, the rising sun formed a massive pyramid-shaped shadow across the Ecuador Plateau nearly twelve thousand feet below us. We were exhausted, but adrenaline pushed us forward.

We arrived at the false summit, a quarter mile from the main summit, and to our relief, the path down and back up through the summit crater was full of snow. Most years, the main summit of Chimborazo is guarded by a massive bergschrund that prevents climbers from attaining the true summit. Most are content to thus climb the slightly lower false summit; we were not contented enough to accept the same. With the path across clearly open, we glided down from the false summit on our skis, and then shouldered them for the two-hundred-foot climb to the main summit.

On top, we were completely depleted; the night and morning had taken a toll on us physically. Steve was particularly gassed, claiming the climb to be his limit, the summit a godsend. For the first time we looked at the view behind us, to see what we had climbed. A neighboring peak was blowing volcanic dust well into the atmosphere, but the clouds and mist from the previous days were completely gone, leaving us with late morning sun that warmed our bodies as we climbed out of the shadows onto the sunny summit. Our next concern was the steep snow slope and possible avalanches, so we didn't waste much time refueling. In no time we were on the lip of the main summit heading back to the false summit.

The first turns were enough to get our ski legs back, but the slight climb back up to the false summit was extraordinarily difficult due to fatigue. But soon we were on the lip of the false summit looking down the nearly perfect snow slopes back to the col. I filmed the team skiing, with a backdrop well below that included the massive Carrell Hut where we started, which ironically looked like a small speck. The ranchlands below were lined with tiny roads. Beyond, the massive and uninhabited plateau of Ecuador was flat and endless.

The skiing was, in fact, nearly perfect, with soft flaky snow providing for near effortless turns. The slope did have cracks beneath the snow, so we had to pay attention, but for the most part, the conditions offered some of the best high-altitude skiing we had ever experienced. But all good things come to an end, and soon we were back at the ice slopes where the light of day highlighted some large crevasses we hadn't seen during the ascent. We belayed ourselves down the slopes to the col, and the next issue was how to get off the peak and back to the refuge. By this time, the sun had warmed the face of the peak. Small rocks were flying as the ice holding them melted. It left us wondering how the peak had anything left to even be a peak; it sounded like a large rainstorm—the rocks flying like raindrops. The line of ascent was clearly not safe or possible. We decided to descend the rocky ridge on the opposite side of the col and headed down carefully on talus slopes that were steep but ice-free. The going was not conventional or obvious, but we soon intersected the trail below and casually walked back to the refuge where we started the adventure nearly fifteen hours before. The guardian had iced tea and food waiting for us.

Chimborazo exceeded our ambition to fill a void after the debacle on Mustagh Atta a few months before. Again, in a natural progression, we came to the peak with a desire to learn what we were capable of. The idea that we could climb that far and long and high without the normal camps was a quick thought heading in, but it ended up being one of the coolest experiences of our lives. The irony was clear: we had enough experience to know we could at least attempt it but not enough experience to know that if we were successful, it would serve to become one of the more memorable trips in our careers. It never dawned on us that what we saw as a temporary quick fix could be so satisfying. This parlayed into a great confidence that we would take with us to China the following January. With nothing much to plan, we were free before the trip to just enjoy life with the satisfaction of knowing we had a great adventure all in place. We joked that this is what most people experience when climbing with commercial expeditions.

A process takes place before any trip, and many climbers don't get to experience that. People often refer to mountaineering as a game of checks and balances; someone writes a check, another deposits it and balances the bank account. What is missed in this all-to-common approach is the buildup of an expedition that vests people who must go through all the logistics and planning. For us, this part of a trip was a source of anxiety with all that needs to be accomplished—everything from getting to and from the peak to what to put in a medical kit to whether or not you can purchase gas for the stoves in far-off-city nowhere. What's the food situation? What will the logistics agent have? What can we buy on arrival? With new baggage restrictions, you can't just throw everything in a haul bag and go. Flying is expensive and limited as to what the airlines will allow you to take. In all, what you end up with is a lot of looking ahead and planning. With this done, we were left with open schedules. For the first time, we had free time to fill. What to do?

Over the years, we had generated very solid relationships with sponsors for virtually everything we needed for any expedition. We worked diligently to do all we could in return, but given the nature of what we did—high-altitude climbing and skiing—our efforts were not terribly marketable. With the evolution of the internet, we found ourselves in a here-and-now environment where the next generation of adventurers was using social media and the internet whereby they could go out and with an iPhone post their adventures in real time. The "rad" factor was enormous, and marketing people harped on the value—more was better. Over the years we attempted to figure out ways to use SAT phone technology from base camp to accomplish the same, but the reality of what we were doing was extremely limiting.

We found the setup of the technology to be draining, both financially and from a time perspective. But the reality was that we could not compete visually with someone skiing powder back home after a big storm. (For us, in fact, powder was mostly nonexistent and avoided when possible for fear of avalanches and exposure.) It was nearly impossible to communicate the background of what we were doing, and our content was considered boring. But also, as the world of instantaneous posts on social media grew, we found the self-promotional aspect of it nauseating at best; everyone was posting photos every second of every day. While at base camp, after a long haul or tough day, the last thing anyone felt like doing was hooking up the SAT phone to fight through the technical difficulties of connecting to the internet when the only thing you felt like doing was eating and sleeping. Personally, just capturing the expedition on video—charging batteries, keeping the equipment running, and then lugging the gear—was a massive burden. And while I relished getting the shot, any other notion of the technical world of computers and phones was too much. It was all just a pain in the ass on top of the stress normally accompanied with climbing and skiing the highest peaks. So, we avoided it as much as possible.

Our routine of capturing the expeditions—snapping photos, shooting video—was thus rendered irrelevant by sponsors upon getting home, and subsequently, while we found that we had great relationships with all our sponsors, we rarely found them interested in what we presented from the trips. I continued to make films, would add credits for sponsors, and over time, we asked for and received gear, but we were never remotely pressed for anything in return. On one level, it was a dream come true. Manufacturers were sending gear by the truckload. But it also was a source of frustration.

As noted, major magazines were tapping into "The Three Amigos" story from time to time, and the lack of promotion generated subtitles like, "The most accomplished ski mountaineers you've probably never heard of." The reality was, to this point, outside of just climbing and skiing as often as we could, we never really paid attention to the past; our efforts were always pointed toward the next trip and the next step in our process. We were in it for the sheer fun. We still feared self-promotion to a certain degree, and what efforts we did make through the films coupled to create, especially locally, a scenario where people saw us as Everest wannabes. And because we didn't tell the world our story, most people had no clue of what we had accomplished. To that point, we never even kept track of all we did.

In the climbing world, it's common for climbers to keep journals of not just expeditions but daily climbs. The editor of this book highlighted a find he came across of one climber who had passed away and donated his life's work, volumes of journals, depicting literally every day with minute details down to holds on routes. It was a work of genius. That was not the case for us, and factually we never accounted for the hundreds of forays locally let alone the long line of expeditions over the past thirty years. In fact, when pressed, I found it nearly impossible to make a list of expeditions and likened it to asking a golfer to list his major golf vacations over the past twenty-five-plus years. It just wasn't something we thought about.

Nor did we have a bucket list of things we wanted to accomplish in the future. Rather, it was just a matter of what could we do next, the only criteria being to see another cool place and do something that would push our experience a bit further. It's ironic that except for Shishapangma, where we did realize it would be a notable first, our list contains many first ski descents, but all were known only long after the fact. And even for Shish, the first recollection of skiing there came long before we knew it would be notable, and only after our first experience with the internet where the other feted Americans had produce probably the first ever expedition website in history. We were just guys out climbing and skiing. There was no plan or effort to be famous, and the reality was, even as adults, there were a few guys out doing things in the high peaks that we looked up to but never past.

That said, here we were, looking ahead to a great adventure in less than a year, with a rare commodity: time. There was a desire to "do something with all of this"—to try for the first time to capitalize on it. Through our CPA practices, Steve and I had done accounting for a handful of other adventurers who were doing such, and the numbers were large. We asked, "Why not us? Why not try?" We could never understand why these gear companies never capitalized on our efforts, and we began to understand that if we didn't fully grasp it, if it was difficult for us to realize it all in a list, how could they find the value? For the first time, the contrast of the world of self-promotion came clearly into view, and we realized—despite the local flavor that we were glory hounds and massive self-promoters—outside of our little world in Aspen, no one had a clue who we were or what we were all about. We turned our frustration to action and set out to prove that we had a story, and we were going to use it. More on that later.

The summer rolled into autumn, and by late fall 2012, we were in the best shape of our lives and ready to head to China. As the ski lifts opened, we found ourselves getting our ski legs into shape and organizing life at home and at work. As the new year dawned, we were packed and ready to go. Before we knew it, we found ourselves at the foot of Mustagh Atta. This time, there was not a soul to be found; the military holed up far from the Tibetan Plateau. The cold was enormous as we set off on the day trek to base camp—so cold we had to walk in altitude boots brought in addition to our AT boots. By this time, we had worked out the kinks in the heated insoles, a minor point in the grand scheme of things but one that gave us great confidence for the effort. We had obtained new chem packs for our hands, which were reported to work much better in thin air. And to better accommodate the base camp staff, we put together warm kits of clothing to improve their lives as they hung around in the deathly cold conditions. We took the failed attempt and did all we could to improve on the situation. We arrived at base camp at about thirteen thousand feet under clear but breezy conditions. We had to set up the large base camp dome, which we would use for sleeping, eating, and generally hanging out—our haven for retreat. Upon arrival, the first niggling problem was to fix the two gas heaters we'd brought from the States.

The Asian connections to the gas tanks were not compatible for the American units, and using a combination of elbow grease, candle wax, and plyers, we managed to jam the system in place without any leaks. All was great; we were finally on the expedition. It was not nearly as windy as the previous season, something that further bolstered our confidence. We rested the next day to acclimate to our haven, and on the third day prepared to head up to Camp 1. At this point, the first of many problems reared its ugly head.

Doug Dolginow, the doctor, had accompanied us on the trip, and over coffee he brought up the subject of the heated insoles. He explained that he didn't want to be the downer of the day, but "last night I was fiddling with my insoles, and I can't get them to work at all." We wondered what was up, and immediately brought all our units out. None of the units was heating up. We reasoned that the nonlithium batteries were the culprit, and we attempted to warm up the batteries.

The temperature outside was near minus forty, and upon testing all the battery packs, we concluded that the batteries had frozen solid. We warmed them to no avail. It was so cold that the batteries were rendered useless. We tried warming them, recharging them, and taking them apart. Nothing worked. Frustration turned to anger, but it never ceases to amaze me what the atmosphere of an expedition does to help you forget about things out of your control.

We discussed climbing in our altitude boots but decided if we were going to ski, we needed to see how well the AT boots and overboots worked. But the first part of the trail was over scree, and it was impossible to use overboots. Overboots are neoprene booties that you put your entire boot into. They then zip and snap up, protecting the entire boot, including the sole. You then attach your crampon to your boot and the metal spikes and frame protect the material covering the sole. They function well on snow and ice only, so for the first part of the climb, we did not have that extra layer they provide for warmth and had no idea how it would go without. We were clad in our down suits and face gear, leaving no skin exposed to the elements. Our warming bodies prompted us to unzip our suits to prevent saturating our down suits with perspiration, and it was impressive that as cold as it was, by simply climbing, we could stay warm. Keeping the core warm translated to better circulation for our fingers and toes, keeping them warmer than expected, which was a nice surprise. But without the overboots, and the simple fact that when climbing in AT ski boots you undo your buckles for better movement, it felt as if we had holes in our shoes. The wind penetrated every opening. This required us to buckle the boots a bit tighter than we normally would, but the tiniest cracks exposed us to the ever-permeating cold. Our toes soon numbed, so we had to concentrate on wiggling them to prevent them from freezing, but if we were on the move, while cold, it was not cold enough to prevent us from continuing.

As we slowly climbed to Camp 1, all was fine, and we managed to stay warm. But upon arrival, and within only a few minutes, our heated bodies succumbed to the cold. It happened extraordinarily quickly. We zipped up our suits and maintained enough warmth for our bodies to function, but our feet almost immediately started to freeze. We quickly set up camp, including a tent to store our food cache, but it was not without constant movement. There was no sitting down to take a breather. Our water bottles—which were in our packs and wrapped in puff coats—were nearly frozen solid, and we quickly realized that even at the lower altitudes we needed to keep our water bottles in our suits. We laughed at how quickly we established the camp, and upon its completion we spontaneously turned around to get to the relative warmth of base camp.

On the way down, our minds raced with the experience, and when we were back at the tent below, the discussion immediately turned toward the next steps. There was a great emphasis on the cold and what we needed to do in order to survive the higher elevations. It was painfully clear that we would never be able to put in all the camps normally required. We had anticipated this, but now the notion was confirmed. But other issues came up—primarily, the footgear. Our suits worked well, maybe too well; we climbed out of them and found even with the venting, they needed to be hung up to dry out. Doug's climbing partner, Bo Parfet, had battled with the venting, not wanting to overexpose his body, and his suit was soaking wet. Down loses its insulating ability drastically when wet, and we knew that we had to pay attention to this; erring on the side of cold, a frightful thought given how cold it was and knowing that pushing the venting too far could be, literally, fatal.

The second and bigger issue was the footgear. While moving, we were able to regulate circulation, and although our feet were never toasty warm, we all agreed that while moving, we could feel our toes. From Camp 1 up, we would be able to use the overboots, which would help. But the main worry was that the temperature at Camp 1, about three thousand feet higher, was fifteen degrees colder than the temperature at base camp. Base camp temperatures were ranging from minus fifteen with no wind to minus twenty-five, but at Camp 1, were hovering around minus forty and later even got to minus sixty. Above that, the weather stations were reporting nearly minus one hundred—not considering wind chill. Overboots are tested to eliminate roughly thirty degrees, so we knew we could go higher, but without a source of additional heat, we silently knew the prospects of a summit bid were drastically reduced.

The issues were pondered and discussed, but when some issue was resolved, another would come up. It was clear that what we were taking on was drastically different than anything we had ever attempted. The Himalaya in the winter had—so far—required every bit of our experience just to get to the peak, and as we slowly settled into camp life, we realized that we were at the beginning of a wholly new activity, not unlike our first forays into large peaks twenty years before. This was, for us, a completely new sport.

But the issues, and they were constant, were not a source of angst or despair. Rather, this new activity, something we pondered but never fully anticipated, became a source of great interest. We fell back into the normal base camp routine, told the same stories, argued politics, discussed religion, family life, and "sex, drugs, and rock and roll"—all the standard diversions. But we had fresh discussions on how we were going to simply get up the peak.

The new hurdles, the problem-solving, the logistics of this peak at this time of year was the overriding discussion, and it was fascinating. It's not to say that at times it didn't generate pure fear—it most definitely did—but in the discussion, the reasoning revolved around problem-solving and paying attention. We took great pride in where we were and what we were doing. The reality of the slim chance of summiting was circumvented with a constant discussion of the next day, and what we needed to do just to survive moment by moment had become an unforeseen source of energy and excitement. For the first time in our lives, we had no previous experience to take on what few if any ever had. We were literally in an environment that had seen fewer people than had set foot on the moon.

The summit faded behind the next step, the next camp, and the next day. We had a great desire to experience as much of this peak as possible, and the process superseded everything. It did not go unnoticed that when here during the normal climbing season several years before, there were hundreds of people hanging around. And yet this time, the only signs of civilization were the transport trucks slowly inching their way along the Karakorum highway nearly twenty miles away. To use a phrase that we picked up from local guide Steve Gall, we were most definitely "logarithmically out there!"

There were some similarities with normal climbing—one being the need to acclimate. This was magnified by the fact that, as I have noted, the intense cold effectively raised the altitude by roughly fifteen hundred feet compared to when we stood at the base of the peak several years before. We could feel it just walking about camp, and we knew we needed to be extremely careful. After the initial push to Camp 1, we rested another day and made plans to head up and sleep high the following day. The blue sky turned to gray, and along with it, the winds picked up. It was odd, however, that with the slight cloud cover, temperature did not fluctuate. In fact, the temperature didn't even fluctuate between night and day. It was just flat-out cold 24/7 with little or no ambient change. With the winds, the chill factor was tremendous. The winds just above the protection of a moraine above camp were roughly twenty miles per hour—conditions we deemed climbable, but only because we knew our camp above was fairly well protected. We had a haven. We also reasoned that if things got out of control, we could always turn around. This was a discussion that you'd never have in the normal season. The breeze that did flow through base camp was enough to make us realize that we needed to anticipate what it would be like higher.

Camp 1 was set, and on this trip up, we would carry the ski gear and our extra sleeping bags to spend the night. As we set out, with the wind, the comfort of the down suits was welcomed. As we pierced the protection of the base camp moraine, the wind was frigid, but with the circulation provided by movement, the climbing was pleasant. Our loads were a bit heavier than the first leg a few days prior, but the acclimation process had thickened our blood, and we started the normal process of rhythm for the expedition. The climber's trance set in, and step by step we ascended smoothly, our trances broken only by the occasional gusts that would interrupt progress as they hit the skis and whipped us out of step. But even there, you could hear the wind on a ridge a mile away, and after a few of the gusts washed past, the brief interruptions were calculated and became part of the rhythm.

We arrived at Camp 1 and began settling in. Upon stopping, the cold began to seep through even the loft of the down, and within minutes, fingers and toes were numb. Steve immediately unloaded his pack, secured his gear with rocks so the gusts would not blow it away, and got in and started the stove to warm the tent and begin the endless effort to melt snow for the brews our bodies required. Jim danced from foot to foot, swinging his arms to stay warm, and as soon as Steve was settled, he crawled into the tent. While they were settling, I busied myself with chipping snow and ice into a stuff sack, making sure I gathered enough for the evening as well as the next morning. Grabbing the metal shaft of my axe, the heat was sucked from my hand through my mitten with bewildering speed. I immediately opened some chem packs, which allowed me to chip the hard snow. The wind had blown any loose snow from the slopes around camp, leaving old snow and ice that was as hard as any frozen water I had ever seen. The pick of my ax barely broke through, and the normal chore of filling the snow bag became a major job. I finished with what I thought would be enough and headed into the tent.

We were using a new brand of single-wall tents for the expedition, and when looking in, despite the three-man description in the brochure, it was clear there was not enough room. But the tents were superlight and durable, and along with the tent we set up, we had hauled up two additional two-man units for higher up. I set one of them up, brought out an additional cook set, and soon had my own shelter. I crawled in, zipped up the door, and tried to regain feeling in my fingers so I could fire up the stove. The chem packs soon brought dexterity back to my digits, and the stove blared in the little tent. I was still in my down suit and let the stove's flame warm the inside of the tent, which was soon engulfed in a cloud of condensation. I unzipped he door a bit to let the steam escape and then dumped the remaining water from my water bottle into the pot to brew a cup of coffee.

As the pot struggled to boil, the next issue was to get out of my boots and into my down booties. The plastic shells were rock hard. I struggled, huffing and puffing, exerting until I was dizzy, but I could not get the boots to open wide enough to pull them off. I stood up awkwardly in the small tent and somehow managed to leverage my foot out of one boot and then the other. This became the next obvious issue in my mind: how was I going to get my feet back in the next morning? Too tired at that moment to contemplate the problem, I pushed the boots aside and put my feet into my down booties, the split seconds between boots and booties numbing all feeling out of my toes. I massaged the circulation back and sat dazed as the purr of the stove mesmerized me. Outside, it was minus sixty, and although the tent felt warm and cozy, I was amazed that it was still minus twenty inside. I had never imagined it would be that cold in a tent, but I was in down booties, a fully zipped down suit, and wearing mittens.

The lack of boil became an issue; the water was tepid at most. I reached outside the tent to find rocks to put around the stove to absorb and reflect more heat toward the pot and was happy with the results. It took for what seemed forever, but I had my hot cup of coffee. I began to think about the boot issue and the prospects of getting them on the next morning. I figured I would have to sleep with the shells in my sleeping bag. I had become accustomed to sleeping with my boot liners but never the shells. I became extremely cognizant of many issues that needed to be dealt with, but Steve and Jim were not near enough to chat, so I wrote mental notes of the issues and would bring them up in the warmth of base camp after what I realized was going to be a miserable night.

I managed to hydrate until the dark of night forced me to give up and attempt to get some sleep. I pulled out my sleeping bag and crawled out of my suit and into the cozy bag. Warmth immediately surrounded my body, and all was good. When warm enough, I decided to arrange the booties in the bottom of my bag. Then, I had to figure out the shells. This became more of an issue than I anticipated—the bulky boots taking up much more room than was available. The sleeping bag was designed for a human body with enough loft for good air circulation, but it did not leave me with much room for the shells. I managed to place one on my side, and the other on my stomach. While this worked, soon I needed to shift to my side, and quickly realized the shells had to go. I figured I would have to heat them up with the flame of the stove. I was too tired then to deal with it and discarded them to the end of the tent.

Sleeping at altitude the first time is always a frustrating proposition, the body working overtime to create circulation in the thin air, and a general discomfort takes over. Sleep is hard to come by. By three in the morning, I did manage to drift off, and it felt good when I did open my eyes to the light of day. In my bag, I was toasty warm, but upon opening my zipper slightly, the rush of cold hit me in the chest, and I quickly zipped it back up. I fumbled for the small thermometer and was amazed even more to see that without the stove, it was minus twenty-five. My boots were covered in a layer of white frost, and I knew I had to get up and get to work. I jumped out of the bag and into my down suit, which was frightfully cold from sitting overnight. I did sleep with my down booties and light gloves and managed to zip the suit up, which slowly warmed with my body heat. I fired up the stove and sat waiting for the heat. I was disappointed and knew immediately that in that environment, especially with only one person, the single-wall tents were not providing enough insulation compared to the double-wall tents we had used on expeditions to that point. I was hoping that Steve and Jim had had better luck.

I fumbled for my boot shells and held the cuffs over the flame. I rotated them and as soon as I grabbed one and set the other down, it cooled immediately. I put a liner on one foot, held the related shell over the flame, and after ten minutes was able to warm up the plastic enough to jam my foot in. Then I repeated the process with the other shell. By the time I was in my boots, my feet were numb. I gave up on the long-anticipated hot drink and packed up. All I wanted was to get off the peak, back to base camp where I knew it was warm and the coffee would flow. Steve and Jim had the same notion, and with few words spoken, we secured camp and found ourselves heading down the scree fields toward breakfast. The jaunt soon warmed our cold bodies, and our minds raced with all the newly found issues from our first winter night high on a peak in the Himalaya. The issues were serious, and as I marched down, I started the process of figuring out what could be done.

Back in the dome tent at base camp, we hung up gear to dry out and over coffee discussed the past couple days. The main issue besides the footgear was the tents. It was painfully obvious that single-wall tents at altitude in extreme cold were not a great thing. The energy saved on weight was more than offset by the misery of minus twenty temps inside; they didn't retain nearly enough heat. While we had not been in temperatures that cold before, our experience was close, and double-wall tents were infinitely warmer. The night was miserable at best. We realized we had to make do with all we had and that meant cold nights up high. We chalked it up to a lesson learned. As we talked, the sky turned gray, and the wind picked up. A halo around the weak sun told us that there was a front moving through, and a giant lenticular formed over the summit. With a needed rest day and hot coffee in hand, we welcomed the storm. It fit well with our schedule, and we would rest and wait for better weather.

Despite all the hard lessons learned, the mood was positive, and while the insole failure diminished severely our notion of getting to the top, we were still engaged mentally to give the peak 100 percent effort. A calm period with no wind was not out of reason, and we looked forward to a major effort as soon as the front moved out. We knew that we would have to eliminate a third camp, but in our previous normal attempt we proved our mettle to climb the great distance and justified the difficult effort knowing the decision was mandatory for a winter attempt, taking the question out of our minds; it would be tough, but we knew we couldn't stop due to the cold and accepted it as the ultimate challenge of our careers.

Then the weather became an issue. One day rolled into another, and another, and another. There was no meaningful accumulation of snow—we reasoned it was too cold to snow—but the peak from just above base camp to the summit was hidden in a cloud of spindrift. Off the left side of a high ridge, the snow blew as far as what we estimated to be a mile or two out over the valley. We were comfortable in our large tent, but the wind outside was fierce. There was a large weather station with a massive windmill to generate electricity for the weather stations on the peak, and the props whirred loudly in the gusts, an irritating sound that became so familiar we could gauge the strength of the wind by sound; it roared 24/7 during the storm. After a week, there was no letup. By this point, time was painting us into a corner.

Finally, around the eighth day, the wind subsided significantly. We immediately rushed up to Camp 1. We had to put in a second camp if we were to have any shot at the summit. After working the sedentary lethargy out of our aching bodies, it felt great to be moving again. We had no loads and merely had to attain Camp 1. The next day we hoped to climb to as close to twenty-one thousand feet as possible to put in a second camp. We arrived at Camp 1, went through the agonizing process of settling in, and, to our delight, the wind subsided almost completely.

But it was cold—cold beyond anything we had experienced. I jammed myself into the single-wall tent and tried to rest. The sun set over the plateau below, and soon the golden glow on the peak dissipated, and I tried to find comfort. The minutes ticked like hours, all night long. I couldn't sleep to save my life. I also developed a severe sore throat and cough, and the next morning there was no question—I had to descend. Steve and Jim took on the extra weight I was to carry and set off to get as high as possible. The day was nearly perfect, albeit cold, and soon I found myself at base camp sitting in my down suit watching the two through a telephoto lens on my video camera as they slowly moved upward. They were moving at a snail's pace. Later I would learn that although the slopes were not steep, they were rock hard. They struggled to skin upward, and while not steep, the slopes were so smooth and icy that a fall—where there was zero ability to stop a slide—could have been lethal. Soon they found themselves carrying their skis on top of already heavy loads, their crampons failing to gain comfortable purchase. They proceeded to just over twenty thousand feet and found themselves only two thousand feet above Camp 1, completely gassed and way too tired to proceed.

They clicked into their skis, which had razor sharp edges and proceeded to ski cautiously back down. To the skier's left, there was a large gully that had filled in with soft snow. It ended close to base camp, and I filmed their descent. They arrived in camp at 5:00 p.m. where they were excited but also disappointed. They had really wanted to gain another thousand feet for the camp, but the exertion in the cold fried their lungs and left them totally depleted.

At base camp, Steve and Jim's disappointment at not attaining the height they'd hoped for was overshadowed by the reality that, for the first time, we did something of the goal—skiing. On top of that, anytime you get a ski from above six thousand meters, that's a victory. Only later would we realize this was a first and a record ski descent from above twenty thousand feet in the winter. There is a helicopter skiing operation in the Annapurna region of the Himalaya where they ski around fifteen thousand feet, but to our knowledge, this was the record. It wasn't pretty skiing, but it was skiing nonetheless, and that's what we were there to do. This, along with the magnificent weather of the day, provided a great boost to morale and amped everyone for a summit push. We basked in the lightness the success brought, and for an afternoon and evening, all was cool. We laughed and forgot for the moment of the difficulties and the precariousness of what we were doing and where we were.

It's difficult to explain the mood swings of an expedition or the impact that seemingly small accomplishments have on setting the tone. When you place yourself in these environments, the main objective is survival. Then, if you're lucky, well-being. You don't sit around talking about the worst-case scenario, and you don't concentrate on the bad things that could happen, but in the discussion that drives the logistics, it is fundamental. So, it's not all doom and gloom, but everything is driven first and foremost by the worst-case scenario. It becomes part of your conscience. This is part of why the challenge and success in overcoming the altitude or the extreme cold derives a fantastic sense of satisfaction. And at times you can't help but fear it all. At those times, you must concentrate on controlling the fear, because fear is what depletes a climber most. Fear takes physical energy in that it creates the spikes in adrenaline, but it drains you mentally, too. So, when you click into skis, or even watch your buddies skiing, I think the combination of the familiarity of the sport and the understanding that it's the main focus becomes a massive boost mentally and physically. I've said it a thousand times; it doesn't matter how bad the snow is or how difficult the expedition has been—illness, weather, bad food, or missing loved ones—when you click into skis in the high mountains, everything is cool. Everything makes sense, and everything is worth it. In the comfort of our dome tent, we let our guard down for a fleeting moment. We relaxed. The food tasted better. With the knowledge that the next day was a rest day, we all slept deeply.

But all good things come to an end, and the next day reality blew in, literally. The perfect weather deteriorated into another storm, and the wind and cold outside soon woke us up from sleep. The well-being from the success did carry over, and we chalked up the bad weather to being the norm for a huge mountain in Asia. We tried to get back into climbing mode, the logistics of a final effort squarely in our brains, but time was not on our side. The storm continued to rage, and a few days later, we were still tent bound. The agony of the wait was getting old, and not even the skiing of a few days before offered comfort. With the days clicking by, we were running out of time.

The weather on the lower slopes was not so bad that we could not climb, and we decided that the next day, regardless, we would go for the summit. With the cache for Camp 2 only a couple thousand feet above Camp 1, and being extremely acclimated to the peak, we would head up very early, bypass Camp 1, and go straight to the Camp 2 cache and use it as a pilot camp to brew up and rest for a few hours. Then, we would simply climb as high the following night and day as was possible. The weather held us at bay for a couple more days, but we were out of time. At a minimum we had to pull the camps, and we vowed that, regardless, the next day we would make a go of it. We woke up, and the wind had subdued drastically, but with the sky a bleak gray, we had no idea if this was the eye or the end. With little said, we brewed up, filled water bottles, and hit the trail. Again, it felt good to be moving.

As we climbed, the sun made an appearance and the wind was minimal, giving us a bit of added energy at the prospects of making something out of this last-ditch effort. The night before, we discussed the matter; we recognized that the summit was just over nine thousand feet above, a challenge that would take us to new personal levels, as we had never gained that much height in a single push. But I did mention that my personal climbing in a twenty-four-hour up-and-down AT ski race netted me over thirty thousand total feet. This was at eight thousand feet, and we were heading to just under twenty-five thousand, but with nothing more to hang our hats on, we reconciled that thirty thousand feet was drastically more than nine thousand feet. If we took our time, and the weather held, we might just be able to pull this off. Also, while our previous expeditions on peaks like Norjin and Chimborazo added confidence, we realized that with the conditions as they were, the likelihood of success for what we were attempting was remote, but with a bit of luck, we knew it was possible. We talked ourselves into believing we could do it, and the challenge presented an opportunity to push ourselves further in our careers. We were there, we were out of options, and we would do the only thing we could—give it our best shot. We took great pride in where we were, and even the growth of the past few weeks had netted us an experience that was ultimately satisfying, regardless. But added to the equation—and it was massively important—the route was a ski tour and we were familiar with the terrain. If we ran out of energy or got to cold, all we had to do was to stop, click into our skis, and slide back to the safety of either of the camps we had established. So, it was not foolhardy grasping at straws but a methodically well-thought-out plan that fit within our own physical and safety metrics given the circumstances we were facing.

As I climbed that morning, I felt a great sense of accomplishment, which fueled my effort. As a mountaineer, especially a ski mountaineer, you go into all expeditions with a sense of reality, knowing that climbing and skiing the high peaks is difficult at best. This was a winter attempt on a peak that had never been climbed in winter, and all the experience we had to that point painted a very realistic picture of how difficult this attempt would be. Everything was stacked against us. But, oddly, this didn't dissuade or discourage us. To the contrary, just being there, all alone, figuring it all out, putting one foot in front of the other but keeping a keen eye on everything going on, gave me an enormous sense of pride. I thought about all the naysayers over the years, and although by this time we had developed a strong conviction to eliminate the negative feelings surrounding all that, I did think about what I was doing then and there, and what they were doing. It was not that I was looking down my nose or anything like that. Rather, I had this overwhelming feeling that I had turned all those negative feelings into something positive. Everything—the trips, the constant state of training, the organization over the years, and even the negative vibes—had played a part in getting me to where I was at the moment, putting one foot in front of the other, in January, in the Himalaya. All the experiences played a part in giving me the opportunity and the desire to be doing something that was outrageous by any definition. As I slowly climbed, I made sure to stop and look occasionally, to try to comprehend it all. And despite the miserable state of it all, I was completely content; I was able to enjoy what I was doing despite the obvious hurdles of the day and all the hardships endured in the past.

There was no doubt in my mind that I had gone well beyond where I ever imagined I would or could. I didn't have a feeling that I was the ultimate mountaineer or anything like that; I didn't see myself any differently than I ever did, and I still looked up to so many mountaineers. It was not an ego trip but a sense of personal accomplishment. And for the first time, I realized that the summit was not necessarily a point on a mountain but, in fact, a place in my mind. On that peak, it was clear, just being there and surviving was the ultimate victory. As I huffed and puffed, the ice built up around the mouth of my balaclava and fogged my goggles. But even that didn't stop me. I tilted my head just right so that the lens was cleared by the wind. I had adopted a mentality to accept the situation for all that it was and to simply give my best effort regardless. The satisfaction was enormous, to concentrate on what I had control over and to let go of what I didn't.

Slowly we proceeded upward. As we ascended above the protection of the moraine above base camp, the wind picked up substantially, causing a bit of anxiety as it was not a great sign. It was not so drastic that we could not climb, so we continued. Moving slowly in anticipation of an extremely long effort, we finally arrived at Camp 1. It was barely 8:00 a.m. The wind became a torrent. A massive lenticular cloud had grown over the peak, appearing to suck all other clouds up from the valley below. There were streaks of sunshine in the sky, but the wind was horrendous, blowing a cloud of spindrift into the atmosphere across a glacier flowing out of a canyon to our left. To our right, just above our tent, the wind was blowing a wave of constant snow up from the lower slopes, across the face, and we were thankful our tent was somewhat protected.

Climbing higher was out of the question. The bid was over. The next issue became retrieving the cache up at twenty thousand feet. The prospects of retrieving that were dismal, but we vowed to hang out for a few hours to see if the wind would abate. The cold from inaction in the tent was overpowering. Our feet started to freeze. We fired up the small stove and hoped the flame would displace a bit of the cold. The wind hammered at the walls of the small tent. We sat in silence pondering nothing. The purr of the stove was mesmerizing between the gusts that flapped the tent with a roar that superseded normal conversation. Jim blurted out simply, "Boys, there's a reason this mountain has never been climbed in the winter." Steve responded, "This is a different level, a different sport."

We awaited the morning crammed in the tent, and the storm continued to build. Any thought of retrieving the gear vanished.

We were now concerned with merely getting off the mountain. Even during the normal climbing season, parties had been completely blown off the slopes of Mustagh Atta, and we realized we needed to get going. We rallied to pull the camp and loaded everything we had, including the skis, in a harrowing retreat. Our packs were massive, which aided in stabilizing us in the wind. As the wind continued to increase, we descended knowing we had narrowly escaped its wrath. Again, there was satisfaction even in descent, hauling massive loads, surviving arguably the harshest environment on the face of the earth.

By this time, I was struggling to keep my feet from going numb. The only consolation was that they hurt like never before; pain was a good sign at this stage because I knew they were not frozen. But the exertion of the trip and the ski boots and no heat had taken a toll. Every effort resulted in frost nip, which exposed all our toes to the hammering of climbing but especially during the descending.

I had experienced this on Everest when, at twenty-eight thousand feet, they were frost nipped, but never before or after until this trip. My nails were completely black, and in the weeks after the expedition, I lost every nail. I struggled mentally at camps when my socks were crusty red with blood and puss, relegating them to the base camp latrine, which we later lit on fire to get rid of items that would not degrade in that environment. But at this stage, the pain was welcomed; my toes were not frozen.

The other nagging issue, small but irritating, was the loss of our cache. Granted it was small—a tent, some food, and a cook set—but in all the expeditions, except for a picket left on Broad Peak, we had adhered to never leaving a trace of our existence. Over the years, we had hauled off everything we carried up, and in some cases, trash left by others, and to be leaving our cache on Mustagh Atta meant not only a loss of valuable gear but a shirk of our responsibility. But even then, we told our base camp staff where we left it, and that it was theirs if they wanted to climb up and get it another time. (We found out later they did, a few months later.) We regrouped at base camp later that day and, after warming up, started the task of pulling up the camp. The next morning, we packed up and headed home.

By the standard definition of mountaineering success, we had failed miserably. But the lessons learned made it, in our minds, a major success. Even before we arrived back in Kashgar, our minds were racing: "This worked; this didn't; we need to do this; what about that ..." We knew we had to return, and before we arrived home, we had started planning the next expedition. One thing that played into our thinking was the simple fact that outside of our sponsors and family, no one had any idea of what we were up to with the winter aspect of our ski mountaineering. There was no formal plan to keep it a secret but rather a reality that we knew what we were attempting was substantial. I think I speak for Steve and Jim when I admit that we didn't tell anyone of our ambitions because our egos couldn't handle the potential scoffing and opinions.

Relating back to previous discussion, the idea was so outlandish that it was akin to when we started out. There was an unknown aspect about it that completely humbled us into submission. We didn't talk about it because it was too scary to hear what people would say, pointing out the obvious and potentially not-so-obvious realities. So, it was not by some altruistic method that we avoided the discussion publicly, but rather we just didn't feel the urge to do so. So often in climbing, a badge of honor is placed on a climber's ability to avoid recognition or promotion. As we aged into the sport, we realized that this was not a great attribute but instead a guise for truly talented climbers that didn't know how to promote themselves to gain recognition of sorts in other ways. Inevitably, the accolades for both climbing and being quiet about it were described as "humble and respectful," and that would come out, but it's not necessarily as great as pop culture interprets it in my view.

Part of the human experience is to seek success, and part of the reason is that it's natural to want recognition. It's painful to see people that have accomplished great deeds in the mountains that fail to get their due. They struggle until someone else claims their accomplishment for them in the name of their humility, but it comes with a downside. Until the accolade manifests, it fuels the fire to put down those that also accomplish great things and can promote themselves. In the crossfire, climbers become bitter, and I really believe the situation creates the constant infighting in the sport. Throw in sponsorships and dollars, and people feel cheated and degraded, all the while not admitting it's only because they lack the skill to capitalize as others do. In our view, it's healthier to accept and enjoy—to share if you will—accomplishments, if only because beyond the fodder of tea houses, pubs, and gear shops, there are so many people that live vicariously through others' adventures that don't have the gift to do what so many climbers are able to do. A balancing act is involved and a point where celebrating becomes bragging, but even there, the impact of backing off on the celebration is much easier to accommodate mentally than being the poor bastard who just soloed the north face of this or that peak for a first that hasn't a clue how to obtain recognition; embarrassment is much easier to combat than the massive chip on a shoulder that results from lack of recognition. The list of climbers who succeeded in sport but failed in recognition has resulted in drug abuse, failed marriages, alcoholism, and even suicidal efforts within this sport and others. When one celebrates accomplishment, if nothing else, it breeds perspective that allows one to move past the climbing with confidence. Success breeds self-confidence and an ability to separate climbing from real life. It is a natural release to obtain recognition that allows a climber to grow. Not obtaining it creates a need to do more, to push harder within the sport, often at unnatural levels. I look back at my own career, and, trust me, I speak from experience.

I was promoting our new business, 8kpeak.com, on social media in a post discussing some gear we were selling and describing our use of it on our expeditions. Despite the local sentiment that we were overhyped self-promoters, the reality of our situation was painfully clear. Beyond our small town, no one knew who or what we were all about. Our goal was to figure out how to leverage our story to simply sell gear. I reached out to marketing friends who taught me what to say, how to say it, and how to use social media to obtain the results we were seeking. I was not terribly comfortable with the idea of what I was attempting, but I gradually learned to set up the posts and hit return. A noted ski mountaineer responded with a slam. I was brought up to not slam back. Then he did it again, and then again. I bit my tongue. But it bothered me. So, I reached out to him and blasted away privately. His response was simple: "You come across as a bit more of an expert than you are, and it's irritating people." I proceeded to barrage him with my accomplishments, to which he, the owner of a competing company replied, "Mike, it's a small pool out there, and you are competition. Get used to it."

The conversation fueled my inclination to stop caring. I took to heart what every marketing person told me: post regularly, post about what we had done, and post photos and short blips to educate "the small pool" of who we were and what we had accomplished. I slowly started to build a following of people who really enjoyed my posts and literally "had no clue" about who we were and what we had been doing all those years. We were primarily known as those guys who skied Everest, but people had zero knowledge of all the other trips and accomplishments, and rightly so. Until I started to compile the list, no small task, we didn't even know all we had done. As I suggested earlier, the task was akin to asking a golfer to compile a list of all his major golf vacations for a period of twenty-five years. Seems like no big deal, but you finish the list and remember this trip or that one that you completely forgot about. But in the process, I gained recognition. It was as if a large rock was being whittled down. And a beautiful thing happened. It should not come as a surprise that as soon as you gain recognition, you stop seeking it. I quickly stopped caring what the local climbing community thought, or rather what I perceived they thought of me. I learned that people enjoyed living vicariously through my stories, my films, my posts, and even my rants. In effect, I took what is arguably a very selfish sport and softened that aspect of what I was doing by sharing with anyone who wanted to read my posts or watch my films. I gravitated toward the positive and let go of the negative. The occasional slam would come without question, but it never ceased to register in my mind that I was "just like that guy." I looked at myself as "that guy with a massive chip on his shoulder," and I didn't like what I saw. I was fortunately always very careful never to share my negative attitude beyond Steve and Jim, but even there, the normal rants subsided into the past, and for the first time, I genuinely climbed for the right reasons. Don't get me wrong; I have always enjoyed climbing and skiing, but this new evolution allowed me to let go of aspects of the sport that once held me captive; if I didn't make a summit, I found the process of failing not a source of regret but an experience that would allow me to do better the next time. I cared less about the materialism of what I was doing and enjoyed the process regardless. Another fantastic aspect to my new headspace came in the form of something I never really struggled with but now really could celebrate: other people's successes. The lesson was clear, and it was important. Accept what you have done and know it is enough.

In that bus, our defiance to promote our project was thus not about being cool or politically correct, but rather there simply was no need to hype what we were up to or what we had just accomplished. We were satisfied with the effort and all we had learned, and we simply wanted to go about our business and try it again.

The major lesson fit well into our recent long pushes in the Andes (on Corapuna) and in Asia (on Norjin Kansang) and was validated with the climbing lesson we learned on Mustagh Atta. It was very clear we needed to force ourselves to do even longer pushes and eliminate camps, and the reality was that the climbing windows in the winter Himalaya were even smaller than we expected. We formulated a plan to head to Bolivia that spring to take on a peak that had eluded us for sixteen years, 21,150-foot Illimani. Not mentioned in this story were a dozen or so trips to South America, including three to this jewel of the Cordillera Real. On our first attempt, we were thwarted by illness. For the next two attempts, weather, the only weather we had experienced in several trips to Bolivia, caught us at midmountain with no time to wait it out. We really wanted to climb and ski it.

Illimani is the king peak in the area and is blatantly visible from every other summit we had reached in Bolivia, as well as from neighboring peaks in Peru. It's even visible from nearly every street in the capital city of La Paz. It is a spectacular mass that rises ten thousand feet above its base and offers sustained steep slopes with great exposure. The upper slopes are steep and generally very icy, so we were not certain it would offer much skiing. However, having been on the peak multiple times, we knew that if we arrived earlier than the normal climbing season—before the storm season snows had melted or been blown away—it would offer a unique and incredible line for a ski descent. Based on what we could find, no one had ever skied the peak, which was a fun tidbit but also a source of anxiety. We would head to the peak not unlike some of the other mentioned "tests" to really push ourselves. We looked forward to a late April trip and spent the winter with continued training and preparation.

By late April we had all our logistics in place for a quick ten-day trip. We were met by our longtime friend Nestor Lora, who owned a hotel in La Paz and had run his own guide company for more than twenty years. By this time, Nestor was aging out of the game, but he opened for our business and provided us with a base camp cook/guardian, as well as transportation for the five-hour drive to the peak.

At fourteen thousand feet, La Paz is the highest metropolitan city in the world, and we spent the next day acclimating with sightseeing and messing around on the main street of the town. With many trips to La Paz in our past, it was fun to walk into restaurants and see people that we had met before. None of them knew our names or had ever known our names, of course, but they greeted us with smiles and salutations. We were eager to get to the peak, and on the morning of the second day we loaded up into the same red Land Cruiser that greeted us in 1996 for our first Bolivian adventure.

The drive was familiar and beautiful as we passed under nineteen-thousand-foot Murrata, a peak we had climbed and skied two years previously. Now and then we caught glimpses of the massive objective, Illimani. At a small village at the end of the road, we were dropped off, and soon a herd of horses arrived at the normal starting ground, a soccer field in the middle of town. We walked several hours to our base camp just below fourteen thousand feet and enjoyed expansive views of the canyon that separated us from the Altiplano and the city of La Paz, some forty miles distant. The base camp was empty at that time of year except for the herds of alpaca and llamas that roamed the sprawling bench of seemingly manicured grass. Clear, cold streams, fed by the massive glaciers that blanketed Illimani, trickled through the grass. The snow line was extremely low due to heavier-than-normal snowfall during the stormy season. And although we were a few weeks early for the climbing season, it served our purposes well, offering more skiing terrain than we had ever seen on the peak—much more than we had expected. We were very excited but also concerned about avalanche conditions.

Already acclimated to fourteen thousand feet, we prepared to haul equipment to the Condor's Nest, a midmountain camp at about eighteen thousand feet. The trail from base camp to the route is a few miles and includes about two thousand feet of elevation gain up and over three massive, buttress-like moraines, making it a complicated approach. There is no trail, and it is difficult to follow the route, so we marked it with rock cairns. The climb to this camp is on steep talus with significant exposure as the route follows a buttress that narrows to a ridge. It is not difficult climbing, but it requires one's full attention, as a slip would be deadly. The route has claimed the lives of more than a dozen unfortunate climbers over the years.

The plan was to haul a camp to this spot, rest, and then take the normal two days to climb the peak. Carrying skis would make the normally long and difficult route more demanding, but we drooled at the prospects of skiing the slopes we could see from base camp. In the morning, however, as we started to load our packs, Pablo, our cook/guardian inquired about our plan and explained that someone had to stay with the camp or the local banditos would scurry up the rocks in the night and take everything.

This was a new development in the area. The locals were surviving on meager agriculture labor wages. Seeing an inventory of gear they could possibly sell in La Paz for what would amount to an annual salary for most people—well, it was worth the risk. This threw a wrench into our plan, and we pondered our options. One was to rest a day, then take the peak on alpine style. This was possible, but the reality of no acclimation combined with hauling heavy loads to camp and then hauling skis up the rest of the peak the following day didn't sound all that fun. It even sounded dangerous. Then, we dreaded the thought of carrying everything—camp and skis—off the last day. It would probably require climbing back up and an additional day to break up the effort. The second was just as unattractive, but it fit into our previous expedition goals to really push ourselves in preparation for the winter Himalayan project. We sat over coffee and discussed just going for it with a base-camp-to-summit-and-back blitz. At first, this was so outlandish we kind of laughed. With the up and down getting to the route, and the actual seven-thousand-foot relief of the peak, we were looking at a nine-thousand-foot summit push, totally unacclimated. But as we sat there, the time factor came into play, and we really didn't have time for option one. Our minds raced at option two, and the more we sat around, the more we talked ourselves into it. We did reason that we needed to at least climb once to the camp at eighteen thousand feet to give ourselves a chance and decided that we should risk leaving the skis. We laughed that the banditos probably would have no idea what ski gear was, but we could easily hide them in the rocks as a precaution. Within an hour, we had talked ourselves into the blitz concept, loaded the ski gear on our packs, and leisurely headed up.

We ascended to the drop-off in about five hours, feeling the eighteen-thousand-foot altitude but gaining valuable acclimation for a summit bid. The day was bright and clear, no wind, and we climbed in light jackets. We slowed our normal pace to accommodate active acclimation and tried to preserve our energy for what would be a massively big effort. At the camp, we were dizzy with hypoxia, but we realized from all the previous expeditions that was to be expected and that the next trip up would be significantly easier. We carefully descended back to base camp, taking a different route down on the steep slopes that were, for the first time on our trips to Illimani, graced with snow. The slopes had frozen during the night and offered a much easier descent, which avoided a lot of the precarious spots on the ridge above. This bolstered our confidence in that we realized with skis the descent would be that much quicker with more skiing than expected. Enthusiasm was running high, and our desire to take the peak on with this great style was becoming extremely attractive.

Back at base camp, Pablo had a great meal prepared, and we enjoyed a beautiful evening. We knew we had to rest the next day, and for the moment, we put the climb out of our minds and relaxed with the knowledge that we would be able to sleep in the next day. The night before a known rest day is one of the greatest feelings a climber will ever experience. It doesn't matter what peak you are on. As soon as you get to base camp, your adrenaline rises. You may get a break here and there, but whenever you look up at the objective, anticipation rises, and your heart beats a bit quicker. The risks you will face are a big part of it, but then there is also the fact that no matter how easy you take it on, you are going to feel the pain of exertion from climbing, altitude, the weather, everything.

It is not unlike the feeling one can take on before a big bike or foot race; your nerves get frayed at the prospects of what you are choosing to take on. Over the years, you learn that when you have a rest day, the best thing to do is to let your guard down and enjoy the experience and to put the climb out of your mind. You can never totally avoid these butterflies, but with a rest day to look forward to, it becomes the same sensation as the end of a workweek anticipating a weekend. We spent that night bullshitting in the small meal tent Pablo set up for us, complete with a table, chairs, and comfort food (cookies, crackers, and even a bowl of apples). Pablo had been on all our Bolivian trips, and he knew our routine and what we liked, and he took great care in making sure we were comfortable. We communicated our plan and he, also being a climber with experience on Illimani many times, encouraged us, but it was not without raised eyebrows and a chuckle.

We slept well that night and woke up after the sun was relatively high and started to hydrate immediately, as well as to load up on carbohydrates for the push. We planned to depart at 10:00 p.m. That would give us enough time to climb and ski the peak and return roughly fifteen hours after that. We needed to descend before the sun melted the snow into sloppy slush and avalanche conditions worsened, especially on the lower slopes. We ate lunch and tried to sleep the rest of the afternoon.

At about 9:00 p.m. we were all dressed and ready to go. We headed back to the mess tent for a small meal and to fill our water bottles. We tried to keep the mood light with jokes and small talk, but the tension was running thick. Steve mentioned that he thought we could be at midmountain in four hours and then at the summit in another four, to which Jim replied that he thought that was "a bit ambitious." We finished our meal, loaded up, grouped together with a "hand in the middle," and as we had grown accustomed to, said a Hail Mary, and asked the good Lord to be with us, to protect us, and to allow us to have a great day.

The time taken two days before to set cairns was noted, and although the walking was not rhythmic across the scree slopes, we made good progress. Once rubber hits the trail, there is always a great relief, and we had to concentrate and communicate about the pace, paying attention not to get ahead of ourselves. We climbed up and down the large moraine slopes, and soon came to an old sign, "Stairway to Heaven," which marked the line of ascent for this route. A ways up, we veered off the normal trail to the bottom of the snow slopes and were excited to find steep hard snow, the cold of night having done its job to aid in a more direct line of ascent compared to the gnarly and exposed rocky ridge. We stepped into our crampons and climbed straight up. Here we were able to gain the desired climber's trance, and soon our steps coincided with our breathing, and we gained an endorphin state of flow. The minutes ticked by like seconds.

Soon, we found ourselves at the midmountain camp, albeit an hour longer than expected (at five hours), where we uncovered our ski gear. We loaded the skis on our backs, roped up to cross the crevasse-riddled slopes above, and after a drink and bite were off again. It was still dark, and the added weight of the ski gear combined with the altitude slowed the pace drastically. But soon our rhythm returned, only to be broken for the occasional view below us that included the lights of La Paz, which took on an odd shade of orange far in the distance with occasional lights of small villages and even single homes dotting the black valley between. The view was beautiful but odd, with the memory of being there looking at where we were now in the middle of the dark night. The dim light of the night allowed us to see the silhouette of the peak, which we viewed with hands over our headlamps to keep us moving in the general direction of the main ridge off to our left.

We had scoped the route enough in the light to know approximately where to go, and higher up found a trail left by an expedition that had climbed when the snow was softer. For us, the snow was hard, perfect for our crampons. As we climbed, the angle grew steeper. We had expected the upper slopes to be steep, and from information from friends who had climbed the route before us, we knew that the upper headwall was more than a thousand feet at forty-five to fifty degrees. We had also been told that the upper slopes were generally "total ice," which was an additional source of anxiety. As we ascended, the ice never materialized, and as the skyline in the direction of the sunrise took on a magenta hue, it became both a great source of excitement and power.

We climbed on, and when we finally reached the steepest slopes, the day had begun. The slopes were still in the shade, but far above we could see the sun gracing the upper slopes. The snow was nearly perfect for climbing, and with that, we also knew we had hit Illimani at the right time for nearly perfect skiing conditions as well. Again, we had to control our excitement and not climb past the next step too quickly. We still had a long climb to the summit. Each step drew us up and closer to the objective. At a slight dip in the middle of the face, before it steepened again, Steve, who was at the front of the rope, asked Jim and me if we needed a picket for a running belay to protect a potential fall. But the snow was so perfect we opted for none. We just wanted to keep going. The exposure was great, but we were very comfortable with the climbing.

I was on the end of the rope, and near the top of the headwall, I had to jerk it to slow Steve and Jim. They were just cruising toward the summit. I had literally and figuratively hit the wall. My pace slowed down the entire team. As I crested the flatter terrain between the top of the headwall and the bergschrund guarding the final summit slopes, Steve and Jim searched for a snow bridge. I gulped down the remainder of the Gatorade in my first water bottle, knowing I still had a full bottle left, then slammed a couple of caffeinated packets of energy goo to keep me going. The summit was within striking distance, and although I was running on fumes, nothing was going to prevent me from getting to the top. Steve and Jim found a usable snow bridge, and we carefully crossed the steep short pitch to the summit ridge, which was a long but gentle stroll to the summit.

I kept talking to myself to the very end: "All I have to do is keep up with that rope, just walk two football fields, that's it." It was agonizing for me for obvious reasons. My depleted situation was complicated by the reality that the very close summit ahead fueled Steve and Jim to want to go faster. I yelled at them to slow down, and they acquiesced. Twenty minutes later, there was nothing but perfectly blue sky in every direction. Steve's prediction of eight hours was, in fact, a bit optimistic, but after ten hours, we were on top.

At the summit, we could see the Altiplano behind La Paz, and, beyond that, the entire Cordillera Real, where we had often climbed. Closest to us was the massif of Murrata, which had the longest glacier in northern South America. To the north, we could see the solo white pyramid of the highest peak in Bolivia, Sajama, and the expanse of the Punta Atacama Desert. The summit was flat, which allowed us to relax. But there was a cornice toward our line of descent, so we had to pay attention not to get too close to the edge, which prevented us from looking down the face we had just climbed.

We spent fifteen minutes on top, and not being acclimated, the altitude crept into our heads leaving us dizzy with hypoxia. My eyes were completely dilated—my body's warning sign that I needed to descend quickly. Steve coiled the rope and stowed it in his pack, and we clicked into our skis. The gentle summit ridge was easy skiing on nearly perfect snow. I skied first and got to the spot where we would regain the face so that I could film the guys skiing off the summit. The first turns as you regain your ski legs are always a source of anxiety—for me that day, even more so. I was beyond exhausted. But after a few sliding turns, I gained my composure and relaxed to find gravity was working, and I was skiing at 21,150 feet. The skiing was on a slight crust, which would normally be of no concern, but in my debilitated state I had to concentrate. Nonetheless, the reality of skiing was overwhelming. Steve and Jim followed, and at the edge we peered down the route, now completely in the light of day. The distance we had covered from base camp was so great we could not find the small tents. We sidestepped down the near-vertical ice cliff and let our skis run across the snow bridge, knowing we were not roped and hoping if it broke, our momentum would carry us to the opposite side. Once we were all safely on the other side of the snow bridge, the snow was soft enough that the steepness was of little concern. We spoke of paying attention. A fall was not an option, but in general, the skiing was anticipated with excitement, not fear.

Steve and Jim were faring better than I was that day, and while I enjoyed the skiing immensely, I was completely gassed. My legs ached, and I had to rest every dozen or so turns. Controlling my descent on the crust was taxing my quadriceps and core muscles, and my body screamed in agony at times. Skiing is most definitely a quicker way to get off a peak, but that doesn't translate to easier. To the contrary, it is infinitely more difficult physically. It's a simple reality that when people tax themselves while skiing at altitude, they shoulder their skis and descend on foot with the safety of crampons. Granted, on Illimani, I was not having my greatest day for whatever reason—I honestly don't know why—but the climb is the culprit for a ski mountaineer. When one reads of climbing epics, it is amazing how often climbers get on a summit push and in an effort to make the work less strenuous, they will cache a headlamp and extra gloves, a water bottle, and bit of food in order to shed weight. At altitude, the difference between reaching a summit or not is often decided by the difference of a pound or less; dumping it allows a climber to succeed.

In Andrew Lock's biography, he describes how on one of his summits he cached a pair of gloves, goggles, and a water bottle on his way to the summit and how he felt that only a pound or so of weight out of his pack left him feeling like he was "floating to the summit." Weight is a big deal at altitude. For a ski mountaineer, the additional weight of ski boots and the weight of the skis, bindings, skins, and ski crampons all amounts to twenty pounds or more! And because ski mountaineering is more about skiing, one would never dream of dropping that additional weight. What this amounts to is an entirely different sport. For nine thousand feet, every step on the ascent entailed pushing that weight up that mountain. To do that, and then ski, an anaerobic sport where at an altitude you can't go anaerobic, I was at my limit. Steve and Jim were faring better, but we all had to stop often to lean over our ski poles and let our strength catch up with our bodies. It's the most difficult skiing there is—combined with various places where a fall was simply not acceptable, even more so.

We slowly proceeded, turn by turn, down the mountain, passing the midmountain camp and getting a bit farther down due to the low snow line. We were now a few hours beyond what we anticipated, and the lower slopes were turning to slush. We decided to get back on the ridge and descend on the exposed ridge to avoid possible snow slides. The shady side of the ridge had a few spots of hard snow and precarious down climbing, but because of our past experiences, nothing that remotely demanded a belay. That day, however, in our tired state, we did slow down to belay in a few spots as we were extremely debilitated from the climbing and skiing. We'd taken only fifteen minutes of material rest the whole day; we had been on the go continuously. We reached the bottom of the route and then walked up and over the large moraine ridges, which slowed us to a crawl. Just over sixteen hours later, we were finally back at base camp.

Pablo handed us each a large bottle of Coke and dragged the mess tent chairs out so we could take off our boots. The afternoon sun was gloriously warm, and there was no wind. We marveled at the day, talked about the satisfaction of getting it done and felt a great sense of pride. Another expedition arrived and, upon hearing of our success and the manner in which we accomplished it, we were greeted by their local guides with mui fuente and congratulations. Garnering the respect of local guides is a rare and wonderful thing! I ate a small sandwich, my stomach and body aching beyond hunger, when all I really wanted was hydration. Despite the warm day, my body shivered from a lack of fluids. I grabbed another liter of Coke, headed to my tent, crawled out of my climbing clothes, and relaxed. I drank the entire bottle, and the next thing I realized was the sun was warming my tent, and it was morning.

Illimani filled a massive gap in our brains after the beating we took on Mustagh Atta, and we savored the personal victory in the weeks after the trip. Illimani is by no means in and of itself a monumental mountaineering achievement. It is a fairly standard peak for climbers and sees many guided ascents. The fact that it was one of our first major peaks in 1996 shows that it is not a massive objective by any definition. But it is high, and its reputation has fallen victim to the evolution of mountaineering in general, whereby the notion of style comes into play. There is great disparity between how people view a peak from their couch versus standing at the bottom of it. This is further complicated by the style in which you stand at the base looking at a given peak, and the frailty of human existence comes into play.

Many people have climbed Everest, but not a lot about their accounts can be even remotely related to Reinhold Messner's experience as he climbed the exact same route for the first time without supplemental oxygen, porters, or fixed lines. Such was the case for us on Illimani. Few people had tried to carry ski gear up the peak, and only later did we discover there was only one known ski descent before us. And certainly no one had ever carried skis up the 8,990 feet of total ascent and skied down in the same day. Few if any attempt Illimani without first acclimating on other lesser peaks in the area. We knew this, and in the days before we did it, it is difficult to express the gnawing fear that this generated for us. There was a bit of finality in that fear, but it was more fear of failure and arriving at a point in our careers where we had topped out, so to speak, and were on the "other side." This was exacerbated by the fact that we had failed on the peak in the past.

To finally pull it off was a massive shot in the arm in terms of confidence. It left us with an experience that defined further not who we were but what we were capable of. We didn't put it into the perspective of what others could or couldn't do but correlated directly into our individual progress. Illimani was a drastic step ahead of the pace that we had achieved to that point. While what we did was remarkable, in our minds we knew it was not something that would register much with many others. This furthered our ability to detach from the strings of our egos in that the experience was so overwhelming in our minds that we realized attempting to explain it was impossible, rendering it beyond any need for recognition. Bluntly, it was one of the greatest days of our careers, and that was enough.

A common thread in this story has been the need to feel acceptance and the need to be appreciated by peers. It's a natural and normal desire. While the desire to be acknowledged had evaporated over time, as we walked away from Illimani—the trip being so different to all the previous experiences, and us pushing ourselves so far beyond what we thought we were capable of—nothing else mattered. Illimani was thus, at age forty-eight no less, a massive turning point for us as a trio.

We marched onward not as arrogant ski mountaineers riding on Cloud Nine and looking at ourselves as badasses but rather as three guys that knew enough about themselves to know nothing else mattered. We had most definitely not topped out in our careers and in fact were looking forward to our newly found passion to climb and ski in the Himalaya in the winter. Before we arrived back home, we mapped out a plan to return to Mustagh Atta with the knowledge that we were capable of more than we realized before our previous attempts. We enjoyed a sort of liberation in that there was no need to hype anything, no need for validation, but also, no need to hide from the discussion if it came up, and no need to expand on anything other than working toward the common goal—to get back to China as soon as possible.

Steve, Jim, and I were all reaching middle age, and with that, the nagging aches and pains that come with age became a source of irritation. Up until that time, we had trained as we always had, with a desire for new ideas on how to train and an enjoyment from putting them into action. Steve and I had been passionate mountain bikers all our lives, and we spent hours every day riding as much as we could. Much of this was driven by our annual pilgrimage to race in the Leadville 100, but after thirteen trips on that course, I had had enough. The endless hours bent over my handlebars combined with the jarring that comes with riding a mountain bike had taken its toll. Steve experienced major back issues as well, and we realized something had to give. We couldn't push ourselves that hard over the summer if we were to expect any results climbing in the Himalaya in winter. So, we dropped our emphasis on racing bikes, and took up lots of speed hiking, taking on the thirty-one hundred feet of altitude gain that Aspen Mountain offered for lunch breaks and after-work routines.

We backed off from daily training to training five days a week. We also adhered to the saying that at age forty it's use it or lose it; we continued our resistance training in the gym to maintain muscle integrity. Our training took on a power and endurance effort that mixed up our routines. The beauty of having a large expedition looming is that it lights a fire under a guy to put in the time. This was further advanced by being able to train in the mountains, which also offered a test to see the results. By the fall season, as the snow accumulated into early winter, we found ourselves climbing and skiing as often as possible on the ski slopes, in particular Snowmass ski area, which offered more than four thousand feet of slogging to thirteen thousand feet, which we could easily accommodate before or after work in a few-hour workout door to door.

Jim had a similar arena on the front range near Denver. By December, we were hitting these routes a couple times per week, and the summer's effort paid off. We were as ready physically as we had ever been for a return to Mustagh Atta.

The need for cash was obvious, and over the summer I was responsible for raising the $30,000 required for the trip. With such short notice, that was a difficult proposition, but by piecing together contacts and using a film project, *Beyond Skiing Everest*, I found our sponsors and friends were more than happy to offer support. I was able to raise all but our airline tickets.

We headed off to Kashgar mid-January for another attempt at climbing and skiing the yet-to-be-climbed-in-the-winter peak. The definition of insanity—that is, trying the same thing over and over and getting the same result—was the furthest thing from our minds as we headed toward the beastly objective with the increased experience, improved footgear, and a year's worth of additional training under our belts. One way or another, we were going to conquer this beast, and we were excited and confident for another try. At this juncture, I could suggest you reread the previous account of the trip because although we were vastly improved on all levels, we experienced an almost identical scenario on this attempt. But it does warrant a description of a few details in that although the scenario was almost identical, the expedition was a massive step in furthering our development as ski mountaineers.

With the experience we gained on Illimani, we decided that we had to move the first camp a thousand feet farther up the mountain to accommodate a slightly different plan. We had no doubt that for any reasonable success, the summit effort would play out from Camp 1. The idea was to put in a single tent and stove three thousand feet above Camp 1 as a "soup camp"; we would not be sleeping or staying the night, but rather rehydrating a few hours on our journey toward the summit. This would break up the nearly ten thousand feet into basically two legs and would limit our time at altitude as well as exposure to the cold. The plan was sound and really the only feasible way of attempting the peak in our view. So, we set out accordingly, and gave it our best effort.

But Mustagh Atta is a very large mountain, and as mountains go, they don't sit in a vacuum; from season to season and year to year, conditions can change drastically. The temperature this year was significantly warmer than on our two previous attempts, albeit still extremely cold. Obviously, this buoyed our confidence. Instead of minus sixty at Camp 1, it was a balmy minus forty. But with the warmer temperature came a devastating wind. From above the moraine above base camp, the wind was constantly strong enough to make walking without ski poles impossible. We acclimated to the fact that it was a lot windier and eventually found success putting in Camp 1 a bit higher, but by the third climb to that camp, we had lost as many tents. We did bring double-walled tents for this expedition, which offered more wind stability, but our quiver of inventory for these tents was slowly being shredded. In all our previous expeditions using similar tents—including a windy month that one tent spent at the north col on Everest—we had never shredded one of these tents. Poles were snapped, and eventually the serrated points of the fractures ripped the tents and overlaying flies. This was not good at all.

By the end of the expedition, we had never gotten above our Camp 1, and except for a single very pleasant night sleeping there, the wind raged constantly. We found ourselves looking once again at a blitz attempt to get as high as possible.

As we set off, the wind hammered us, blowing us off balance. We arrived at Camp 1 to yet another shredded tent and knew the game was over. As we pulled the camp, the wind—seemingly out of nowhere—unleashed its fury. We loaded our packs, strapped on the skis, and hefted our packs (about seventy pounds apiece) onto our backs. As I waited for Steve to get his pack on, I leaned on my poles. As I turned slightly to start heading down, the wind caught my skis and pack and whipped me to my knees. This was going to be a brutal descent. I started to inch forward on my poles, trying to find the angle where the wind had the least resistance. The trail to Camp 1 is a well-beaten path of switchbacks during the normal climbing season, and at least one direction offered less resistance than the other, but the turns were something that required a bit of getting used to. The wind would blow us to our knees, and it was not letting up. I was down farther than Steve, and after a while I took a knee and a break. I was sweating profusely, and the cold and wind was freezing my suit and pack straps. I was not cold and knew I would be back at base camp soon. I had no alternative.

I sat there not even able to hear myself breathe, for moments wondering how we were going to get off this peak. Then, out of the corner of my eye, I saw that Steve was cartwheeling across the slope, the wind blowing him like a rag doll. I instinctively stood up to run up to him, and as I raised myself to a standing position, the wind caught me square on my front side, and I was completely airborne, flying. I landed several yards off the trail, thankfully on my pack. I looked up, and Steve waved that he was okay. I rolled onto my stomach to catch my breath.

Ground effect is a term used in aviation whereby wind over a slope ceases at a level where enough physical masses break it up. On the talus slope, there were rocks about one to two feet high, and I found that on my stomach, I was out of the wind. I was glad I was not a few hundred feet farther up the glacier; a smooth glacier offers no ground effect, and we would have without question been blown completely off the peak. I crawled back to the trail, found coverage behind a large rock, and waited for Steve and Jim to catch me. I noticed that the wind was constant, but if I held my head just right, I could hear the large gusts hitting the ridge across from us. Several seconds later it would reach us. I had to listen and slither, hitting the deck when I heard the gusts. Fear was superseded by the intense concentration required to slowly descend, literally inch by inch, often in a crawl.

What took us a few hours to ascend after being acclimated took us seven hours to descend. I finally found myself at a point just above base camp, below the nearby moraine, and the wind was blocked for a reprieve. I sat on a rock and waited. Jim is about thirty pounds lighter than Steve and me, and the difference made his descent even more difficult. The wind thrashed Jim into submission; when he finally reached me sitting on the rock, he was white as a sheet and running on fumes. The terror of the descent in that wind forced us to sit for a moment to regroup, despite the short walk back to the base camp dome.

As we sat and regained a bit of our sanity, the relief of being down washed over us. We had never remotely experienced a day like that during any of our trips. Our bodies slumped as the adrenalin left our blood, leaving us standing in the cold, drenched with sweat that crusted into ice. As the cold seeped back into our bodies after the exertion, we realized for the first time how incredibly cold it really was. Ironically, during the battle to get down, cold was the least of our concerns despite the wind chill from the storm. We checked each other for frost nip and noted that all our fingers and toes were oddly warm. We became conscious of the power of the mind in such circumstances. The reality is that this was probably the most dangerous day in our entire careers, yet in the battle to survive, there was some power beyond consciousness that allowed our bodies to survive, a power that superseded any thought; we were on auto pilot—concentrating without thinking. As we loaded our packs on our backs and plodded back to the tent, we were conscious of where we were, what we had done, and that we had survived. There was no need to celebrate. We didn't even have a sense of relief. Rather, a feeling of gratitude and satisfaction came over us. The feeling redefined the term *success* whereby the feeling also exceeded any past experience as a source of accomplishment. We were three men, three ski mountaineers, situated in arguably the most difficult environment in the world, and we were experiencing it all at that moment. There was no further need to look for beta on climbing and skiing in the Himalaya in the winter. There was no need to compare ourselves to anyone or to compare Mustagh Atta to any mountain. We had summited a psychological mountain, and survival was the success. Mustagh Atta in the winter had pushed us to our physical, mental, and spiritual limits, and we had succeeded. All the trips before, all the preparation for that trip had paid off.

Back home, we recovered from the expedition and life slowly resumed its normal course. But the experience had humbled us.

We had pushed ourselves to the limit and survived, which was slowly accepted with relief. That relief, however, was not at the expense of our desire to continue with our effort to climb and ski in the high Himalaya in the winter. But the experience left a massive impression. It was an experience we had no desire to repeat. We didn't want to get caught in the wind on Mustagh Atta again. Indeed, we, made a conscious decision to do whatever we could to avoid such exposure.

First, that included an acceptance that Mustagh Atta in winter would remain unclimbed—let alone skied—by us. Enough was enough; three times was most definitely not a charm. But the experience also painted a picture in our minds of places where we could more realistically take our experience and use the natural landscape to help avoid the issues that prevented us from obtaining a greater success. Namely, we realized that Mustagh Atta was a stand-alone windsock, with nothing to block the fierce winds from all directions. We realized we needed to find a peak buried in a range between large peaks where the winter winds would be more broken up. Again, we reached out to Kari Kobler and asked him to figure out a seven-thousand-meter peak that was more shielded, which would give us a better chance.

While the cold was obviously something we couldn't avoid, by reviewing data on the internet, we learned the more southern regions of the Himalaya, toward Nepal, were nearly twenty degrees warmer than what we experienced on Mustagh Atta. Also, being farther north, the days on Mustagh Atta were much shorter. The dark of night didn't allow the sun's rays to penetrate nearly to the extent that it did on peaks like Shishapangma and even Everest, which were situated at nearly the same latitude as Miami. We could expect temperatures at seven thousand meters to be minus sixty or so, but there was no evidence of what we saw on Mustagh Atta, where temperatures ranged from minus sixty to minus ninety—and on a few days to minus triple digits. We could handle the pure cold. The wind was the bigger issue, and if we could solve that, a bit warmer would give us an even better shot at what we were looking for—a winter ski descent from above seven thousand meters.

Kari initially suggested we return to Norjin Kansang, which was also on our radar. We knew the peak, and it was a more realistic objective. Then the Chinese Mountaineering Association quashed that idea when they informed us that Tibet was closed in the winter from October to March. Kari got back to us a few weeks later with another suggestion, a seven-thousand-meter peak located in the Annapurna region that was located between Annapurna itself, and another high seven-thousand-meter peak. The issue was access, and without a helicopter—an added cost of nearly $15,000—it was not possible.

But a review of the peak suggested that it was a great objective that fell within our criteria, and we set out to see if we could raise the funds. By this time in our careers, we were all fifty years old, and the pitch was not easy; our gear manufacturers didn't see the marketability of our ugly mugs combined with the extreme nature of what we were attempting. Even if it there was no age discrimination, it was difficult to reconcile old dogs having any reasonable chance for success. It was extremely difficult to educate them that the irony of climbing let alone skiing in the winter Himalaya was not a young man's game if only because the main ingredient for success was experience.

Experience was required just to realistically take it on. Looking back at our careers, until we found ourselves in the winter Himalaya, it was difficult to imagine being there any earlier than we were. I leveraged this concept, and while the arm-twisting was extreme, we found success with our clothing manufacturer, Mammut. Mammut was in the process of working with a North American down gear-maker, Feathered Friends, to rebrand Mammut's need for more available down products for its North American line. They had down suits produced for the expedition and threw a bit of cash toward the effort with the idea that they could use the project to market it all.

We had also formed a relationship with the manufacturer of our heated insoles, Thermacell. They were already using our images, and with the notion that I had started a sequel to *Skiing Everest*, which I would call *Beyond Skiing Everest*, they defrayed the bulk of the financial burden. Then, a helicopter company in Nepal threw a curveball at us under the guise of "increased fuel costs"—simply, an additional $12,000 for the long chopper ride. This was probably an unscrupulous manager trying to plug a hole in his cash flow, the winter being an extremely slow time of year for the helicopter industry, but he had us over a barrel. I went back to work finding the additional funding.

As luck would have it, I met a family friend, a wealthy individual who also had an enormous passion for mountain culture, and in a fifteen-minute gondola ride, I explained the situation. I was by no means making a pitch and would have never hinted at asking him for any funding, but apparently my heartfelt despair resonated. The next day, he showed up at my office and explained he wanted to help us "achieve our dreams." I explained that our conversation was not even remotely an appeal to get him to write a check, which he confirmed was not how he interpreted the conversation. He later said he saw us as guys doing remarkable things in the mountains through which many others could vicariously live, especially if a film was involved. He added that he wanted no acknowledgement for the contribution and that it was a deeply personal gift. He said that he could easily afford it and that it would bring Steve, Jim, and me a great opportunity. Wow!

I called Steve and Jim, who were simply speechless at the prospects of being able to proceed with a project that was pretty much dead just the day before. Steve called Kari, and three days later we wired funds to his Swiss bank account. The trip was a go.

Over the years, we had learned not to let ourselves get too far ahead of anything, whether it was the next camp or even the next flight. We had a few weeks to get everything in order. Work—dealing with year-end tax returns, tax planning, and just wrapping up clients' accounting—was difficult. Steve and I had to basically cram two months of normal year-end work into twenty days. Jim on the other hand worked at Wells Fargo Bank as a programmer, and in the corporate world he merely scheduled his vacation and worked status quo, not wanting to leave his team in the lurch with his absence but knowing it really didn't matter; this was his time.

I envied Jim a bit during these pretrip moments—my name and reputation being on the line and not wanting to let anyone down. But the push also served a purpose. It was money in the bank to pay all the bills while I was gone, and then all the bills that had to be paid immediately on my return; there is no vacation pay for a business owner. The contrast between being a corporate employee and the freedom of running my own business was worth the effort. The other peripheral benefit was that by the time

Steve and I wrapped everything up, we relished the thought of the thirty-odd-hour flight to get to Asia. After the tearful goodbyes, we could walk out the ramp and take our seats, and there was nothing to worry about. If we missed something, it had to wait. We were comforted by the fact that after having done this for so many trips in the past, we had it all down. Occasionally I would experience an "oh, shit" moment, but it was soon forgotten, trumped by the ultimate excuse that it must wait.

Our itinerary ultimately brought us to Kathmandu, and upon arrival at our hotel, we headed to the Nepal Mountaineering Association office to pick up our permit and meet our mandatory liaison, a stoic lady who clearly had zero desire to accompany us to base camp during the winter and after the meeting was never seen again. She was on the ultimate vacation and with a wink and a kiss left us to not blow her cover. We were also introduced to two Sherpa—Sherpa being now required by the Nepal Department of Tourism to accompany all teams climbing in Nepal after a series of tragedies on Everest. These guys were super expensive but part of the requirement. We were not interested in having them porter our gear up Himlung, but they were extremely eager to make a winter ascent of a seven-thousand-meter peak, a massive résumé-builder for their careers. We figured we would climb with them to accommodate their goals.

Dorji Sherpa and Lundup Sherpa were extraordinarily strong members of Kari's staff, great guys with the mind-set to fit in with the three of us—they understood our ribbing and joking around. They were also super strong. We welcomed them, and we made it clear that if there was a summit to be made, they could snag the first winter ascent (Himlung had never been climbed in winter). We would be more than happy with a first descent. The gesture was taken by Dorji and Lundup graciously, and with a bit of disbelief, but we made it clear that they were part of our team and not working for us in the normal way Himalayan expeditions evolved. We had mutual respect.

We loaded into a bus the next day and headed back to the airport. Our bags were searched, and after the discovery of our satellite phone, for which we had no permit, we were hit with a $1,500 ticket. With a wad of cash, the bribe was made, and we were off to the tarmac. We quickly learned that we were about fifty pounds too heavy for the comfort of the pilot, and we discarded bits and pieces of luxury gear. We were soon aloft, flying over Kathmandu toward the Himalaya, towering above the clouds. I had never been in a helicopter before that, and the sensation was odd, but soon I relaxed and gazed in a daze as the whiteness of the mountains drew closer and closer. We flew for an hour or so and descended into a deep valley to a small village where a person was standing next to several large gas cans. The helicopter had to land to refuel. After twenty minutes, we were airborne again and flying through a deep canyon. Around a corner, the pyramid of Himlung loomed ahead, and we could see plumes of snow blowing into the deep blue sky. It was not massive wind but rather typical alpine spindrift from the constant summit breeze. Below, we could see a yellow tent and knew this was base camp, albeit the location slightly higher than we had anticipated.

We landed, and our altimeters registered fifteen thousand feet, a thousand feet higher than we were told to expect. We worked quickly to unload all the gear as the helicopter idled. As soon as the last bag was off, the pilot gunned the machine, and it immediately launched into the air. We snapped photos of the helicopter as it flew down the valley and became difficult to see, giving contrast to the vastness of the terrain and environment where we found ourselves. The cold was immediate, but there was no wind, and the radiant heat was welcomed.

Our initial concern of going from five thousand feet to fifteen thousand feet was soon confirmed. We were led to the double-walled insulated base camp tent where a heater was warming the small space. A thermos of hot tea and cookies was set on a table. As we sat—after the hurry of organizing the loads—our heads began to spin. We were high, perhaps too high for comfort. My reaction was to immediately walk outside and see if there was any way to access a lower elevation. From what I could tell, there was no feasible place farther down the valley to set up an acclimation camp. My heart raced in fear. I could barely stand with hypoxia taking over and destroying much of my physical equilibrium. I quieted my panic with the notion that I just needed to sit and catch my breath. I asked for coffee in order to get a bit of caffeine into my blood, which would increase circulation and supply the needed oxygen. Then I tried to make myself as still as possible.

None of us had any mountain sickness at the moment—no nausea or headaches—and we vowed to let time heal the immediate wound. We would sit for the next few days to acclimate, and if we needed more time, we would take it.

Over the next few days, our bodies slowly adjusted, and we laughed at the thought of where we were. To that point, getting to fifteen thousand feet was always a weeklong process of hiking in to a base camp or at least hanging out at lower altitudes, regardless if the upward progress was slow. It was eye-opening to subject ourselves to altitude that quickly, and we were astonished at what we experienced. Fifteen thousand feet is not much higher than where we had been training, but the reality of not slowly attaining that altitude, as in all previous trips, was interesting—a lesson learned better late than never. Base camp was our refuge for additional altitude problems, and we took the time to hang out and give ourselves the window of safety we badly needed. We agreed the valley was one of if not the most beautiful place we had ever been. It was vast and wide and surrounded by no less than four seven-thousand-meter nearly vertical peaks. With the clear weather, it was beyond description, looking almost fake it was so magnificent. Soon, however, with acclimation taking hold, we found ourselves ready to hit the trail and experience more of it.

Our initial plan was to climb Himlung via a standard ridge route, but it was clear from the snow conditions, as well as a handful of recent naturally released avalanches, that the snow conditions were dismally bad. The ridge route was a death trap. The season before, Lundup had put in a route from the valley floor below, and while it was extremely long, he said it was possible. It was our only option. We were glad that he had previous experience, and he became the point person for logistics moving forward. Regardless, we knew we were in for a bit more adventure than we had planned for.

At camp, we studied the route, which would lead across a massive glacier. This would involve getting from where we were down a cliff to the glacier three hundred feet below. We fixed a line to rappel down, and then, with a handful of wands, set across the dry glacier, often using the position of the sun to keep us moving in the general direction of another cliff on the opposite side. The glacier was a jumble of ridges and cliffs, lakes, and frozen glacier-melt streams. We would head in one direction only to find it impossible to proceed. Then we would backtrack and head in another direction. The distance was only three or four miles as the crow flies, but the glacier features created a maze. After a long day, we had found a route through to the other side where we were confronted by a cliff like the one that we'd descended. We climbed it to get to the base of the route.

We did not have any fixed line for this section, but it was not vertical. It was, however, very steep and covered with dirt and talus—easy enough to climb, but it was treacherous to descend unprotected—a fall being fatal. The wall was also longer and higher, and for five hundred feet of it, you had to really concentrate on each step. With the anticipated back and forth, it was a gnawing obstacle that we dreaded. If we weren't fearing a slip and fall, the constant rock fall, ranging from pebbles to house-sized boulders, was enough to ruin the sanctity of the place. On the first carry, we climbed the cliff and cached our loads at the lip. Putting the route in had taken its toll, and we were too tired to climb farther to Camp 1. We carefully descended the cliff to the glacier below and followed our newly marked route back to base camp.

After a rest day we headed back across the glacier and proceeded to climb the gentle slopes to just under eighteen thousand feet. The snow was horrifically rotten, and we were glad we were not up on the ridge. The crust was not strong enough to support us until about halfway, where it became a mix of sastrugi lips and ledges with rotten deep snow between. But the day was windless, there were no clouds, and although the air was cold, for the first time on any winter trip, the exertion allowed us to ascend in relatively normal gear—our shells over underlayers. The quiet was deafening, and the mass of the peak lay before us, the contrast of the rock and snow against the deep blue sky making the scene distant but close.

Our Camp 1 was perched on a knoll above a long precarious ridge that required taking the skis off, as it had been blown free of snow, making for awkward travel with the deep snow between the talus rocks. Our loads were huge, but with no time limit, we proceeded slowly. Dorje and Lundup did not have skis, and they struggled through the deep snow with a power and agility only Sherpa exhibit. We reasoned the spot was protected from the wind, set up the camp, and carefully descended back to the valley below. The skiing was marginal, and with the soft, deep, hidden spots between the rock-hard patches, it was more sliding with skis on our feet than actual skiing, but we did manage to make ski turns, which "made everything cool." We arrived back at base camp under a calm sky. We needed to rest for a push to the new camp the next night. We didn't let our guard down in the sense that we realized we were in the Himalaya in winter, but we savored the incredible day and relaxed evening.

The next morning, we awoke to fresh snow and a strong wind. We would stay put at base camp for the next few days while the storm, which really caught us by surprise, raged on. The wind at base camp was powerful, so we knew it would be worse higher up. However, the conditions were still not nearly as severe as our previous experiences. We took advantage of the days off, and on the third day gave our extra ski gear to the Sherpa and watched them ski on the gentle slopes behind camp. Skiing is a universally loved sport, and although the Sherpa flailed, they couldn't get enough. Lundup requested the skis for his next journey to our camp, and promised that if the slopes became too much, he would take them off and carry them down; we didn't need a blown knee or other injury.

The morning of our departure back to Camp 1 came with perfect weather, and we set out at a reasonable hour with lighter loads. We felt strong from the acclimation and rest. At the cache where we left our skis at the other side of the glacier, we clicked into our skis—including Lundup—and proceeded up the slopes, which had a blanket of new snow. On the steeper sections, Lundup could not get a grip on the hard snow. He left the skis and proceeded on by foot, but we ascended with much greater ease than on the previous trip. We arrived at Camp 1, where the wind was, not surprisingly, more forceful than at base camp. One of our tents was shredded, a pole broken and ripping through the nylon. Unknown to us, Dorji had carried an extra tent for the summit push, and we set it up for the night. But looking at the tent was a reminder to us all of where we were and what we were attempting. Flashbacks of Mustagh Atta raced through our minds, but with a beautiful afternoon ahead of us, it was soon forgotten. We spent a comfortable night and headed back to base camp the next day, excited that the next push would be for the summit.

The plan was to get back to base camp, rest for a couple of days, then head back up to Camp 1, then carry gear to a spot for a second camp, and then attempt the summit. We rested for two days, and the weather changed. By this time, we had burned through a week. The extra days to acclimate at the beginning, and then the few days of the first storm were lost, and the prospects for the summit bid were, again, painting us into a corner. We had budgeted two weeks for the climbing, and at this stage, we were a solid week behind that schedule.

The storm was not a snowstorm, but rather a wind event. Another day turned into a few more days, and we found ourselves in the same position as on Mustagh Atta—at the end of our trip. The only difference was that on Himlung, we were at the end of the good weather envelope. While there was no way to predict the start of the spring monsoon, it was a rule of thumb that anyone climbing in that part of the range really needed to be out by February 20. We were seeing changes in the weather, and they were for the worse.

Finally, with three days left to spare, the day dawned perfect. We didn't have time to establish a Camp 2, but we reasoned we had Camp 1 in a great place at eighteen thousand feet, and if we could get to it by afternoon, then spend three or four hours brewing up and resting, the prospects of attaining the summit were good. Lundup said it was entirely possible for our team based on how well we had performed up to that point. The route was superlong but not nearly as long as the route on Mustagh Atta, and the summit was nearly a thousand feet lower. The day was perfect, with zero wind, and we were excited with the plan to blitz the peak as we had on Illimani. On Illimani we'd tackled nine thousand feet of climbing in a day—Himlung would require a thousand feet less than that. Overall, Himlung was two thousand feet higher than Illimani, but we were completely acclimated to eighteen thousand feet, and it all played into our psychology to know we were going to be taking on the largest day in our lives. We had progressed to this point, and we had the confidence to take on the task at hand.

With no loads, we set off at 11:00 p.m. and settled into a very slow and reasonable pace, one that would conserve our energy. I will never forget the peaceful feeling of the moment as we crossed the now fairly well-beaten path across the glacier. Even the cliffs guarding camp from the glacier and the route on the other side had been traveled enough to become if not familiar, not the dreaded death track they were when we first scaled them. We were on autopilot, in the climber's trance, wandering along a set path toward an objective we had the confidence for. With little said, we found ourselves at Camp 1 and crawled into the tents to brew up. Being in the bottom of the valley, the sun began to set on us. We rested peacefully. Jim later recalled that he even heard snoring.

At 9:00 p.m., we got up and put our boots on. The night was beyond cold. Stars dotted the sky, and we could see the faint lights of base camp across the valley. We were in our down suits, with our heated insoles turned on, following Lundup who became a guide as he was the only one who knew the route from this point. The slopes from here up three thousand feet were on the steep left side of the ridge we had avoided to begin with, the objective being to skirt around a massive icefall that threatened the upper cwm slopes that led above to the summit pyramid of Himlung. The climbing was on the same rotten snow, which had seen a fresh layer added during the storms that set us back, and the climbing was massively difficult. Crampons were a hindrance in the deep snow and talus, so we took them off despite the steepness of the slope. We took turns breaking trail, stopping at wide avalanche-prone gullies and crossing one at a time. After several hours, the sky started to brighten with the dawn of another day, and we found ourselves on a high ledge looking ahead to the top of the ice fall.

Lundup was uncertain if the route was climbable as we proceeded to a crux of sorts, a traverse on sloping talus and ice that skirted around a buttress a thousand feet above the glacier. It was dark enough so that we didn't fully appreciate the exposure, but on Lundup's previous attempt, this section was fully fixed to prevent a fall, the consequence of which was certain death. There was a narrow ledge that held snow, and to our relief, it was frozen solid. We used ski poles to carefully balance step by step across the ledge—three hundred to four hundred feet or so—praying the snow would not come loose and fall off the sloping rocks. We fully realized that there was nothing to grab if it did, and nothing to arrest on between the trail and the abyss. We proceeded, tapping the snow with our feet to test its integrity.

At the end of the traverse, there was a cave formed by rock on one side and ice from the glacier on the other. Above that was a jumble of seracs and crevasses, then a smooth glacier above. We put on our crampons and roped up. Lundup and Dorji were now moving much quicker than the three of us as we were carrying skis, and they rushed ahead with a small spool of rope to fix a few ice steps. We followed their lead quickly, and the brief stop to rope up allowed the cold to seep into our bodies; we had to keep moving.

The sky grew lighter, but we were in the shade. Still, the sun blanketed the peaks on the other side and the higher reaches of Himlung, which gave us a mental boost. By this time, several hours out from Camp 1, our heated insole batteries were done. We had planned to spot heat through the night, but the cold was too much, so we held them on high as long as they would go, hoping the light of day would be enough to finish without freezing our feet. The chem packs in our mittens were still putting out heat, but with the constant gripping of ski poles and metal ice axes, our fingers were growing numb. Fortunately, if we kept moving, the cold could not supersede the warmth in our down suits. We were by no means toasty warm, but we weren't shivering from the cold either. We moved our toes and fingers in our boots and mittens as we plodded along.

The top of the icefall was a broken jumbled mess of seracs and crevasses, which demanded respect and our attention as we climbed through it. After negotiating a last large crack, we looked forward to a gently sloping cwm that lead to the summit ridge. The path looked short until we saw Dorji and Lundup as dots far ahead. But with the gentle slope we could take our skis off our packs and skin the terrain. We quickly transitioned to our skis and were off, again staying one step ahead of the extreme cold. It felt great to take the weight off our shoulders, and although there were still crevasses along the way, the freedom to be on skis was comforting and the movement efficient.

We plodded along in the shade, but with the growing light could finally see the slopes to our left, up to the avalanche-prone ridge. For the first time, we could see the reality of the route, and it was not comforting. We had climbed the entire night directly below massive ice cliffs and a collection of odd five-hundred-foot pillars of ice. There were remnants along the entire way—massive ice seracs that had fallen across our path—with no way to skirt out of the line of fire. At this altitude, the ridge and slopes were void of snow, the wind having blasted them down to cold blue ice. The situation was so dangerous that it made us shake. We had been rolling the dice, almost the entire way. Knowing this, we started moving faster than normal, and we had to control our pace to not wear ourselves out. We quickly caught Dorjee and Lundup, who were stopped at the only safe spot, a point where fifty-degree ice led above them a couple of rope lengths to the summit ridge. At a distance, this didn't seem a problem, and with the summit only fifteen hundred feet up another lesser ridge, we were excited. We gave each other the thumbs-up; the prospects of topping out were great. As we approached the Sherpa, however, we couldn't figure out what was going on.

Lundup was standing one foot on the short face leading to the ridge, fumbling with an ice screw to fix a small vertical bulge before the lesser terrain above. He tried hammering the screw in. He switched out screws. Then, he tried to climb a bit higher, and his crampons slid down the ice like roller skates. As we pulled in to Dorji, he looked at us and threw his hands up in despair. We unroped and walked over to the slope to check things out. He said the ice was too cold and hard to get any protection in, but worse, he could not get his crampons to bite, nor could he swing his axe hard enough to gain purchase.

I swung my axe into the ice, and it pinged off, barely scratching the surface as if I had been hitting solid granite. I had heard of glacier ice so hardened by the cold and wind that it was not climbable, but I always thought it was a bit of a myth. How could solid steel not penetrate ice? But here we were, experiencing what in our climbing career was the irony of all experiences; the ice was so hard we could not protect the climbing with titanium ice screws. Axes would bounce off, and crampons skated off the ice like sneakers. Yet moments later after we took our skins off our skis, the cold almost prevented them from gliding. We made a few efforts to find softer ice so we could get to the ridge but to no avail. We had topped out ready and able to reach the summit, but Mother Nature had other plans. We had no choice but to turn around. We also realized that even had we been able to ascend farther, the entire pyramid of Himlung was ice—there was nothing higher to ski. In these moments of a climb, justification comes in small doses but doses nonetheless help soothe wounds.

By the time we had explored the options, we had been standing around for the better part of twenty minutes. I looked at a thermometer attached to my pack, which ended at minus thirty. Based on our experience with a lower thermometer on our previous trip, we reckoned the temperature was about minus sixty, and our altimeters placed us at 21,165 feet. Fortunately, there was little wind, but the altitude impaired our circulation drastically, and the brief stop allowed for any bit of heat to escape our bodies. Our fingers and toes were completely numb, and the warmth of exertion was completely gone despite our layers and down suits. We were as cold as we had ever been. To make matters worse, Lundup was gloveless on his right hand, which was buried in the cuff of his suit. He had dropped the glove while trying to climb the slope and lost it. We reached into our packs for an extra pair of gloves for just the occasion and persuaded him his mistake was just that—it could happen to anyone. That's why we bring extras. We gave him shit to offset his embarrassment, and all was fine. We clicked into our skis and despite the downward slope, used our poles to break up the sticky cold suction that held us back.

The skiing was not steep, and the snow was awkwardly cold and sticky. But to be sliding down the peak from what we realized was an improvement over our last high-point winter ski, once again made everything cool. It was not the greatest skiing, but it was familiar, and we realized the effort of hauling the gear was worth it. We gazed down the valley toward the high peaks, which were now blanketed in the sun's rays. The morning light was transforming the unique magenta hue on the horizon, where it was still dark and early. But we had little time to enjoy the view. The overhanging ice cliffs left little room for anything other than a rapid descent back to our crampon transition point, which we knew was sheltered from ice fall.

We soon found ourselves at that point of refuge, with the sun finally breaking through a valley and lifting our spirits. The day was cold but with no wind. We faced the sun and absorbed its energy. Our toes and feet warmed, causing excruciating pain as the blood rushed to our extremities. We strapped our crampons on if only for the harrowing traverse, which sloped slightly down and was something that kept our guards up. Soon we transitioned and were off. The traverse in light was even more menacing than at night, and as I watched small snowballs bouncing into the abyss, I tried to focus on each next step, leaving me to fight the urge to peer over. Once we all were across, we took off our crampons and with tired clumsiness descended the steep powdery talus slopes back to camp.

At camp, the sun was in full force, and the lower slopes were warm. We sat dazed, in complete and utter exhaustion, while Dorji and Lundup followed, their progress lacking the quick descent aided by our skis. Except for the few hours spent at camp the day before, we had been on the go for twenty-seven hours. We sat wordless, too tired to talk. We fired up the stove and hydrated, and we ate energy goos and power bars to recover as best we could. We still had to pack up the entire camp, ski down to the edge of the glacier on dicey slab-ridden snow, walk back across the glacier, and then climb up the cliff on the other side—all with massive loads. In past journeys across, this was a five-hour effort. With massive loads, after twenty-seven hours climbing to over twenty-one thousand feet all night, we had no idea how long it would take.

After forty-five minutes, we packed everything up, divided the loads among the five of us and were off. The journey back was easily the most difficult physical and mental task any of us had ever experienced. The skiing was nearly impossible. At one point, Steve fell flat on his face, the first time in nearly thirty years of ski expeditions. As he lay there, on his stomach, we couldn't hold back the laughter, but we were relieved when he moved after a minute of what he called "sleep." Walking back across the glacier, our toes and joints screamed with pain. When we arrived at the cliff, we took a few breaths and vowed to get it over with. Climbing up with the aid of the rope, it felt like a summit of summits. At the top, we were only a quarter mile of flat easy walking to base camp, but we had to stop frequently to rest. We finally arrived back at camp, crawled into the base camp tent, and took a coffee break, noting we had been on the go for almost thirty-six straight hours. It was, by leaps and bounds, the longest, most grueling effort in our entire careers. But we had survived!

The weather the next day showed signs of change, and our base camp cook woke us up early with the news that the helicopter was on its way—along with a massive storm. We rose with an adrenaline rush, knowing we were pushing up against some unwritten rules of getting out and wanted to take no chances of getting caught. Despite our aching and tired bodies, we packed up our personal gear immediately. We all then jumped in to pack up the group tents and gear and to get all the bags and equipment to the landing site near camp. It was the quickest pack up we had ever experienced, and we finished just as the whoop-whoop of the helicopter echoed in the valley below. The sky was starting to turn dark, and the wind blew long streams of snow off all the peaks above us.

Soon we were airborne, buzzing down the valley and on our way home. As we flew out of the mountains, the clouds buried the peaks in all directions—we had just made it out. Over the next several days, we heard reports about another expedition on the adjacent peak, Annapurna. That crew survived a dump of nearly fifteen feet of snow. We had made it out just in time. Another day would have pinned us at base camp for the next two weeks. What we lacked in a summit was more than made up for with luck and our ability to plan. As we lofted down out of the Himalaya and over the villages and farmland, the fresh scent of the green valleys and the warmth of the air at the lower elevation enveloped us even in the helicopter. As we drew close to Kathmandu, the scent of lush vegetation was overwhelmed by the smell of the city. It was the familiar but repugnant smell of pollution. After Himlung, however, we welcomed it. It was a testament to what we had achieved. No, we had not attained a summit or even a seven-thousand-meter winter ski descent. What we achieved was not something many people will ever have the chance to experience. It was not just a single experience from a single expedition but rather a culmination of a lifetime experience of natural progression that included dozens of expeditions where we slowly proceeded step by step, moment by moment, into what could only be known by wanting to know, and making a decision to try.

Postscript

After we left Himlung in 2015, we went back to what had become our norm. But in retrospect, when I look back at that expedition, there is a satisfaction that needs to be understood, a satisfaction that even today I am continuing to digest. Shortly after the trip, a writer for *Backcountry* (ski) *Magazine*, who had been following my posts on social media, called me. She had obviously done her homework in the limited way that she could, on the internet. She recounted what she had compiled. In short, she told me she had been in an editorial meeting pitching various stories, and the subject of the "the Marolt brothers" had come up. The consensus was "How could these guys have flown under the radar so long considering the climbing and skiing they have done over a period lasting over three decades?"

To that point, none of us had ever kept a list of all the expeditions and peaks, nor have I expanded on most of them in this essay. She ended up writing a piece titled "The Three Amigos," profiling Steve, Jim, and me, which people seemed to enjoy based on the comments I received after the piece came out. But at this stage, while the ego was pumped, the effect was not something that validated us merely because we had grown past needing or caring about that kind of stuff. But the piece did get me thinking. Why hadn't we ever kept track, and why didn't we leverage our story more than we did?

I put pen to paper and tried to compile the list one lazy afternoon. What surprised me most was how difficult it was. I'd finish what I thought was the list, and wake up in the middle of the night with an "Oh, shit, what about that trip to Peru?" Often, I couldn't even remember the names and heights of the peaks.

After a few attempts, I simply gave up. It struck me as odd that at this stage, in my midfifties, I couldn't care less.

Then locally, the sport of climbing thirteen-thousand-and fourteen-thousand-foot peaks became vogue in the ski mountaineering world. People were keeping track of everything, even going so far as to set up websites so others could track their progress. It never dawned on us to keep track of our days out on Colorado peaks, and we rarely carried cameras on local forays. Our focus was always the next peak in some exotic range, and after each trip, we left with great memories, but we never thought to keep track other than that.

I conservatively estimated that we had several hundred local peaks under our belts, but it was never about anything other than having fun. The local peaks were the ultimate training for our real passion: the high peaks of the greater ranges. We kept track of the larger peaks only from the point of view that it was the accumulation of everything we had done to that point. As each trip ended, it became the basis for figuring out what to do the next—a natural progression that provided a basis for taking on a bit more each time we sat down to plan another adventure. Thus, Himlung was not the end. It was a foundation for the future. There was no need to keep a list of all that led to that point; we always were and still are only focused on the next trip.

One important thing about not achieving the goal of a major project on the scale of what we were doing—to climb and ski from above seven thousand meters in the winter—is that it leaves the door open for finishing unfinished business. If you would have asked me fifteen or twenty years ago if we would still be climbing and skiing in the greater ranges at fifty-five years of age, I would have laughed. Back then, no one at this age was still at this game at the ultimate levels—the high Himalaya in winter. At least I was not aware of anyone. But in our careers, we seem to have hit things perfectly.

When we started, we were strong, passionate, and, in our young minds, unstoppable. It was a period where the gear was extremely heavy and rudimentary. I often wonder how we carried that gear up Shishapangma or any of those high peaks, let alone click in and ski down. It's crazy! But since then, the AT ski industry has grown dramatically, and in turn, the manufacturers have spent millions of dollars on research and development to make the gear significantly lighter and better performing—things we couldn't have dreamed of twenty-five years ago. The development of this gear has exceeded our unmitigated aging. When you combine the gear with our still strong desire to continue climbing and skiing and throw in the added improvements in physical training for an aging population, here we are, at our age, still hungry for adventure. The winter project has thus become a well-calculated endeavor where our experience allows us to progress and not scare ourselves out of the game. Rather, our winter endeavors have allowed us to really understand the cold environment and adapt to it. Thus, my comment made to the author of "The Three Amigos" piece makes sense: "Climbing and skiing in the winter Himalaya is the most miserable but satisfying ski mountaineering we have ever experienced."

Our desire since then has been always to return. The peaks of Nepal in the winter are guarded by heavy snows, making the peaks extremely difficult to access, let alone climb. Tibet is thus a better alternative. But in Tibet, since 2015, the Chinese have closed the region for tourism in the winter. The Tibetan Plateau is devoid of tourists in winter, and the revenue for permits doesn't justify the expense of manning all the border crossings. Our question is that if there are no people, why do you need to man the borders, but that's an argument that can't be taken on let alone won. So, we have continued to twist their arms, and for a brief period in 2016, we were told to "come on in." This was rescinded shortly thereafter, but the process has provided a relationship with the Chinese Mountaineering Association, and they, being climbers, understand our desires, and we are hopeful.

Our ultimate desire is to head back to Cho Oyu for a winter attempt. The chances of climbing Cho—given it has only seen one winter ascent—are minimal, but the terrain is familiar, and the nature of the peak offers a very good chance of a seven-thousand-meter ski. And, with a bit of luck and a warm spell, we might even be able to pull off the ultimate: a winter eight-thousand-meter ski. In the meantime, we have continued to climb and ski, obtaining a couple six-thousand-meter peak first ski descents in the Occidental Range of Peru, as well as an easy gem of a ski off the 18,491-foot El Pico de Orizaba in Mexico. Most recently, in 2019, we found a tiny forty-mile range also in Peru, which to our amazement we had never heard of—not many had—where there are four six-thousand-meter peaks and many five-thousand-meter peaks. We achieved another milestone of sorts with our twentieth ski descent from six thousand meters. We are heading back in spring of 2020 as a training expedition to bag a couple more of those peaks with a goal to then head east in early 2021 to make another attempt at climbing and skiing from above seven thousand meters in the winter on a peak in the Dhaulagiri region of Nepal. No, we are not done yet! Our passion still exists to continue with our adventures, and as Jim was quoted in the article, "we love to climb and ski, and we will continue to climb and ski the highest peaks in the world until we decide we don't want to."

Passion is a strange thing. Don't let anyone tell you something is too dangerous, or that you are not capable, or whatever. Follow your passion to its end. And remember that the ultimate gift is not the objective but who you are with. And above all, passion is not mental. The greatest gift is understanding that you are supposed to follow your passion—do it. One thing I have learned—contrary to what people tell you—is that you can't do whatever you want. That is, by leaps and bounds, far from the truth that is more than clear by this essay. But I can guarantee one thing without question: if you get out and try, you will find you can do a lot more than you ever thought you could.

Steve Marolt skiing off Cayambe, Ecuador Photo Jim Gile >

Mike Marolt skiing Illimani, Bolivia. That was a flash ascent descent netting 9,000 feet of climbing and skiing in a single 17 hour base to base effort. I regard this as one of the largest accomplishments of our careers. We were the first to climb and ski the peak in a single day. Photo Steve Marolt

Mike Marolt skiing Illimani, Bolivia Photo Jim Gile

Steve and Jim descending Mt. Logan in Canada. At that time, circa 1990, we climbed and skied in climbing boots. With massive loads, it was difficult descending at best. Photo Mike Marolt

Mike and Steve Marolt after successfully evacuating Pat Callahan from Mt. Logan. With Jim we managed "slotorama" an all-night push to get from the peak back into Alaska where we had a radio to call for the airplane to get Pat out. photo Mike Marolt

A battered tent on Himlung. During our winter attempts, we lost not less than a half dozen tents to the intense combination of cold which made poles brittle and the high winds common in the winter Himalaya. Photo Jim Gile

2019, on route to a first descent of 20,150 foot Chumpe, Peru. In our mid 50's, we still have gas in the tank. Photo Jim Gile

2017, Steve Marolt on route to a first descent of 20,500 foot Ampato, Peru. Photo Jim Gile

2018 Jim Gile snapped this photo of Steve Marolt, Mike Maple, and myself on 20,000 foot Parincota, Bolivia. We had ferocious weather that year, but with time running out attempted to climb the peak. Maple's fingers started to freeze at this point and we turned around.

2018, we decided on a Monday to head to Mexico to climb and ski 18,500 foot Orizaba. Conditions were wet and rainy until the last day. We skied powder from the summit. Photo Jim Gile

Mike Marolt skiing powder on Orizaba, Mexico. Photo Jim Gile

Mike Marolt climbing on belay over the lip of
Cayambe, Ecuador, 2008. Photo Steve Marolt

2008, Summit of Cotopoxi, Ecuador, Mike Marolt ascents the final steps. Cotopoxi was a gem of a climb and ski, albeit steep incredibly dangerous hard snow and ice. Photo Steve Marolt

2007, Mike Marolt skiing corn snow off the North Col of Everest. Photo Steve Marolt

2016, Steve Marolt ascending the lower slopes of Himlung, Nepal in late January. Photo Jim Gile

2016 our turn-around point on Himlung at just over 21,000 feet. The temp per my thermometer bottomed out at -30. It was probably -60 creating an irony of our climbing career. Ice axes pinged off the cold ice and skis barely slid. We could not set ice screws in the cold ice, nor would our crampons bite for the last steep pitch to the summit. There was no skiing on the icy slope above so that and the ferocious cold made the turning back a no-brainer. Photo Jim Gile

1997, high on Broad Peak. I snapped our mentor, Bob "Sloman" Slozen waking up. Photo Mike Marolt

Steve Marolt approaching 7000 meters on Broad Peak. Photo Mike Marolt

Mike Marolt skiing off Ampato, Peru for the first ski
descent of the peak. Photo Steve Marolt

Mike Marolt sparking arcs in the Elks Range near
home in Aspen. Photo Steve Marolt

2009, Steve Marolt preparing to click into his skis at over 23,000 feet on Norjin Kansang, Tibet. Photo Mike Marolt

2007 Mike Marolt ahead of Jim Gile just above the gold band on Cho Oyu. Cho was an acclimation peak for another attempt at Everest. Steve and I attained our second 8000 meter peak ski and became only the 5th people ever to attain multiple 8k skis. Jim got his first. It was an important benchmark for us in that it proved our ski descent off Shish was not a fluke. Photo Steve Marolt

Mike Marolt on steep terrain at 23,000 feet on Cho. This day was our first high carry so we were not acclimated. Our loads were huge and it ranks as one of the most difficult days I've ever had in the high peaks. Photo Steve Marolt

2007, high on the north ridge of Everest. It's interesting to note that our gear was not much different than we use at home in the Elks Range. Others were clad in down suits, sucking oxygen and struggling. We were just having a good day. Photo Steve Marolt

Steve Marolt and Mike Maple high on Norjin Kansang. Norjin was tough in that the crevasses were long and plentiful. We had massive route finding on our summit day. Photo Mike Marolt

Mike Marolt arcing turns on the lower glacier with Norjin Kansang summit in the background. Photo Steve Marolt

Steve Marolt, Jim Gile, and Maxut Zhumayev contemplating Shishapanma. This was the moment that Steve proclaimed "if I stand on top I will do it on my skis." Max became the youngest climber from Kazakhstan to climb and 8000 meter peak and would go on to become one of the greatest climbers from his country climbing all 14 without supplemental oxygen. Photo Mike Marolt

Mike Marolt at pilot camp after skiing Shishapangma. Photo Steve Marolt

Steve Marolt at about 20,000 feet on Mustagh Atta in our second attempt at the peak. This was the only sunny day. Temps per the weather station on the summit recorded at -100 degrees. It was cold and windy beyond comprehension on that peak. Photo Jim Gile

Steve Marolt making nice turns on fantastic snow on Manaslu. However, in all our expeditions, Manaslu is the only peak I could never recommend. It is an avalanche chute from a to z. Photo Jim Gile

Mike Marolt fighting wind and cold on Mustagh
Atta in the winter. Photo Steve Marolt

Steve Marolt skiing past climbers at 25,000 feet on the North
Ridge of Mt. Everest. They were clad head to foot in down and
sucking supplemental oxygen. The looks on their faces as we skied
by was as if they had seen flying frogs. Photo Mike Marolt

2000, Steve Marolt making last steps to the Centeral Summit of Shishapangma. He proclaimed if he stood on top he'd stand on skis. He made good on that! Photo Mike Marolt

Steve Marolt high on Shishapangma on our summit bid. 20 minutes later we found ourselves in high wind and whiteout conditions. At that moment, however, it was a glorious view. I remember telling myself as we picked up from this rest, "this is what it's all about!" That moment sealed my fate; I became a high altitude skier. Photo Mike Marolt

Steve Marolt in front with skis, followed by Jim Gile at just over 7000 meters on Shishapangma. Just up the ridge, I asked Steve is we should drop our skis and he looked at me as if I just insulted our mother and continued on not missing a step. I followed. Photo Mike Marolt

Team photo Shishapanma. Maxut Zhumayev, Koonte ??, Jim Gile, Vadim Khaibullin, Steve Marolt, Cherie Silvera, Mike Marolt, Pat Morrow Photo Mike Marolt

Tres Amigos, Mike Marolt, Steve Marolt, Jim Gile 2007 Everest basecamp.

Max Marolt, Montezuma Basin circa 1964. This is where
Dad had a racing camp in the cirque of a 14er Castle Peak.
It is where he would teach us how to climb and ski.

Tres Amigos, 2019, after a first ski descent of 20,150 foot Chumpe, Peru. We met at age 5, and have spent over 30 years climbing and skiing in the 5000 meter to 8000 meter peak arena. I've never had to find partners to go on adventures with, a huge aspect to our success.

Mike Marolt sitting down to film Steve Marolt
on the North Ridge of Mt Everest